AUSTRALIAN MADE
A MULTICULTURAL READER

EDITED BY SONIA MYCAK AND AMIT SARWAL

SYDNEY UNIVERSITY PRESS

Published 2010 by SYDNEY UNIVERSITY PRESS
Fisher Library, University of Sydney
sydney.edu.au/sup

National Library of Australia Cataloguing-in-Publication entry
Title: Australian made : a multicultural reader / edited by Sonia
            Mycak and Amit Sarwal.
ISBN: 9781920899363 (pbk.)
Notes: Includes bibliographical references.
Subjects: Australian literature--Minority authors.
            Ethnic groups--Australia--Literary collections.
            Immigrants' writings--Australia.
            Minorities--Australia--Literary collections.
Other Authors/Contributors:
            Mycak, Sonia.
            Sarwal, Amit.
Dewey Number:
            A820.80355

Cover design by Miguel Yamin, the University Publishing Service

TABLE OF CONTENTS

INTRODUCTION

The voices in this collection of essays are many. Some of the contributors reside in Australia, some write from countries elsewhere in the world. Some contributors speak from the academy, some are members of culturally and linguistically diverse communities, some occupy a place in both. Sometimes the voices describe, sometimes they analyse, sometimes they theorise. Given the different positions from whence these voices come, not surprisingly, their tone and intent varies. But they are all engaged in the same important enterprise: to shed light on the writers, the readers and the texts of multicultural Australia.

A single all-encompassing way to understand this literary field is not possible, given the complexity and multifaceted nature of culturally and linguistically diverse writing in Australia. The aim of this collection is therefore not to provide a definitive statement about multicultural literature in Australia. Nor is it to encompass all forms of that writing and all forms of authorship. No single volume could do such a thing. But what a collection like this can do is to open another space for debate. And given the nature of multicultural literary production in Australia, it is imperative that that debate includes as many types of analysis – as many voices – as possible.

The collection opens with an essay by Alison Bartlett. She discusses *Neem Dreams*, a novel by Inez Baranay published in India, which is 'acutely aware of the cultural politics of representation'. The broader focus, however, is upon Baranay as a multicultural writer as she engages with the institution of Australian literary criticism, the academy, and the critical theory that informs much of the work undertaken in that environment.

In discussing the literary career of Inez Baranay in relation to 'shifting cultural formations', Bartlett does not shy away from her own involvement in 'the matrix of relations' that has constructed Baranay's career, saying 'I had more than a passing interest in Baranay, so I feel obliged to introduce myself as a character in this story of critics, crucibles and literary careers.' With great insight she goes on to examine the 'Australian literary politics' and 'shifts in institutional and political discourses' that underpin the reception of Baranay's writing and her reputation as a writer.

Similarly focused upon one author and her oeuvre, Anne Brewster looks at the writing and reception of Anna Couani's work produced from 1977 to 1989. Brewster theorises the generic conventions of experimental writing and Couani's specific use of textual strategies such as first person narration and quotidian description to create anti-realist texts which posit a fragmented subjectivity and exemplify 'the condition of cultural/ethnic minoritisation'.

If Couani's writing foregrounds 'the lived contexts of events', Brewster's analysis skilfully reads Couani's career through a biographical and chronological perspective which contextualises it within the author's own 'ethnic and gendered difference'. She finds that during the 1970s and 1980s Couani's experimental writing defied the exclusions of mainstream white Australian culture, particularly within the publishing and literary industries.

Debra Dudek is motivated by a strong belief that multiculturalism can and should be more proactive against racism. She contends it is crucial to understand how the concept of race 'anchors' multiculturalism in order to more effectively combat racism. She therefore argues for a 'critical multiculturalism' which would acknowledge how race underpins multiculturalism and in turn allow for radical and racial difference.

Dudek employs the notion of 'critical multiculturalism' to read two texts written for children. She finds that the representation of multicultural issues in Shaun Tan's *The Lost Thing* and Ranulfo Concon's

Nirvana's Children offers a critique of hegemonic multiculturalism. She concludes that 'critics must put to work critical multiculturalism as a reading and writing strategy' when studying multicultural literature in order to 'shift discourses of multiculturalism from cultural difference to racial difference and therein to work against racism'.

Konstandina Dounis gives an account of Greek-Australian women's writing, paying special attention to intergenerational differences, relationships between mother and child, and connections to homeland(s). She begins with her own biography which she deftly interweaves with the development of Greek-Australian literary criticism and the trajectory it took through the 1990s.

Dounis' voice is of the critic who is herself 'bilingual and bicultural', addressing the sombre reality that multicultural women writers continue to be marginalised. Believing literary translation into English to be the vehicle for the necessary 'transferrings across' that will allow such writers to participate in the mainstream literary arena, she interprets the works of Greek-Australian women like herself. Indeed throughout her analysis her personal perspective is striking: she writes as one of those writers and one of those 'second generation daughters'. In her own life, and her mother's life, she finds 'crystallised' many of the 'thematic preoccupations' she identifies in the works written by other Greek-Australian women.

An intensely and intentionally subjective voice is heard as Hoa Pham, together with Scott Brook, speaks about herself and fellow Vietnamese-Australian writers. Based upon interviews with Dominic Golding, David Nguyen, Chi Vu, Tony Le Nguyen and Binh Duy Ta, the focus of this paper is the '1.5 generation' – those born in Vietnam and raised in Australia. These are young people who are 'between' the 'parent culture' of first-generation migrants and the 'host culture' of the adopted country. They are 'cultural intermediaries' who mediate public perceptions of the Vietnamese-Australian community and representations of contemporary Vietnam for non-Vietnamese audiences.

Pham and Brook find that 'the idea of an experience that is specific to a 1.5 generation has been a powerful metaphor for catalysing the arts of young Vietnamese'. Identifying a number of concerns – living between two cultures, notions of home, return narratives, and sense of self – they conclude that: 'the ongoing search for Vietnamese-Australian identity and the return home is a pressing tension for Vietnamese-Australian artists of the 1.5 generation and features strongly in Vietnamese-Australian works'.

Nijmeh Hajjar also provides a poignant and personal perspective as she reviews the most recent novel by Jad El Hage. Tracing themes of hope, idealism and pacifism, she writes not only as a literary scholar but as an immigrant to Australia originally from Lebanon, the country in which the novel is set.

Hajjar's critical perspective is informed by her own experience of Lebanon. She contends that the author's point of view is also inextricably connected to Lebanese heritage, saying 'Let's remember, Jad is first an Arab novelist.' This touches upon the complex issue of how multicultural writers should be positioned. Her lament that the novel is not written in 'our beautiful Arabic tongue' bespeaks the multicultural reader who enacts a bicultural and bilingual reading strategy.

So personal is Hajjar's response that she likens the protagonist of the novel to her own brother. And she relates the title of the novel – *The Myrtle Tree* – to her own recent experience of eating the hinblass berry while in Lebanon. This reflects on her intention to 'emphasise the role of the reader in the creation of the text'.

Sonia Mycak provides an overview of a specific body of multicultural writing but in doing so offers an empirical approach. Interested in the question of how literary activity is enacted within culturally and linguistically diverse communities in Australia, she employs an institutional approach based on field theory. Drawing upon the work of Dutch scholar Kees van Rees on the contemporary literary field in Western European countries, Mycak theorises a model which illustrates the structure by which literature is produced, circulated and consumed within the Ukrainian community in Australia.

This is part of a larger project to study the literary cultures of communities and writers who migrated to Australia as so-called Displaced Persons immediately after the Second World War. It is hoped this model of Ukrainian-Australian literary production will have a wider applicability as a study of immigrant community writing in Australia and can reflect upon other community-based culturally and linguistically diverse literary fields.

Igor Maver's overview of Slovenian writing in Australia shows a similar focus upon community, in that he begins by outlining the history of Slovenian migration to Australia and the cultural and literary infrastructure which has supported 'the literary creativity of Slovenian migrants in Australia'. His comprehensive survey of Slovenian-Australian writers comes to rest upon the poetry of Jože Žohar, a writer who 'deserves special attention' for the innovative quality of his work.

Maver's work provides an opportunity to hear an important viewpoint: analysis of a migrant literature from a source country perspective. Undertaking his analysis from 'here in Slovenia', he finds these works 'transcend the thematisation of the Slovenian migrant experience in Australia and adopt a cosmopolitan existential stance which addresses readers internationally'. Maver concludes that the texts enrich both the 'source' and the 'target' cultures alike while the authors are ' "transcultural" writers in the best sense of the word' whose 'literary voice and vision have pluralised and globalised Australian as well as Slovenian literary production'.

Harriclea Zengos undertakes a detailed survey of Greek-Australian poetry, prose and drama, finding that it has 'undergone profound developments in the last two decades'. She notes that the term 'Greek-Australian' as applied to writers and literature is 'difficult to define'. Zengos nonetheless traces 'two types of writers' and 'two streams of literature'. She differentiates between the first-generation migrants who came to Australia as adults and write in Greek, and the second generation who were born in Australia of Greek immigrant parents or came to Australia as young children. 'This dichotomy in Greek-Australian literature also gives rise to a duality of theme.' The former are preoccupied with exile, the lost homeland and the foreignness of the new world; the latter are concerned with ethnicity, identity and hybridity.

Zengos concludes that such categories are now being 'redefined'. Since work is now being accepted by mainstream publishers, she feels it 'has moved from the margins' and 'Greek-Australian writers have become a part of the Australian literary scene.'

Sissy Helff is concerned with the positioning of culturally and linguistically diverse literature, particularly within a national context of multiculturalism. She first discusses the problems inherent within existing terminology such as 'migrant writing' or 'multicultural literature'. Then she invites us to consider an alternative term 'transcultural literature', arguing that 'seeing Australian mainstream culture and national identity through a transcultural lens might open up new avenues of coming to terms with the complex category of national literature'.

Applying her argument to Indo-Australian literature, Helff questions the label 'Asian-Australian writing' as a category which constructs homogeneity without respecting the differences between South-Asian, South-East Asian and East-Asian literatures. Exploring to what extent Indo-Australian writing should be considered part of Australian literature, Helff embarks upon a close reading of Suneeta Peres da Costa's *Homework* and Bem Le Hunte's *There, Where the Pepper Grows*, two novels which she considers imagine multicultural Australia in very different ways.

One of the texts Sissy Helff looks at deals with 'the predicaments of growing up in an immigrant family in contemporary multicultural Australia'. Such a focus is shared by Mary Besemeres who considers the cross-cultural dimension of relations between children and parents in immigrant families, an issue which is evident in a large number of intercultural narratives. Beginning with the question of how child rearing practices construct a certain 'cultural self', Besemeres comes to address the wider issue of cross-cultural families as they impact upon the formation of cross-cultural subjectivity.

Drawing upon works of psychological anthropology to theorise the relationship between culture and self, she interprets two novels both of which are by Australian Jewish writers whose parents emigrated from Eastern Europe but published 35 years apart: *Whole Life* by Morris Lurie published in 1987, and *Alien Son* by Judah Waten published in 1952. She finds

> what narratives like Waten's and Lurie's can add to our understanding of the influence of particular cultural patterns of child rearing on individuals is the light they shed on the development of a person's 'cultural self' – or conflicting 'cultural selves' – from the inside. (p. 43)

Christine Sun interrogates the representation of Chinese cultural identity in writings produced by five Australian authors with Chinese ancestry. Given that migrants of Chinese descent come not only from China but also from Malaysia, Singapore, Hong Kong, Taiwan and other South-East Asian countries, Sun reminds us that regional, linguistic, gender, political, socio-economic and ethnic differences emerge when considering 'Chinese' cultural identity. As she states, ' "Chineseness" in Australia is and will continue to be a site of contested meanings'.

Sun differentiates between 'reductive and essentialist ways of representing 'Chinese' cultural difference in literary texts' and a more 'open-ended cultural expression'. The former constructs a 'universal' or 'global' definition of 'Chineseness' based on certain cultural practices that are stereotypically ascribed to Chinese people. This may ignore 'individual' and 'local' expressions of Chinese identity formed within different types of Chinese culture all over the world. A 'non-essentialist' representation, she finds, is able to demonstrate 'the multiplicity of narratives that construct a sense of cultural identity' and present a diverse and subjective range of cultural experiences.

Deborah Madsen also considers the complexity of Chinese cultural identity. She takes as her focus the body of Chinese-Australian literature which developed in the years following the end of the so-called White Australia policy. She does this because 'despite the presence of Chinese immigrants and Chinese Australian communities since the time of the gold rush, it was only after 1975 that a generation of writers of Chinese heritage began to emerge'.

These decades have seen several waves of 'very different migrations' which 'complicate the history of the Chinese-Australian community'. Such differences and complications are of interest to Madsen as she provides an overview and analysis of the literary texts. As she explains,

> Mapping the impact of these differences upon Chinese-Australian literary production, while attending to points of convergence that allow us to speak of a coherent body of work that would constitute modern Anglophone 'Chinese-Australian Literature' is the aim of this essay.

Gaetano Rando begins with an overview of the corpus of work by first-generation Italian-Australian poets. Noting that these writers are little known outside the Italian-Australian community, he focuses upon the work of one particular poet. Paolo Totaro, Rando explains, 'constitutes an exception for his many years of engagement in "mainstream" political, cultural and intellectual endeavours'. Thus begins Rando's analysis of the poetry of 'an Italian intellectual [who] became a pioneer of multiculturalism' in Australia.

Among Totaro's many achievements is the fact that his 1978 publication *Participation* was 'instrumental in determining for the first time multicultural policy' in several Australian states. However Rando's appreciation of Totaro's work here is primarily literary. He quotes at some length from the poetry, which is necessary given Totaro's collection of more than 100 poems is largely unpublished. Rando finds the 'plurilinguistic lyric experimentation' particularly interesting and concludes that Totaro is able to present the 'recesses of his soul as well as the collective experience of the migrant diaspora'.

Robert Pickering analyses *Days in Sydney* by Didier Coste, a novel in which 'bilingualism would seem to be a fundamental prerequisite' in the attempt to 'seize the contemporary contours' of a multicultural society. This is a text which enacts cultural difference not through translation but by alternating two languages in a 'properly organic' relationship between English and French. Language, however, is comprehended both as a 'living presence' and in its 'opacity' and 'elusiveness'. Experimental in structure and narrative technique, this novel posits 'the problematic of identity' which 'is articulated through a questioning of the very adequacy of language, style and form to give it presence and meaning'.

Pickering's paper bespeaks the question of how to define an Australian text. The novel is an 'account of life and love in Sydney' and grapples with 'what it means to live in contemporary Australia'. Yet it was neither published in Australia nor written by a person permanently based here. Nonetheless, as Pickering argues, the work is 'of remarkable resonance and depth, which adds a distinctly new dimension to Australian creative writing'.

Dennis Haskell addresses the concept of national identity and the way national identities determine personal and cultural selves. He does this by analysing two Australian films, both of which are 'concerned with national mythologies that inform the personalities of the central characters'. Despite this collection of essays having an overt literary focus, Haskell's paper was included to remind us that the multicultural text in Australia can be, and very often is, a film. And just as a multicultural literary text can interrogate notions of national, cultural and personal identity, so too do *The Goddess of 1967* and *Japanese Story* contribute to such a debate.

Maintaining that Australian identity has undergone a process of 'revaluation' in the last thirty years, Haskell addresses the 'reconsideration of Australia's relationships with Asia' specifically in relation to Japan. Tracing the depictions of (and differences between) Australian and Japanese cultures, Haskell finds that 'Australian identity is unfolded partly through comparison with Japanese identity ... in re-envisioning the Japanese, these films re-envision Australians.' He contends that 'both films portray complex, internationalised situations' that reflect the transition Australian national identity has undergone in recent decades.

Despite the different approaches they take, together these essays converge upon a number of important questions.

How does multiculturalism intersect with different genres and generic conventions? How is cultural diversity expressed and enacted within life writing, women's writing, experimental writing, children's literature, poetry, prose and film?

What does it mean to be a 'multicultural writer' in Australia today? Is it a biographically determined category – does one need to be born outside of Australia or born of immigrant parents? Is it a self-identified category or a definition of authorship that is imposed by readers and critics? Does the multicultural writer occupy an enunciative position which is limiting or liberating? Many of the authors whose works are here reviewed show that multicultural authorship can be a fleeting or strategic form of identity a writer enacts at certain points in his or her career, and that while ethno-cultural and linguistic differences and influences can inform the creation of a text so too do other personal, social and cultural contexts come into play.

What is a 'multicultural text'? The essays in this collection show that defining such a text invokes various possibilities: a text published in Australia or published overseas; a work written in one language or bilingual; a narrative set in Australia or located in another place; a narrative depicting culturally and/or linguistically diverse characters and settings.

In addressing such questions, the perspectives and points of interrogation are many.

The concept of multiculturalism itself comes under scrutiny, particularly the shortcomings of an Australian multiculturalism which has not yet resulted in a fully inclusive cultural field but has left many a fine writer little known outside of his or her own ethno-cultural community.

Terminology such as 'migrant writing' or 'multicultural literature' is queried, as we are invited to consider other terms such as 'transcultural' and 'transnational', which might better encompass the global nature of literary production today.

The construction of ethno-cultural identity is investigated, particularly as it is represented within literary texts. Different frames of reference are employed: intergenerational differences, bicultural and hybrid identity, bilingualism, and cross-cultural subjectivity.

Inherently, the notion of an Australian national and cultural identity is challenged, as are national mythologies as they impact upon the representation of individuals. There is a wariness of stereotypical attributes which essentialise identity. There is attention to global dimensions which admit cultural difference.

Such complications and contestations are welcome and implied in the very title of this book. To Australian readers the term 'Australian made' might evoke certain associations. As a label it most often refers to goods and services in an attempt to circumscribe their origins. But there are disputed meanings of an 'Australian made' product found on a supermarket shelf. Was the item packaged and distributed in Australia, does it contain ingredients from abroad? All these connotations were considered in formulating the title of this book. Certain implications we thought would prove fruitful: the text as a commodity which is distributed and consumed; the text as a product of institutional forces as well as individual agencies. Contestations also exist when labelling a text as 'Australian literature' – was it written, published, distributed, received in Australia? Did any of these processes occur overseas? To what extent do international influences create any Australian literary text?

Presenting the work of critics and scholars from both Australia and abroad, this collection creates a synergy between local and international perspectives as it explores what it means for a writer or reader to be 'Australian' and a text to be 'Australian made'.

Sonia Mycak and Amit Sarwal

1

CRITICS, CRUCIBLES, AND A LITERARY CAREER: INEZ BARANAY AND HER INDIAN NOVEL, *NEEM DREAMS*[1]

ALISON BARTLETT

Inez Baranay has been publishing in Australia for almost twenty years, but her seventh novel, *Neem Dreams* (2003), was published in India, indicating a shift in her publishing career. While *Neem Dreams* continues Baranay's interest in issues of Third World development and Western tourism, travel and trade, in this paper I propose that it also engages with the institution of Australian literary criticism especially in postcolonial debates. *Neem Dreams* was released almost a decade after Baranay's non-fiction text, *Rascal Rain* (1994), which met with fierce criticism, and it has been a decade in which Baranay has been variously addressing that criticism, contemporary theory and the academy. I therefore argue that *Neem Dreams* signals Baranay's uneasy relationship with 'Australian' writing, publishing and identity, as well as her changed relation to the academy and to contemporary theory. While the back-cover blurb of *Neem Dreams* alerts us to the neem tree 'acting as a kind of crucible for India', I want to argue that in many ways, postcolonial theory is the crucible for this book. In this chapter then, I read this latter part of Baranay's literary career over the last decade through its encounters with

---

[1] This article was first published in *Antipodes* December 2007: 15–19, and is reproduced with permission. Web addresses have been updated.

the academy, with *Rascal Rain* and *Neem Dreams* operating as bookends. Such a substantial and productive career means that shifts in institutional and political discourses become evident in tracing the ways in which Baranay's texts and career are read (and written). I am interested in the kinds of questions such a career raises about the imbrication of theory and fiction, and the circulation of authority between writers, critics and the academy.

Neem Dreams

Neem Dreams was published in India by Rupa & Co. In many ways this is fitting, as the novel mainly revolves around the lives of four characters in India. Pandora is an Australian whose PhD was on women and development in the Third World. She is an ecofeminist and wants to write about the local women's project which involves the collection of neem seeds. This project has been organised by Maneeksha, an Indian woman who was educated in the United States and has recently returned to India to be married to Prashant. Prashant and his cousin run the local neem factory, producing skincare products which Jade, another Australian, wants to buy in bulk. She works for an upmarket store in SoHo named Orientalisme, which offers urban-bound New Yorkers the commodities of the East. Jade is particularly attracted to the marketability of the raw brown paper wrapping of the neem soap. Andy, a gay English lawyer, is in India to cast his lover's ashes into the Ganges and to find out more about neem as a potential answer to AIDS. The collision of these lives with the politics of globalisation, rural aid, trade agreements, corporate greed, packaging, traditional knowledge and ownership, and postcolonialism all spiral around the neem tree, 'a kind of crucible', the back cover calls it, and a symbol of India itself. The narrative structure is sophisticated, repeating the same few days from different narrative points of view, and covering continents as personal histories are filled in. Interspersed are seven chapters on the myths, remedies, folklore, business, politics and potential patents of the neem tree.

The book was released in September 2003 and reviews from India were glowing. Almost all of them admire Baranay's skill as a foreigner to capture an authentic 'India'. For example, Eugenie Pinto's review in *Crossings* (2003) claims that 'Inez Baranay's perception of India is truly amazing. She has put her finger on the pulse of the country – nothing has escaped her keen observation.' Meenakshi Kumar in the *Hindustan Times* (4 September 2003) is slightly more hesitant at giving out accolades to a foreigner writing about India:

> Like most foreigners who are bitten by the India bug, Australian writer Inez Baranay too, is in love with the country. But unlike most foreigners, it's not the unwashed sadhus, bedecked elephants or snake charmers who fascinate her or form a part of her writing. Her latest book, *Neem Dreams*, steers clear of dishing out an exotic India.

Swati Pal, in *The Sunday Pioneer* (14 September 2003), another Indian newspaper, is similarly happy that 'the writer does not use India as an exotic backdrop', while Padmini Devarajan in *The Hindu* (2 November 2003) raises the possibility that gender is another potential hurdle which Baranay overcomes: 'Baranay has risen above her feminine voice and foreigner perspective to strike a neutral unbiased language as far as basic values and issues are concerned.' Pal claims that Baranay 'uncannily conjures splashes of Indian reactions, attitudes or relationships with as much authenticity as she does the American, Australian and British ethos'. Reviewers highlighted the fact that this novel was published initially in India, perhaps as evidence of Baranay's commitment to the Indian literary establishment, authenticating her involvement in Indian cultural life which the reviews applaud in 'getting it right'. But it is also an aspect of representation which Baranay argues is rooted in shared class and cultural values. Outlining her immersion in Indian novels, newspapers, magazines, music, conversations, as well as travels in India while preparing the manuscript, Baranay suggests that 'the middle classes have a culture that overlaps several other categories of cultural identity such as nationality and ethnicity' ('It's the Other Who Makes My Portrait' 2004). On this basis, she suggests that the educated middle-class Indian characters she writes are probably closer to her own cultural identity and sense of self than an Australian woman of a class and life experience different to herself. While this argument is crucial to Baranay's critical position in 'representing' India, it does not explain why this novel was barely received in Australia. There has only been one online review on an Australian site by an Indian reviewer (API Review of Books) – two years after publication (see Prasad 2005). While *Neem Dreams* continues Baranay's enduring interest in travel, tourism, and development, in other more complex ways it marks her active engagement with academic criticism and postcolonial theory.

Critics

Neem Dreams comes almost a decade after the publication of *Rascal Rain*, which narrates her experience as an Australian Volunteer Abroad with a women's development project in Papua New Guinea. In contrast to the strong reception given to her previous fiction, *Rascal Rain* was not well received in reviews, which focused on its cultural politics as if it were 'a defence of imperialist projects and attitudes' (Baranay, 'Fraught Territory' 224). One critical article which appeared in the regional journal *LiNQ* (1997) explored the shortcomings of the book in detail (see Ash, 44–54). Interested in the discourses which operate to construct the tourist, the traveller and the aid worker, Susan Ash's article notes that Baranay 'conspicuously demonstrates political and personal awareness. For example, she recognises the travel industry's slogan 'Papua New Guinea is for travellers not tourists', as nothing but a "wise-ass distinction" ' (47). Ash then asks, 'can [Baranay] avoid colonizing, exoticizing operations in language? The answer is emphatically no, but what does surprise is the degree and intensity to which she employs "staggeringly" ... offensive images of local people' (47). The article then lists examples, including one description of a young boy as a 'beautiful ... fine-boned black-skinned just-out-of-childhood beauty' (*Rascal Rain*, 1). Ash critiques this by writing,

> She calls him a 'young god.' (1) In other words, here we have the stock aestheticised, eroticised and sexualised body of the native … In fact, [Baranay] subjects everybody she meets to this penetrating inspection by the Western eye, selecting and filtering the visible for signs which, when translated into narrative, will enter a web of signification already familiar to the Western reader. (48)

In short, Ash concludes that 'the resulting narrative invokes base, derogatory stereotypes' (49).

In the next issue of the journal *LiNQ* (1998), Baranay wrote a reply to Susan Ash titled, 'Theory Couldn't Help Me', rebuking many of the points Ash made and repositioning herself as a creative writer who does 'know' theory but does not find it helpful in her writing. In telling the story of her year in New Guinea, Baranay argues that *Rascal Rain* was,

> a strenuous attempt to make sense of the experience, while looking at ideas of what is a story, woman, race, culture, postcolonialism, development/aid and so on, and whether so-called women's development in third world countries – these terms I use in implicit multiple inverted commas – obligatory po-mo irony – is feminism or not or should it be or must it not be. (54)

In protesting her position as knowing subject rather than naïve writer, Baranay mobilises satire and allusion in her angry defence: 'to scold about … the "Western eye" is ludicrous. What are writers supposed to do, put out our eyes? To not ever write anything about non-Western people?' (54–55).

Around this time I had more than a passing interest in Baranay, so I feel obliged to introduce myself as a character in this story of critics, crucibles and literary careers.

This part of the story begins in 1992 when, as a beginning graduate student, I wrote to Baranay asking for an interview as part of my doctoral work which sought to position the writer as knowing subject, as theorist of her own work. Baranay was still living in New Guinea. We corresponded briefly. She was moving to Cairns in North Queensland where I had lived and asks advice on where to live. A couple of years later, we end up living around the corner from each other as I finish writing my PhD, and *Rascal Rain* is published. The interview takes place in March 1993, when Baranay is 'trying to make sense of the chaotic experience of the year before' ('Fraught Territory', 226).

'Send me some theory' she asks, on women's development, on postcolonialism, on the latest feminism. 'I don't have any truck with universities', she tells me, and nor did she have any contact with 'us' academics. She met some academics in Goroka, she tells me, but they were nice people. She isn't joking.

> I went to university [in the sixties] when the English school was extremely conservative. I was much more interested in the sex, drugs and rock'n'roll of that era. But I didn't see that reflected anywhere in the way the classes were conducted or in what we were reading [or] how it was talked about. (Bartlett, 220)

When I ask if she had come across any of the French feminists I was using, she says they were

> just names to me, and they've been on my Must Read This One Day list, but haven't fallen into my lap ... I mean, where do you? You have to go to university don't you, to come across that sort of thing? (Bartlett, 216)

So I sent her some theory. I sent some Irigaray, and some Cixous, and a commentary by Elizabeth Grosz. I sent some Spivak and Chandra Mohanty's 'Under Western Eyes' (1986), which seems to have become an enduring trope in Baranay's institutional reception. This was the theory that 'couldn't help', and maybe it indicates some of the limits of theory for articulating politics that have been lived rather than imagined. Baranay presents a compelling quandary for writers who are informed of theoretical debates of cultural representation. Writing in retrospect in 2003, Baranay suggests that the book's reception was partially overdetermined by the pressing social concerns of the time. It appeared, she reminds us, after the 1988 Bicentennial, which officially celebrated two hundred years of colonisation in Australia and also provoked increased political and social movements to recognise the traumatic Indigenous history this involved. Ash's critical article coincided with the publication of the Stolen Generations report *Bringing Them Home* (1997), which documented the systematic removal of Indigenous children from their parents in order to dilute Indigenous culture. *Rascal Rain* therefore appeared 'in a period of increasing anxiety over Australia's ongoing shame-making history', and many took pains to demonstrate their difference and distance from the increasingly evident racism inherent in the nation's structures' (Baranay, 'Fraught Territory', 227). Baranay still rues the fact that 'the book's serious treatment' of women, race, culture, postcolonialism, development or aid and feminism was 'generally neglected' in its reception ('Fraught Territory', 227).

I feel deeply implicated in the matrix of relations being played out here, and which I now seek to construct as a narrative of a literary career reshaped by changing cultural formations. It is not coincidental that Susan Ash's article was published in *LiNQ* when one of my supervisors was editor, and that Baranay was given the opportunity to respond to that criticism. In a special issue of *Meanjin* in 2003 on Papua New Guinea, editor Drusilla Modjeska attributes Baranay's dilemmas to the genre of memoir. But the cultural politics of representation are also infused in her latest fiction. If the neem tree is 'a crucible for India', then postcolonial criticism and Australian literary politics also function as crucibles for *Neem Dreams*.

Crucibles

Neem Dreams is conscious of its engagement with the fraught politics of postcolonial theory. In one scene, the materialistic Jade wants to talk clothes with Pandora, the highly ethical women's development worker:

> 'I secured a special little selection of *salwaar kameez*, these embroidered ones', [she says] patting her own ample dimensions, 'perfect for a New York summer'.
>
> Pandora didn't say anything. She had emphatically not 'gone Indian' in her own dress, in fact she never wore a dress ... There was an appropriation issue she avoided by dressing as someone who is fine with the way she usually is. (*Neem Dreams*, 186)

The novel touches on *suttee*, the practice of widow burning, by having Pandora think 'that it is too easy to condemn the practices of other cultures by imposing the standards of our own practices of honour' (*Neem Dreams* 205). Local politics and religious loyalties are conveyed as complex mechanisms, as representations of national identities are understood to be multifaceted when Meenaksha tells us, 'She says there is not a single India and I say there is not a single West' (*Neem Dreams*, 223).

The novel, therefore, is acutely aware of the cultural politics of representation. At one particular scene this becomes quite pointed as Pandora – the ethical one – polices herself. Pandora thinks of an Indian boy named Jolly as 'sweet':

> Uh-oh, hang on a minute, she checks herself, am I allowed to think of Jolly as *sweet*? Sweet, that word meaning a gentle, attractive demeanour, you can't call just anyone sweet, sinister meanings are attributed to adjectives applied to identifiable Others. Let's decide, she decides again, that there are sweet people in all the locations of the world and that I mean the same thing by it wherever I am, though that's not the end of it according to the professional perversities of

certain pundits, critics keen to crow over forbidden perceptions, and whatever you might say about Others is forbidden. Never mind.

'The tea's really good' she said. (*Neem Dreams*, 56)

This does not need a 'Dear Susan' for the traces of literary criticism to be read through *Neem Dreams*. In fact Baranay spells it out in the authoritative space of *Meanjin* to say that

Writing this book was, in effect, an answer to, or defiance of, the objections made to my *Rascal Rain* and the foreseeable objections to the very project of writing a novel set in India with Indian characters. ('Fraught Territory', 225)

Neem Dreams seems to offer a responsive example of a text affected by institutionally regulated reading formations, which David Carter (1997) argues can 'govern how texts get to be written and get to be read' (x).

Literary Careers

It is easy to read the last decade of Baranay's career as being driven by the need to defend her writing. But I do not want this to turn into a story of the lone writer accosted by academic critics then spending years in her turret (or travelling the world) writing back to the academy. Instead, I am interested in the shifting cultural formations at work in shaping her writing, reputation and reception. David Carter elegantly articulates the ways in which literary institutions – of writing, of theory, of criticism and publication and reviewing – can

be discovered as textual or narrative effects which in turn will depend for their significance on the institutions governing what counts as literariness, as authorship, as appropriate reading, as a 'serious' career in a specific literary system. (xi)

Such cultural formations cannot be figured, Carter argues, in dichotomous terms like inside-outside, creative-critical, because they generate effects on each other: they form relationships.

Baranay's construction as a writer in the public domain exemplifies this. A decade ago, Baranay's reputation could easily have been read (as I did in my doctoral work) as pivoting on her position as a 'multicultural' and a 'woman' writer at a time when multiculturalism was still a federal directive and feminism a powerful social movement. Small presses actively published such writers. Even though Baranay has been dubious of being labelled in these ways, she also benefitted from their cultural currency, contributing to Sneja Gunew and Jan Mahyuddin's *Beyond the Echo: Multicultural Women's Writing* (1987) and to Sneja Gunew and Anna Couani's *Telling Ways: Australian Women's Experimental Fiction* (1988) a year later. Her biography on the AustLit Website still emphasises her multicultural dimension, saying that she writes in English and that she has worked for the Federal Department of Immigration, among other things (although it only lists her publications up to 1992).

Now, however, when positions like 'multicultural' or 'woman' writer are barely noticed in federal policy or publishing priorities, Baranay's biography demands to be read quite differently. Her own account which appears on her website forms the basis of her biography on the Ozlit site on VicNet, and so suggests that she has a vital role in self-representation. The discursive construction of Baranay's career in such 'official' (web)sites is evidence of the shifting cultural formations which constitute a literary career. Her official biography is written in the third person, and consciously constructs a literary career. It begins by positioning Baranay as only provisionally Australian:

> Inez Baranay was born in Naples, Italy of Hungarian parents who emigrated to Australia when she was a baby. She was educated in the western suburbs of Sydney then moved to the inner city. She lived in Malaya with her parents as a teenager for two years, and began her adult travels with a trip to Bali in the late 1970s. (www.inezbaranay.com)

Note how her parents emigrated rather than immigrated, grammatically locating the subject elsewhere in relation to Australia. This gesture is repeated through listing other international locations for growing up, and a continuing adult life of travel 'beginning' in Bali. Her writing history is also charted through her travels, through her connections with and movement between other places:

> The Edge of Bali (1992) marked the end of 40 years based in Sydney (including travels in south-east Asia, Europe, Morocco and India).
>
> Inez went to Papua New Guinea with Australian Volunteers Abroad in 1992 (the subject of Rascal Rain: A Year in Papua New Guinea (1994).
>
> She lived in Far North Queensland for the next few years, in Cairns and in the Torres Strait Islands. In 1997 Sheila Power was published. During this time she travelled often to the US (mostly New York City, with a stay in 1995 at Yaddo, the artists' colony in Saratoga Springs) and India, where she had been several times to study yoga. Other trips to India have included a period as writer-in-residence at the University of Madras and a Literature Residency granted by Asialink. India is the setting for her recent novel, Neem Dreams (2003) and was published there. (www.inezbaranay.com)

I read this biography as a claim to be much more than an 'Australian' writer. There seems to be a distancing of the writerly self from Australian literature, and more of a positioning as 'global citizen'. Indeed, in an interview for The Hindu (2003), Baranay maintains that 'nativity doesn't define us':

> After World War II, [my parents] happened to land up in Australia with a random throw of the dice. Italy is now just a name to me and being an Australian is only a twist of fate … I became an Australian only by leaving the country. (www.inezbaranay.com)

If 'multicultural' and 'woman' writer are relics of the 1980s publishing and literary worlds, then Baranay seems to have adopted the markers of a newly cosmopolitan globalised economy to position her work and her career.

In this discourse, Baranay's identity and career have been resignified in order to do the work of authorising, as Carter suggests happens continually in the drive to authorise authorship:

> To write involves situating the text in a particular career trajectory the possibilities of which will be determined by the other texts and careers circulating in the relevant literary system ... The writer's own prior texts and careers will be part of what is at stake, part of the structuring context, in any new act of writing; and any new writing which is granted status within the career will work to re-order, to re-write, this prior history. (xii)

This sort of reworking of prior history is evident in granting status to *Neem Dreams*, for while multiculturalism and woman writer are displaced for a more cosmopolitan cultural currency, Baranay mobilises that history in new ways to shore up her engagement with the literary politics of postcolonialism. She argues in a 2004 critical article that while she is so obviously a 'foreigner' in India, it is not a new experience for her: 'I grew up in an Australia where reffos like my family were foreigners, so a sense of foreignness, of parts of myself as essentially Other, had become part of my sense of myself' ('It's the Other Who Makes My Portrait', 2004). Even as she writes this, however, there is still a willingness for shift-shaping again, as she claims 'the writer goes on being shaped and changed by new texts and new characters, both other to and inextricable from, her sense of self' ('It's the Other Who Makes My Portrait', 2004; see also 'Multiculturalism, Globalisation and Worldliness', 2004).

Such a rewriting, or rereading, of Baranay's career, also tacitly suggests a displacement from 'Australian' literary establishments. Indeed, this is evident in her recent relations with Australian publishers, who told Baranay that there was 'no market' for *Neem Dreams* ('Fraught Territory' 228), and that the India and its characters in the book 'were not recognisable to them' ('It's the Other Who Makes My Portrait', 2004). She cannot persuade publishers to reprint her previous works, most of which are out of print (personal communication, 2004). In order to sustain the circulation of her writing, she has consciously taken control of her publishing and distribution. She recently released *Three Sydney Novels* (2004), which packages her previous books, *Pagan* (1990), *Between Careers* (1989), and *Sheila Power* (1997) under one cover. And she is distributing *Neem Dreams* outside of India herself. This perhaps indicates much about the market-driven publishing industry, but also suggests a shift in the business of being a writer, and being an Australian writer. Writers have for some time been obliged to market themselves as commodities, for writers' festivals, for creative writing courses, and Baranay suggests that self-publication and marketing is the next step. But this step also suggests a more conscious control of a career, of rewriting prior texts and future career trajectories. This need not be judged in a cynical or a celebratory way, but seems an extension of narratives of globalised corporations and trade agreements, individual packaging and ownership issues, the very themes which concern *Neem Dreams*.

In addition, Baranay's association with universities has been irrevocably changed in the last decade. Not only has she been writer-in-residence, and taught creative writing at universities, but she has also completed a PhD. Her second book of nonfiction, *Sun Square Moon: Writings on Yoga and Writing* (2005), includes material that began as part of her PhD. Baranay reviews, gives conference papers, and publishes monographs and academic papers, but still consciously positions herself as a creative writer for whom university is one of the fields in which she operates. But if Baranay's literary career has been reshaped through her textual interactions with academia, is the opposite also evident? Does the interaction between creative writing and academic writing as it merges in the form of doctoral graduates disrupt the sedimented divisions between writers and theorists? If Baranay now has academic credentials, does it change how we read her work? Will she receive the 'serious treatment' she imagined for *Rascal Rain*? Can a writer like Baranay be regarded as doing postcolonial work in the form of fiction? Can a writer's ethics and aesthetics be considered as seriously as a critic's? Somehow, I am not so optimistic about these possibilities, although I should be. These questions prod and stretch the institutional formations through which we read and write careers, including our own.

Works Cited

Ash, Susan. 'Aid Work, Travel and Representation: Inez Baranay's *Rascal Rain* and Alice Walker's *Warrior Marks*.' *LiNQ* 24.2 (1997): 44–54.

Baranay, Inez. *Sun Square Moon: Writings on Yoga and Writing*. Sydney: Sun Square Moon, 2005.

——. Personal Communication. 2 February 2004.

——. Inez Baranay Website. 7 June 2004 [Accessed 14 January 2011]. www.inezbaranay.com.

——. 'It's the Other Who Makes My Portrait: Writing Self, Character and the Other.' *TEXT* 8.2 (2004). [Accessed 14 January 2011]. www.textjournal.com.au/oct04/baranay.htm.

——. 'Multiculturalism, Globalisation and Worldliness: Origin and Destination of the Text.' *JASAL* 3 (2004): 117–32.

——. *Three Sydney Novels*. Broadway: The Three Sydney Novels Project, 2004.

——. *Neem Dreams*. Delhi: Rupa, 2003.

——. 'Fraught Territory.' *Meanjin* 62.3 (2003): 223–29.

——. 'Theory Couldn't Help Me.' *LiNQ* 25.1 (1998): 52–56.

——. Review of *Creativity*, by Kevin Brophy. *TEXT* 2.2 (1998). [Accessed 31 May 2004]. www.textjournal.com.au/oct98/baranay.htm.

——. *Sheila Power*. Sydney: Allen & Unwin, 1997.

——. *Rascal Rain: A Year in Papua New Guinea*. Sydney: Angus & Robertson, 1994.

——. *The Edge of Bali,* Sydney: Angus & Robertson, 1992.

——. *Pagan*. Angus & Robertson, 1990.

——. *Between Careers*. 1989. Sydney: William Collins, 2000.

Bartlett, Alison. *Jamming the Machinery: Contemporary Australian Women's Writing*. Toowoomba: ASAL, 1998.

Carter, David. *A Career in Writing: Judah Waten and the Cultural Politics of a Literary Career*. Toowoomba: ASAL, 1997.

Devarajan, Padmini. 'Unbiased Perspective.' Review of *Neem Dreams*, by Inez Baranay. *The Hindu Literary Review* 2 November 2003. [Accessed 29 Jan, 2004]. www.hindu.com/lr/2003/11/02/stories/2003110200100400.htm.

Gunew, Sneja, and Jan Mahyuddin. *Beyond the Echo: Multicultural Women's Writing*. St Lucia: University of Queensland Press, 1987.

Gunew, Sneja, and Anna Couani. *Telling Ways: Australian Women's Experimental Fiction*. Adelaide: Australian Feminist Studies, 1988.

Hafeez, T.A. 'Speaking Through Her Work.' Interview with Inez Baranay. *The Hindu Literary Review* 2 November 2003. [Accessed 28 Jan 2004]. www.hindu.com/thehindu/lr/2003/11/02/stories/2003110200110400.htm.

Human Rights and Equal Opportunity Commission. *Bringing Them Home: Report of the National Inquiry into the Separation of Aboriginal and Torres Strait Islander Children from Their Families*. Sydney: Commonwealth of Australia, 1997.

Kumar, Meenakshi. 'Writer from Down Under Sells.' Review of *Neem Dreams*, by Inez Baranay. *Hindustan Times* 4 September 2003. 28 January 2004

Mohanty, Chandra Talpade. 'Under Western Eyes: Feminist Scholarship and Colonial Discourses.' *Boundary 2* 12.3 (1986): 333–58.

Pal, Swati. Review of *Neem Dreams*, by Inez Baranay. *The Sunday Pioneer* 14 September 2003.

Pinto, Eugenie. 'Indian Dreams.' Review of *Neem Dreams*, by Inez Baranay. *Crossings* 8.3 (2003). [Accessed 14 January 2010]. http://webcache.googleusercontent.com/search?q=cache:ysRTLp8I9 1MJ:www.iasa-

india.org/jan2004.htm+Eugenie+Pinto+%E2%80%9CIndian+Dream
s%E2%80%9D&cd=1&hl=en&ct=clnk&gl=au

Prasad, A. Rajendra. Review of *Neem Dreams*, by Inez Baranay. *API
Review of Books* (June 2005). [Accessed 7 August 2005]. www.api-
network.com/main/index.php?apply=reviews&webpage=api_review
s&flexedit=&flex_password=&menu_label=&menuID=homely&me
nubox=&Review=5429.

2
REMEMBERING TRANSCULTURAL CHILDHOODS: MORRIS LURIE AND JUDAH WATEN

MARY BESEMERES

In this paper I explore an issue that comes to the fore in a large number of intercultural narratives: the cross-cultural dimension of relations between children and parents in immigrant families. I focus here on two such narratives by Australian Jewish writers whose parents emigrated from Eastern Europe: *Whole Life*, by Morris Lurie, and *Alien Son*, by Judah Waten, examining how the authors write about relationships with family members whose cultural worlds were in many ways foreign to their own. There is a clear distance between the texts in terms of style and anticipated audience, attributable partly to generational differences between the authors themselves. *Alien Son*, first published in 1952, has typically been read as realist autobiographical fiction,[1] while *Whole Life*, published in 1987, is both more obviously experimental and unambiguously a work of life writing (the subtitle is 'An Autobiography'). Waten was born in Odessa, Russian Empire, in 1911, into a family that

---

[1] Richard Freadman (2004) notes that *Alien Son* is cast negatively in Sneja Gunew's influential account of Australian immigrant literature, *Framing Marginality* (1994), as a 'paradigmatic' case of 'scholarly identification of migrant writing and realist aesthetics' (28). Freadman argues that Waten's realism is characteristic of Australian Jewish writing and is bound up with the specificity of Jewish historical experience.

settled in Western Australia when he was three, moving to Melbourne when he was fourteen, while Lurie was born in Melbourne in 1938 to recently arrived immigrants from Poland and Palestine. *Alien Son* predates the policies of multiculturalism in Australia by twenty years and is something of a landmark text in Australian literature in focusing on an immigrant community; *Whole Life* was written more than ten years after the rise of multiculturalism as a public discourse, and assumes the inherent interest and value of immigrant experience. Yet, for all the differences between them, there are also revealing parallels between the cross-cultural families – and cross-cultural selves – that emerge in these two narratives.

There has been a revival of interest among anthropologists in the relationship between culture and the self, or culture and individual lives. American scholar Naomi Quinn is at the forefront of recent work on this issue in psychological anthropology. Her articulation of how a person's upbringing contributes to the development of their 'cultural self' connects in interesting ways with the portrayal of cross-cultural childhoods in Lurie's and Waten's narratives. Quinn argues boldly in a recent essay that cultural models of child rearing have the 'greatest influence of all on who we are' (Quinn 2002). She formulates the relationship between self and culture as follows:

> I rely on a contemporary way of thinking about what was once described as 'personality' – and is now generally thought of as 'selfhood' – not as some mono-thematic and fax-like copy of a people's 'culture', but as the characteristic kind of self – notwithstanding all its complexity, inconsistency, and unexpected turns – that results from the experience of growing up and living in a given cultural community, and hence internalizing the cognitive schemas shared as a result of that experience. (2)

She goes on to argue from examples of anthropologists' writings about child rearing in Inuit, Taiwanese, German, Gusii (African), and both working- and middle-class American communities, among others, that child rearing practices result in 'a lifelong, culturally distinctive self, one shared with others who have been raised according to the same cultural model' (48).

While my approach to cross-cultural autobiography is informed by related assumptions to Quinn's, my sense of the concept of the 'cultural self' differs somewhat from hers (for a detailed discussion of questions about the relationship between self, language and culture, see Besemeres, 9–35). In reading autobiographical writing I would give more weight than Quinn does to what she refers to as the 'complexity, inconsistency, and unexpected turns' (2) in the self, and accord what she calls 'the characteristic kind of self that results from the experience of growing up … in a given cultural community' (2) less explanatory power in determining the whole of who someone becomes. This hedge notwithstanding, the texts by Lurie and Waten significantly bear out Quinn's contention that cultural patterns of child rearing in particular communities have a profound impact on the selves that emerge.

In the case of the parents that Quinn refers to, the cultural values underpinning their child rearing practices are shared and reinforced by others in the immediate community in which they live. As exiles, the parents portrayed in Lurie's and Waten's narratives had no such support from teachers or other, non-immigrant parents. While attempting to raise their children within the cultural frameworks they themselves grew up with, they often seem not to have reckoned with the extent to which the children would have to deal with a different cultural outlook at school and on the street. Similarly, the teachers and neighbours who figure in these texts often respond to the parents' behaviour dismissively or with unease, attitudes the authors recall partly internalising as children. Quinn's conception of a 'cultural self' that develops through one's upbringing is complicated, in the case of these writers, by their experiences of growing up within two very different cultures.

In *Whole Life*, Morris Lurie's relations with his parents are portrayed as both shaped and significantly displaced by his relationship with another family member. At times, the text reads like eloquent pages of hate-mail sent to the memory of his parents, for having entrusted him as a small child to the mercies of his tyrannical grandfather. Towards the end of the book we learn indirectly that Lurie's grandfather came from a shtetl[2] near Bialystok, in Poland, and that he later lived in Palestine before joining his son's family in Melbourne. None of this is spelt out explicitly; the psychic drama of the child's interaction with others in the family is deliberately (and compellingly) foregrounded over historical or social reference. The author refers to his grandfather throughout by the Yiddish term *zaydeh*, a word that captures how he was known in the household, and hence how the child Morris thought of him. The following mordant lines are characteristic of Lurie's portrayal of their relationship:

> He was proud of me.
> He praised me to one and all.
> For me he bought a persimmon, the first of the season. For me he cooked the newest potatoes, as small as a single bite, tender in their skins.
> If there was only one banana in the house, a peach, a plum, one last or only anything, it was always for me.
> Whatever was special, whatever was a treat.
> Nothing was too good for me.
> I was the focus of his days.
> The centre of his life.
> I was the light in his eyes, the smile on his lips, the visible pulse that beat in his wrist.
> I wanted him dead. (*Whole Life*, 44)

---

[2] Shtetl is the Yiddish word for 'town'. Shtetls were small towns in pre-Holocaust Eastern Europe which were predominantly Jewish. See Eva Hoffman's *Shtetl: The History of a Small Town and an Extinguished World* (1997) for a social history of Polish 'shtetls', focused on Bransk.

Lurie brilliantly conveys the oppressiveness of *zaydeh*'s presence. 'Had I been to the lavatory? From his cupboard he brought out the *feigen*, the figs, the medicinal figs in a tight solid block from which he cut me an exact measured slice' (*Whole Life*, 43). '*Don't walk so fast! He shouted at me. Don't whistle! Don't swing your arms! Don't scrape your shoes on the ground!* Whatever I did, whatever I wanted to do' (*Whole Life*, 48). Nightmarishly, the hatefulness to Morris of *zaydeh*'s relentless attentions appears for the most part to escape the notice of his parents; the book is partly an intuitive reconstruction of why they allowed his childhood to be blighted in this way. One element in Lurie's piecing together of what happened is his mother's struggle as a first-generation immigrant to save enough money to bring her parents and their extended family out of Hitler's Europe (what Lurie calls the 'classic duty of the oldest child'). The struggle marked her so indelibly that, so the book suggests, she lost any instinct to protect the family she established in Australia from her despotic father-in-law.

And yet an important aspect of Lurie's relationship with his parents and with *der zaydeh* remains largely unexplored in the narrative. The defining impact of shtetl culture on *der zaydeh* is registered in the memoir through his overt cultural observances, such as taking his grandson to the synagogue or 'shul' on 'Shabbos' and on feastdays, initiating him into the religious realm which is such a large part of his life: 'He sat me beside him where he had his regular seat, he pointed out words in his book with his finger, he commented, he explained' (*Whole Life* 44). Characteristically, the intransitive use of the verbs 'commented, explained' implies that *der zaydeh*'s explanation goes over the boy's head because the old man makes no attempt to connect with him, only to impart his knowledge – as if the child were merely a receptacle for learning. Another cultural observance of *zaydeh*'s is making the *lockshen* or noodles for the Sabbath, although the fact that he prepares the food himself in place of a *bobbeh* or grandmother seems strikingly countercultural when compared with recollections of shtetl life like ones cited in Barbara Myerhoff's study of a community of elderly East-European immigrants to America, 'Bobbehs and Zeydes' (Myerhoff et al. 1992). Lurie suggests that his grandfather had an artistic gift, expressed through his culinary creations, which, as nascent writer and artist,[3] Lurie's child self could appreciate; indeed *zaydeh*'s precision and perfectionism are part of his own inheritance, however ambivalently. 'When I write with my fountain pen, when my heart and brain are in balance, … when the letters spring together in flawless accord … when I write like my *zaydeh*, I feel his love.' (*Whole Life*, 176)

But the expression of *zaydeh*'s 'love' for Morris – portrayed in the book as a kind of obsession which bypasses the child himself and objectifies him – is arguably no less redolent of cultural beliefs than his attendance at *shul* or care for the correct preparation of Sabbath meals. At times, Lurie's account hints at this. Insofar as there is an implied framework for understanding the relationship, however, it is psychoanalytical, rather than cultural.[4] The prologue to the memoir ends with a telling mention of the author's psychiatrist – 'the son whose story this is, in hopeless depression, driving to see the psychiatrist who has been trying to help him … for almost two years …' (*Whole Life*, 9). While such explicit references to the psychological aftermath of Lurie's childhood are rare, they create an important frame for understanding what is otherwise evoked in the narrative from the point of view of the child.

When Lurie portrays his mother as failing to recognise that *der zaydeh* was a stifling presence, he appears not to take into account how

---

[3] Lurie became a cartoonist and professional illustrator as well as a writer.

[4] In a fascinating study of shame in Australian autobiography, *Shameful Autobiographies* (1999), Rosamund Dalziell convincingly teases out the Freudian story-behind-the-story of Lurie's relationship with his grandfather and father. She shows how *Whole Life* obliquely conveys that *zaydeh* transferred his love for his first son, who died of cholera, to Morris, who was named after that son, and that this contributed to the bitterness Lurie's father felt, inspiring an ambivalence towards his own child.

far her perception would have been shaped by ways of relating to children familiar to her from her own shtetl upbringing. In a scene where this gap in expectations is particularly evident, the child is sitting in the bath imagining that he is a shipwrecked sailor, mesmerised by the glass-like stillness of the water, when he is interrupted by an outraged *zaydeh*:

> Suddenly there's a noise, the handle rattles, the door crashes open. '*Er zitzt!* …' He sits! He has done nothing! He hasn't even washed! I am caught out, shamed, and before I can say a word seized, ordered this way and that, lift your arm up! lift your foot! (*Whole Life*, 62)

From the kitchen, the mother does not intervene; indeed elsewhere she is described as drying the boy in much the same impatient way, although (unlike *zaydeh*) without hurting him. Just as *zaydeh* 'orders' him to lift his arm, so earlier, the mother 'orders' him to get in the bath. There is no sense for either of them that the child is entitled to 'playtime', an idea that clearly informs the narrator's own perspective. A bath, as they see it, is for the child's health, *gesundheit*.

Drawing on interviews with Jewish immigrants to America, sociologists Mark Zborowski and Elizabeth Herzog (1974) write: 'Growing up is not a transition of the total child through graded phases. There is no nursery life in the shtetl, no kindergarten phase, no recognized period of adolescence' (330). Their account of childhood in the shtetl is of course constructed against the background of late twentieth-century American middle-class perspectives, according to which childhood is a distinctive phase worthy of attention and nurture in its own right. There is, I think, a close parallel to this contrast in the bath scene in *Whole Life*, where Lurie implicitly endorses the right of the child to daydream and repudiates not only his grandfather's rageful indignation, but also his mother's consent that he be interrupted in that way. Remembering her attitude to play, Lurie asks rhetorically, 'So are there games, can there be games? Mixing in a bowl. Taking out the peas. Helping. Helping is the games' (*Whole Life*, 100). *Whole Life* implies that this withholding of undiluted playtime is part of the mother's insatiable drive to work, which borders on the pathological; the interviews cited by Zborowski and Herzog suggest, however, that her approach would not have been idiosyncratic among the mothers she knew as a child.

Lurie evokes a 1940s suburban Australia where children spend most of their hours out of school playing. The contrast with his parents' household is revealing: on a typical afternoon he is 'mucking around' on the street with his friends, kicking stones in a state of 'pleasurable boredom' when a summons comes from the house: '*Ya Mum wants ya!*' When you had to go in. And after the bath, and after, the powder, being powdered – *Die puder!* – under this arm, this arm' (*Whole Life*, 114). Outside, a kid, he does what he feels like doing; inside, he succumbs to being bathed and powdered, something that would look babyish to his friends. In passages like this, Lurie highlights with retrospective irony the cultural differences between the two spaces he grew up in.

In *Alien Son*, Judah Waten, writing about a boyhood lived more than thirty years before Lurie's, recalls a similar tension between his Russian Jewish mother's emphasis on reading and study and Australian children's outdoor culture, tacitly sanctioned by other parents.[5] He describes the strange figure his mother cut as she would fetch him from his games to read to him:

> I liked to hear Mother read, but always she seemed to choose a time for reading that clashed with something or other I was doing in the street ... I would be playing with the boys ... kicking a football or ... flying a kite, when Mother would unexpectedly appear and without even casting a glance at my companions she would ask me to come into the house, saying she wanted to read to me and my sister. Sometimes I was overcome with humiliation and I would stand

---

[5] The scenes in Lurie and Waten's books compare interestingly with Hungarian-born Jewish Australian autobiographer Andrew Riemer's (1992) contrast between the disconcerting freedom of neighbours' children to come and go, and his parents' expectation that children be introduced to one another over cake and coffee by their parents.

listlessly with burning cheeks until she repeated her words. She never reproached me for my disobedience nor did she ever utter a reproof to the boys who taunted me as, crestfallen, I followed her into the house. (*Alien Son*, 171)

The mother's lack of response to her son's taunting friends signals both an otherworldliness and an unmovable quality. We learn that she was raised in a shtetl near Odessa, and in her youth trained as a nurse, joining a medical mission and taking part in the revolutionary movement of 1905. In Australia, she is fiercely opposed to what she sees as the indifference of the surrounding society to her ideals of serving humanity, and of intellectual and moral betterment through education. Waten writes: 'She emanated a kind of certainty in herself, in her view of life, that no opposition or human difficulty could shrivel or destroy' (*Alien Son*, 168). He evokes with humour and a lack of rancour that contrasts with the tone of grievance found at times in Lurie's memoir, what it was like to be caught between his mother's forceful worldview and the strong pull of his friends' more secular world.

The mother in *Alien Son* is a deeply singular character. She is a solitary figure within the Russian Jewish community, in which other mothers 'speak derisively' of her for refusing to settle down (*Alien Son*, 169). Yet her conflicts with the dominant culture outside the immigrant community point to the extent to which her way of being is cultural as well as particular. The following passage captures both these aspects; I quote at some length to give a sense of Waten's engagement with the different cultures of his childhood, and his mother's relationship to them. By way of supplementing her children's education, 'Mother' would take the narrator and his sister to music shops where she would request that records be played for them, ignoring the salesmen's rising impatience:

I was Mother's interpreter and I would ask one of the salesmen to play us a record she had chosen from one of the catalogues. Then I would ask him to play another. It might have been a piece for violin by Tchaikovsky … or an aria sung by Caruso.

With each visit Mother became bolder and several times she asked to have whole symphonies and concertos played to us. We sat for nearly an hour cooped up in a tiny room with the salesman restlessly shuffling his feet, yawning and not knowing what to expect next. Mother pretended he hardly existed and, making herself comfortable in the cane chair, with a determined, intent expression she gazed straight ahead at the whirling disc.

We were soon known to everyone at the shops. Eyes lit up as we walked in, Mother looking neither this way nor that with two children walking in file through the passageway towards the record department. I was very conscious of the humorous glances and the discreet sniggers that followed us and I would sometimes catch hold of Mother's hand and plead with her to leave the shop. But she paid no heed and we continued to our destination. The more often we came the more uncomfortably self-conscious I became and I dreaded the laughing faces round me.

Soon we became something more than a joke. The smiles turned to scowls and the shop attendants refused to play us any more records … Mother was not easily thwarted and without a trace of a smile she said we should talk to the manager. I was filled with a sense of shame and humiliation and with downcast eyes I sidled towards the entrance of the shop.

Mother caught up with me and laying her hand upon my arm, she said, 'What are you afraid of? Your mother won't disgrace you, believe me.' Looking at me in her searching way she went on, 'Think carefully. Who is right – are they or we? Why shouldn't they play for us? Does it cost them anything? By which other way can we ever hope to hear something good? Just because we are poor must we cease our striving?'

She continued to talk in this way until I went back with her. The three of us walked into the manager's office and I translated Mother's words.

The manager was stern, though I imagine he must have had some difficulty in keeping his serious demeanour.

'But do you ever intend to buy any records?' he said after I had spoken.

'If I were a rich woman would you ask me that question?' Mother replied and I repeated her words in a halting voice.

'Speak up to him', she nudged me while I could feel my face fill with hot blood.

The manager repeated his first question and Mother, impatient at my hesitant tone, plunged into a long speech on our right to music and culture and in fact the rights of all men, speaking in her own tongue as though the manager understood every word. It was in vain; he merely shook his head.

We were barred from shop after shop, and in each case Mother made a stand, arguing at length until the man in charge flatly told us not to come back until we could afford to buy records. (*Alien Son*, 183)

In passages like this one, written more than thirty years before works like American author Maxine Hong Kingston's *The Woman Warrior* (1976) established the contemporary genre of cross-cultural autobiography, Waten shows how the child of a transcultural family is forced into the difficult role of translator and go-between. The sense of humiliation he describes is integral to the experience. Critic David Carter (1990) observes that in *Alien Son* self-consciousness is seen as emblematic of the immigrant condition, but it would perhaps be more accurate to say that self-consciousness in the narrative epitomises the position of the child of immigrants (see v–xvi). For Waten's mother, by contrast, embarrassment is a foreign concept. The narrative captures the humour of the situation without diminishing the mother or rendering her eccentric. Indeed, Waten pays tribute to what was inspiring about her stance, while signalling how far the nature of her son's cross-cultural predicament was lost on her.

What narratives like Waten's and Lurie's can add to our understanding of the influence of particular cultural patterns of child rearing on individuals is the light they shed on the development of a person's 'cultural self' – or conflicting 'cultural selves' – from the inside. In different ways, *Whole Life* and *Alien Son* demonstrate the degree to which members of the same family may inhabit culturally different worlds, and how this tension can help to shape both the children's identities and their perceptions of who their parents are.

Works Cited

Besemeres, Mary. *Translating One's Self: Language and Selfhood in Cross-Cultural Autobiography.* Oxford: Peter Lang, 2002.

Carter, David. Introduction in J. Waten. *Alien Son* 1952. North Ryde, NSW: Angus & Robertson, 1990, v–xvi.

Dalziell, Rosamund. *Shameful Autobiographies: Shame in Contemporary Australian Autobiographies and Culture.* Melbourne: Melbourne University Press, 1999.

Freadman, Richard. 'Generational Shifts in Post-Holocaust Australian Jewish Autobiography.' *Life Writing* 1.1 (2004): 21–43.

Gunew, Sneja. *Framing Marginality: Multicultural Literary Studies.* Melbourne: Melbourne University Press, 1994.

Hoffman, Eva. *Shtetl: The History of a Small Town and an Extinguished World.* London: Vintage, 1997.

Kingston, Maxine Hong. *The Woman Warrior: Memoirs of a Girlhood among Ghosts.* New York: Vintage, 1976.

Lurie, Morris. *Whole Life: An Autobiography.* Melbourne: McPhee Gribble, 1987.

Myerhoff, Barbara, Deena Metzger, Jay Ruby, and V. Tufte. *Remembered Lives: The Work of Ritual, Storytelling, and Growing Older.* Ed. Marc Kaminsky. Ann Arbor: University of Michigan Press, 1992.

Quinn, Naomi. 'Child Rearing and Selfhood, or, Culture and Personality.' Paper presentation. Culture and Personality: Renewal and Revision in Contemporary Research. American Anthropological Association, Chicago, Illinois. 19–23 November 2002.

Riemer, Andrew. *Inside Outside*. Pymble, NSW: Angus & Robertson, 1992.

Waten, Judah. *Alien Son*. 1952. North Ryde, NSW: Angus & Robertson, 1990.

Zborowski, Mark, and Elizabeth Herzog. *Life Is with People: The Culture of the Shtetl*. New York: Schocken, 1974.

3

THE RADICAL POETICS OF THE GENDERED URBAN QUOTIDIAN: READING ANNA COUANI'S LITERARY EXPERIMENTALISM OF THE 1970S AND 1980S

ANNE BREWSTER

I

Anna Couani is an important iconoclastic writer whose main body of work, published in the late 1970s and throughout the 1980s, redefined the parameters of the Australian literary field. This article examines Anna Couani's formal experimentation which it locates within the gendered and cultural contexts of minoritisation. It examines how Couani's post-romantic critique of realism constitutes an exploration of subjectivity and identity formation. Her experimental fiction, I argue, in its efforts to defamiliarise reading conventions, articulates a crisis of belonging. In its radical poetics of the gendered everyday it seeks to locate the body in the alternative communities which characterise minority constituencies.

Anna Couani is a third-generation Australian; her parents were of non-Anglo backgrounds but were both born in Australia. Her maternal grandfather was Polish and her father's parents came from Kastellorizo, Greece. Her parents were involved in political activism in Australia and they visited the Soviet Union in the 1960s. Her father was involved in the Atlas Club (a Greek Communist Party club). Couani describes her mother as having an ambivalent relationship with the Greek community

46

because she was Polish and had an independent career. In an interview with Sneja Gunew (2000) Couani describes her mother as being 'assimilated to the point where she likes to believe that she is Anglo-Australian' (unpublished). She suggests that a number of factors, including their complex ethnicity and their understanding of their roles as women, meant that her family, like that of her mother's, were 'isolated'. She describes her own generation as being equivocal about its ethnic background. On the one hand it wanted to conform to the mainstream, and was critical of the traditional Greek community. On the other hand it was not totally accepted by the Anglo community. This made individuals such as herself become pro-Greek and anti-Anglo. She relates in the same interview with Gunew that within her own family there was a division between 'white wog' (her mother's Northern- European Polish side) and 'black wog' (her father's Southern-European Greek side).

Couani has remarked that during the 1960s she was looking for a community to which she could feel a sense of belonging. Her way of doing this was to identify with an alternative arts and literary community. She developed friendships with a number of writers such as Ken Bolton, Kris Hemensley and Robert Kenny and conceptual artists such as Neil Evans, who influenced her development as a writer. During the mid-1970s she was starting to develop her hallmark style as an experimental writer. Hemensley's experimental magazines *The Ear in a Wheatfield* (1972–76) and later *H/ear* (1980s) made a marked impact on Couani's development. Kenny published three of her books in his publishing series Rigmarole Books. In this article I undertake a chronological survey of Couani's *oeuvre* which spans 1977–89.[1] I examine the textual strategies of her literary experimentalism and how, for example, her interest in first-

---

[1] This article emerged from research undertaken for an entry on Couani in the 'Australian Writers 1975–2000' for the *Dictionary of Literary Biography* (Vol. 325) (New York: Thomson Gale, 2006) 53–58. Here, I would like to thank David Jardine for his excellent research assistance.

person and anti-realist modes persisted, albeit in slightly altered forms, throughout this period. In order to situate her experimentalism within the reading conventions of the period, I also survey the reception of her five literary books – *Italy* (1977), *Were All Women Sex-mad? & Other Stories* (1982), *Leaving Queensland and The Train* (1983), *The Harbour Breathes* (1989), and *The Western Horizon* (2004).

II

Her first book, *Italy*, was published by Rigmarole Books in 1977. It was heavily influenced by Couani's interest in the *nouveau roman*. As such it aims to comment upon the tradition of the realist novel. The short pieces discard the conventions of realist narrative and frustrate readerly expectations around closure, characterisation, point of view and description. In drawing on the narratively undramatic material of domestic life they stage a pointedly gendered investigation into and extension of the realist novel's interest in everyday life. If realist prose fiction has drawn on the category of the urban quotidian, and directs its attention to the process of urban modernisation, it does so through the textual elaboration of the interiority of the subject, that is through what one theorist has called the creation of a literary 'affective individualism' (Bell 2000). *Italy* talks to and critiques this tradition of character- and story-based narrative. In its short pieces the descriptive processes of realist fiction are used for very different ends. Realist prose fiction is characterised by an interest in detail, particularly in the expressive actions and vernacular styles of the body. *Italy*, however, mobilises the visual effects of description to produce quite different effects. The 'realism' of the conventional novel invokes truth effects through figural elaborations of concealment and secrecy. In realism the development of the characters' adventures produces in the reader a sense of intimacy with and proximity to them and their unfolding interior lives. However, *Italy's* interest in the visuality of description is quite different. The domestic, urban and coastal scenes, populated by sketchily drawn 'characters' are virtually devoid of plot or story or indeed any trace of narrative significance. Traditional gender roles are evacuated. This overall rhetorical effect of flatness and depthlessness is a feature of the *nouveau roman*. In realist prose fiction descriptive detail is used to invoke the social organisation of detail in the real world. As Susan Stewart (1984) argues, such organisation is always hierarchical (26); it thus works in concert with the teleological drive of narrative. As Stewart suggests, surface detail that is presented to us without hierarchy, as we see in Couani's prose, 'does not tell us enough and yet it tells us too much' (27).

Writing which interrupts the conventions of realist prose fiction exposes how the truth effects of this fiction work. It foregrounds the artefactuality of the genre and, in the process of defamiliarising our reading habits, exposes the *unreality* of realism. As Stewart argues, 'to describe more or less than is socially adequate ... [increases] the unreal effect of the real' (27). *Italy* thus foregrounds the realist strategies of conventional fiction. Pieces such as 'The View', for example, disrupt narrative point-of-view and ideas of looking and perspective. Joan Kirkby (1983), for example, notes in her chapter on Couani, there are many images of windows, balconies, rooms with views, mirrors, and hidden and detached observers in *Italy*. These can be seen to figure the condition of the divided, post-humanist self, and its self-reflective splitting. 'Detective Story' similarly self-consciously employs notions of narrative sense-making, allegories of reading and detection, and imagery of light and shadow (491–98).

Its female narrative pointedly suggests that women are detecting, that is, they are agents of naming and analysis. Another piece, 'what a man', is a repetitious poetic piece which works on sound and semantic strings of association. It activates the seductive lure of narrative as we strive to decipher the contour of a story in this associative list of monosyllabic words. The paratactical structure problematises the narrative closure.

It is clear that Couani's methodology in this first book, then, is self-reflexively literary and that it mobilises the generic conventions of the *nouveau roman* in order to critique realist fiction. During the decade or so of the publication of her literary books, there was a marked lack of engagement on the part of reviewers and essayists with Couani's literary antecedents and a narrow critical lexicon employed to assess Couani's experimentalism. Kirkby, for example, is representative of this period in judging Couani's experimental prose according to the conventions of realist prose, and finding the former inevitably 'constrain[ed]', 'confin[ed]' and 'circumscrib[ed]'. The images of limitation ironically reflect the narrow range of literary generic conventions according to which the work is judged. When Kirkby does refer to the *nouveau roman* it is to mention that it works to 'suppress subjectivity' and 'feelings'. It would be interesting to extend this observation to ask about the political and generic implications of denaturalising subjectivity. Similarly, while Harrison-Ford (1978), in an intelligent and favourable review of *Italy*, comments that the book demonstrates 'how terribly structured much "realist" fiction can be', and imagines that *Italy* functions as a 'corrective' (19), the discussion of the poetics of her experimental prose he does not develop further.

The pieces in *Italy* were written in 1974–75.[2] Many years later, in 1989, Couani described, in 'Author's Statement', her work during this

---

[2] Strangely enough, while *Italy* was inspired by Mediterranean architecture, landscape and light (hence the somewhat randomly chosen title), Couani had not yet travelled to the region when she wrote these pieces. She was to do so in 1978 and her next book, *Were All Women Sex-mad? & Other Stories* (1982), was written during this period of travel. Perhaps the title of this book can best be understood retrospectively, that is, by considering the significance of Italy as a signifier in Couani's later work and commentary. In the title story from *Were All Women Sex-mad? & Other Stories*, for example, Italy has a central symbolic role as the country of origin of the Italian woman unhappily married to the Russian, in Aunty Cis' story about her neighbours. The Italian woman's lover later asks her to meet him in Italy

period as 'striving for an effect of objectivity, perfection and stasis' (Brooks and Walker, 31). She said that 'this style was in some ways a self-protecting reaction to a hostile environment' (Brooks and Walker, 31). The 'hostile environment' no doubt refers both to the literary conservatism of the period and also to her ethnic and gendered difference. She resolved, in her next book, to adopt what she saw as an overtly feminist stance and to 'take the bull by the horns and adopt the maligned "female style" of first person use [and a] subjective/emotional stance' (Brooks and Walker, 31). Couani is, needless to say, careful to insist that the first-person narrative mode does not always 'mean you are writing about yourself' (Brewster, 33). While *Italy* bears traces of Couani's interest in oral genres (for example in the dialogue section of 'Untitled', and her references to family jokes ['Lovers', 48] and childhood stories), the title piece of *Were All Women Sex-mad? & Other Stories* (1982) develops further her interest in the oral genres of a gendered everyday life, particularly conversation.

(*Were All Women Sex-mad?*, 38) and this is the country where she eventually suicides. In this story then, Italy functions as a sign of desire – for a lost homeland or an impossible love. In an unpublished interview with Sneja Gunew in 2000, Couani states that 'I see Europe finishing at Italy … I think Greeks are really middle easterners and not Europeans at all' (*The Harbour Breathes*, 13*). Here Italy is a cypher for Europe. In personal correspondence, Couani has written:

> My actual experience with the Mediterranean countries when I wrote Italy was mostly based on my reading of writers who used that landscape and on my study of architecture … So I found myself with a manuscript which had a Mediterranean feel to it. I didn't really want to refer to any specific place (like Kastellorizo) because the places I described were mostly fictional and I'd never been there. I didn't want to refer to Greece either, so I used the word, Italy … It's a title in the tradition of Joe Brainard and that kind of American ironic thing. Not with a literal meaning, but with layers of meaning and not so serious. (Brewster 2004)

If realist prose fiction maps everyday life, it does so through the reproduction of particular forms of subjectivity. Couani's experimental prose, which also investigates the urban quotidian, produces temporal and spatial maps of urban life which rely more on narrative techniques such as conversation and dialogue than on plot and characterisation, as I suggest above. Her use of dialogue differs from that with which we are familiar in realist fiction. Couani's dialogue does not serve the interests of characterisation but is rather a vehicle for the elaboration of ideas. In the titular piece, for example, although speakers are identified and, as the narrative progresses, are linked in a web of friendships and relationships, they do not develop the 'three-dimensional' depth characteristic of realist fiction.

The dialogues of 'Were All Women Sex-mad?' are in fact more like monologues, in that they are sustained speeches or 'raves'. They focus largely on the gendered world of relationships: on romance, friendship, and the interactions of families and neighbours. The subjects of these relationships variously experience love, loss, migration and travel. Their conversations revolve around histories of intimacy and distantiation. The slowly unfolding web of memories and connections between the speakers constitutes an alternative community which expounds the values of freedom, cosmopolitanism and love, through talk. This alternative community overtly aims to evade the compulsions of reproductive heteronormativity.

This 'new Utopian lifestyle' gives centre stage to 'personal' issues and the development of personal ethics (*Were All Women Sex-mad?*, 49). As one character playfully puts it, their conversations constitute a 'School of Life' (22). One speaker talks about 'learning be independent'; 'making commitments to way of life without realising the consequences of those decisions' and 'doing the right thing with a sense of purpose' (49). Interestingly, these statements are couched retrospectively; the speaker is nostalgically recalling 'those days [when] I was so certain of what I was doing' (49). Nonetheless, the conversations and talk continue to proliferate, even if this 'new' utopianism has been eclipsed within the titular story by the inexorable march of time.

These speakers are immersed in passionate and urgent conversation. Their passion to 'talk about what's going on' (*Were All Women Sex-mad?*, 12) is seen to contrast markedly with the taciturnity, defensiveness, anti-intellectualism and cynicism of mainstream white Australian culture. In mainstream public culture, generally, people 'think conversation on a serious level is a joke' (30), one speaker suggests. If *Were All Women Sex-mad? & Other Stories* imagines a counter public-sphere of passionate, thoughtful talk in its various forms – conversation, gossip, jokes – it is essentially a sphere which foregrounds a self-conscious relationality. The enunciative positions in the titular story, for example, are always defined in relation to other people – in specific, intensely lived and felt engagements.

It is no surprise then that Couani's choice of narrative mode is that of the first person, whether in the form of direct speech, or occasionally (in the *other stories* of the collection) that of an omniscient narrator. Couani (1981) herself has said that she chose to use the first person because she wanted her work 'to feel immediate' (194). Certainly the choice of first person was also a political one; she was making a conscious decision to recuperate a 'maligned "female style" ' (Brooks and Walker, 31) that had been trivialised as 'too subjective, too emotional' (Couani 1981, 194). The personal voice (in its various modes) in *Were All Women Sex-mad? & Other Stories* performs the work of a recognisably *embodied* ethics. It foregrounds the lived contexts of events and the fact that the imperatives issuing from the body are always the products of intercorporeal and intersubjective exchanges.

If the pieces in *Were All Women Sex-mad? & Other Stories* constitute an alternative everyday life, like everyday life many of the conversations and monologues lack closure and continuity. The pieces convey the immediacy, the sense of potentiality and the dynamic, fluid and singular nature of everyday life. One speaker characterises their life as being marked by 'a sense of beginning everything rather than a sense of having to maintain everything' (49–50). Most of the pieces thus foreclose on any neat notion of closure or resolution in the speakers' lives. They remind us of the lack of neat narrative order and the repetitions of everyday life. As one character puts it: 'no-one ever seems to be able to co-ordinate with me so [that] we're both in love at the same time' (14).

By eschewing, in *Were All Women Sex-mad? & Other Stories*, the so-called neutral and objective narration that she employs in *Italy*, Couani nonetheless subscribes to a similar agenda: the intensely and intimately personalised enunciative positions of *Were All Women Sex-mad? & Other Stories* attempt to highlight the gendered and racialised specificities of cultural forms such as literature and to demonstrate that – to borrow Colebrook's (2002) words from another context – there is 'no point of view outside specific contexts and communities, no transcendent point of justification' (691). Yet in contrast with *Italy* – which some critics saw as representing alienation and isolation (Gunew 1994, 120) – *Were All Women Sex-mad? & Other Stories* focuses on the idea of community. It is clear that, during the 1970s and 1980s, Couani's experimental writing posed a critique of the exclusions of mainstream white Australian culture, particularly those of the publishing and literary industries. In convening an alternative literary imaginary she and other writers created alternative and feminist communities to counter their marginalisation, communities which aimed to foreground the cultural and political assumptions discursively reproduced in the reading habits of the mainstream literary community and the academy.

Experimental writing foregrounds the relation between literary producer and consumer, in that it promotes an active, participatory form of reading. Because it defamiliarises reading habits, it foregrounds the reading contract. We are reminded of the relative status, the hierarchy of literary genres and the value generated by different forms of literary production. In this way experimental writing foregrounds the social and material nature of literature – the (discursively and industrially) mediated nature of the relationship between literary producer and consumer. The relation between the two is a self-conscious aspect of Couani's literary practice; she commented that:

> It became obvious to me that reading, editing, book production and promotion, organising, teaching were all integral parts of the discourse and things I should pursue as actively as writing. (Brooks and Walker, 30)

Active participation within alternative literary and feminist communities as editors and small-press publishers, in parallel with their labour as writers, was a feature of other experimental writers' practice during the same period, as we see, for example, with many L=A=N=G=U=A=G=E writers in the United States in the 1970s. The alternative community of talk that Couani figures in *Were All Women Sex-mad? & Other Stories* found its counterpart in the real life community of experimental and feminist writers which she became part of in the 1970s.

During the mid-1970s Couani became committed to small-press publishing as a means of disseminating experimental writing. She edited the magazine of experimental writing, *Magic Sam* (1976–80) with Ken Bolton and a book series (initially also with Bolton) called Sea Cruise Books. From 1976–81 she published single-authored books by Joanne Burns, Ken Bolton, Denis Gallagher, Kris Hemensley, Robert Kenny and Kerry Leves; her own collection with Barbara Brooks, *Leaving Queensland & The Train* (1983); two anthologies of short, experimental Australian prose titled *Island in the Sun* (1980) and *Island in the Sun 2* (1981); and *The Harbour Breathes*, with Peter Lyssiotis, in 1989.[3] All her own books were published by small presses. She has commented that she saw the period between 1972 and 1975 as the heyday of small publishing in Australia and feels very disappointed by the subsequent decline in this

---

[3] This book is unpaginated so I have inserted my own page numbers with an * (asterisk).

industry in Australia (see Couani 1988 and 1990) and the domination of multinational presses.

In 1978 she became involved in the formation of the Poets' Union branch in Sydney. However, she found that this organisation was marked by the exclusion of women. As a result, in the early 1980s she became part of the Sydney Women Writers' Workshop which set itself up in reaction to the male-dominated Poets' Union. This feminist group, which also went by the name of 'No Regrets', produced three anthologies with that title in 1979, 1981 and 1985. It is clear that her feminist concerns inform *Were All Women Sex-mad? & Other Stories*. Couani (1988) has said that in the 1970s it was her and other feminists' goal to 'establish a female presence in print and in production' (10).

III

Just one year after *Were All Women Sex-mad? & Other Stories* her third book, *Leaving Queensland and The Train*, appeared (1983). The first half of the book is a collection of pieces by Barbara Brooks and the second, by Couani. The pieces in *The Train* continue to investigate the concerns of *Were All Women Sex-mad? & Other Stories*, such as Couani's interest in women's first-person narrative modes. In *The Train* these investigations take the form of talk/conversation, diary entries, dreams and first-person narration pieces which she has described as being 'like essays' (1981, 194). Many reflect on the writing process. However, in spite of the apparent transparency of the first-person address, they do not aim to configure a humanist self. They emphasise the performativity and rhetoricity of the self and foreground the link between representation and identity. In 'Talking with Another Writer', for example, the narrator says: 'no matter how you try and sneak up on it or reveal it, your 'self', what you really are, is always elusive' (*The Train*, 51). Language, the tool we wield in order to 'reveal' this self, to 'lay ... character bare' (52), is figured as a train which 'roar[s] past too fast for me to jump on' (52). There's always something left behind in our efforts to fix our experience in language.

In her third book Couani returns to her interest in realist description, in her discussion of the 'facts' that writing putatively records. She points to the crisis of the sign; the gap between signifier and signified. She identifies the function of figurative language in reinforcing the apparent literalness of its opposite, 'factual' language: 'the metaphor shields the facts, preserves them' (*The Train*, 73). In 'The Detective' she turns to the allegory of the detective in her analysis of reading and writing. Although 'there are mysteries in life', the narrator tells us, 'we have evidence if not comprehension of interpretation of the evidence' (56). 'The evidence', the detective-narrator assures us, 'is endless' (57). This narrator 'collects information', just as the writer – both of the realist novel and the *nouveau roman* – compiles description. In literature, description conveys the illusion of reality; by making things visible, as Susan Stewart suggests, narrative shapes the relationship between characters and their environments (25), and organises experience into events (22). The narrator of 'The Detective' parodies the privileging of the scopic regime, gazing at the 'facts' through a range of lenses including a camera, binoculars, opera glasses, spectacles, telescopes, drinking glasses and windows.

The detective is also an allegory of the process of memory. In *The Train* this theme develops into a key concern. Here Couani explores memory through the modes of reminiscence, 'essayistic' writing and dream. An earlier story, 'Were All Women Sex-mad?' is structured in a complex, cyclical form where stories and letters repeat themselves. The characters are travellers, searching (unsuccessfully) for love, a home and a sense of belonging. The past is the realm of travel, and the narrative motifs of repetition and return figure the constitutive reiterations of subject formation. Our relation to the past, as John Frow (1997) reminds us, is one of desire not truth (229). Further, our narratives of reminiscence and history provide a closure that is otherwise absent from experience and, as Stewart argues, outside the temporality of everyday life (Stewart, 22).

The detective, then, as the exemplary reader/writer, mines the everyday and transforms it through narrative. In many ways narrative has an ambivalent relationship with the everyday. The small qualitative changes of the everyday are oppositional to the periodic ruptures of history (Massumi 2002, 3) and the temporality of the novel. The everyday has been the subject of much theoretical investigation. Two other theorists whose mention of the flatness and boredom of everyday life is relevant to my discussion of Couani's anti-realist fiction, are Blanchot (1987) and Colebrook (2002). Claire Colebrook reminds us that everyday life is characterised by inaction, passivity, immobility, inertia and non-being (687–706). Blanchot also defines it as a realm of insignificance and boredom where there is nothing to know and nothing happens (12–20). This idea is playfully articulated in an earlier piece from *Italy*, the 'Starr Report'. Here the glamorous comic-strip journalist-heroine of the 1940s, like the detective, looks for the 'sweep of implication' of things, in other words, for narrative. Her friend, the suburban housewife, Sue-Ellen, by contrast, lives in the narrativeless everyday world of domesticity, surrounded by 'familiar and fond objects and spaces' (*Italy*, 57). Brenda Starr contrasts Sue-Ellen's apparent marginality in the private zone of the domestic with the intrigue, romance and mystery of the public work of investigative journalism. She admires what she imagines is the absence of anything important to describe or document, or indeed to think about, in Sue-Ellen's world: 'Everyday you see something like a row of bottles sitting quietly on a shelf without thinking, Aha! An everyday experience I hardly ever see, I'll note that down' (*Italy*, 57).

It is possible to read the 'Starr Report' on Sue-Ellen's life as a spoof on the reversals of Couani's own 'flat' *nouveau-romanesque* project and its critique of the teleology of realist fiction. Couani is as interested in the mundane, passive, routine aspects of a gendered everyday life as she is in its active aspects, even when they are not assimilated to narrative. Indeed, she is interested in the life of objects and how they affect the body as it occupies space. In her descriptions of objects – in their spatial dimensions, form and colour – Couani shows how they impact upon people, triggering feelings, thoughts, memories, intensities, meanings. She demonstrates the pervasive inter-relations of things and bodies.

Brian Massumi (2000), summarising William James, has commented that the relationality of subjects and objects 'registers materially in the activity of the body before it registers consciously' (196). He also argues that 'our awareness [of objects] is always of an already-ongoing participation in an unfolding relation' (196). I would suggest that the flat *nouveau-romanesque* prose of *Italy* and other pieces throughout Couani's *oeuvre* describe this zone of relationality. If, as Massumi suggests, 'participation precedes recognition' (196) then we can see that Couani's project as a writer is to map this zone of 'participation' and bodily 'awareness'. She is not interested in narratively elaborating the 'recognition' or the 'conscious registering' of objects as a story: this is the *métier* of the realist prose fiction writer. I (and others) have already commented on the predominance of images of looking and observing, through doors, windows, mirrors and rooms with a view in *Italy* and elsewhere in Couani's work. I would like to suggest that, in addition to the active looking of narrators and speakers, the objects which they behold also *actively* affect the reader/beholder. Just as *we* look at objects, so *they* act upon the reader/beholder. Couani's work thus foregrounds the ingressive nature of experience, that is, the quality of our being affected by objects.

Gail Weiss, in *Body Images* (1999), talks about the body's dual inward/outward orientation in terms of Merleau-Ponty's notion of reversibility. The body has both intracorporeal and intercorporeal relations – that is, it has relations with itself (for example between the various senses); it has relations with other bodies; and with its environment. All these relations are reversible. (For example, when we touch someone, we are both touched and touching). I am proposing that

Couani's prose describes the bodily immediacy of the relationality of subjects and objects, and the reversibility of this relationship: the fact that objects act upon us as much as we upon them. If the body is the locus of everyday life, it is also a primary source of 'evidence' about our relations with ourselves and about the world in which we live; in 'Myself' Couani writes 'I begin with my body as you do with yours' (*The Train*, 63). The second section of *The Train* comprises a number of interesting pieces about the reversibility of bodily relations. For example, in 'The Map of the World', she imagines that the body is a 'map of the world' which 'is felt from the inside' (64):

> Reading a globe of the world with its topography is relief. Reading with the fingers as though blind. Feeling it with the back, down the spine. Making contact with the nipples and the nose only. (*The Train*, 64)

This is an interesting moment of intracorporeal reversibility, where we *see* by *touching*, 'reading with the fingers as though blind'. Elsewhere, in 'The Mask', there is an example of the interface of environment and body, where the habits of memory are seen as bodily practices:

> Tonight as I was driving home I took the road I used to take on the way home from work. When I got onto that road, that particular stretch from the training school to the station and the shops, I remembered those times we drove down for lunch, to the pub after work, and all the other routine journeys home. The road now seems touching as though my body was moving along the surface of the road. (*The Train*, 70)

Like bodily relations, the text is reversible in that all textual elements are co-present, and the end is given at the same time as the beginning. (From this point of view the text differs from everyday life which is non-reversible and linear.) Memory, because it is textually mediated (and because it can be forgotten), is also reversible. In the titular piece of *The*

Train Couani deploys the image of the train in her figuring of memory. She describes the train as not just the past but as 'joined together from the past and through the present into the future'; it is 'our lives as they *run* together' (75; my italics). The images of movement, continuity and fluidity are interrupted, however, by imagery of stasis: in her memory/dream the train has stopped; and the phrase 'you can't run away from the past' is reiterated. The uneasy pun in the phrase, 'You said the train always *stands* for the past' (75; my italics), seems to embody this crisis of representation; the past is there but not there. It is static, enduring (fixed in memory, in images, in language) but it is moving (changing and being revised through the interminable transformations of *nachträglichkeit* – everyday life, in effect). This interruption in the figuring of the past is paralleled by the reversibility in *The Train* between sleep and forgetting, on the one hand, and dreaming and remembering on the other. These modes of being are discontinuous, oscillating. The troublingly ambiguous and contradictory figuration of the past is, I suggest, exemplary of the crisis of representation and the repetitions of identity formation. It is no coincidence that Couani earlier deploys the image of the train as a metaphor for the dismaying mobility of language; here 'the train's roaring past too fast for me to jump on' (52).

The Train received mostly negative reviews. For example, Liliana Rydzynski (1983) comments, in *Aspect*, that the language is 'commonplace' and the 'gaps' 'embarrassing' (68). Rydzynski scolds Couani and her writing for being immature, sad, confused, doubtful and uncertain. This kind of affective response is a telling index of the prohibition on straying from the orthodox and the conventional. Similarly Carolyn Gerrish (1983) describes the prose, in *Womanspeak*, as 'self-indulgent to the point of being ludicrous'; she describes it as 'shallow', 'alienating', 'egotistical' and solipsistic (27). Nonetheless, in the year that *The Train* appeared, Couani's work started to attract serious attention. In an article on the direction of short fiction in the 1980s, subtitled 'White Anglo-Celtic Male No More' (1983), Elizabeth Webby refers to a story, 'The Lace Curtain', from *Were All Women Sex-mad? & Other Stories*, as 'one of the best stories I have read for ages' (38) and a few months later in the same journal (*Meanjin*) Joan Kirkby (1983) published the first full-length article on her work titled ' "A Woman is Watching Things": The Work of Anna Couani'.

IV

I would argue that all Couani's work, in its investigation of cultural marginalisation and textual experimentation, exemplifies the condition of cultural/ethnic minoritisation. However, in the 1980s Couani engaged overtly with the politics of discursive multiculturalism.[4] Her fourth book of creative work, *The Harbour Breathes* (1989) combines text by Couani with photo montage by Peter Lyssiotis. It directly addresses issues of the exclusion and marginalisation of ethnic minority communities. Couani describes processes of their ruin, disintegration, displacement and being made invisible:

> Were these the first signs of disintegration or the signs of a community which contained them. The community was containing the changes but not the price rises. The next generation moved out to the west where housing was cheap and our city became the playground of the rich. In the western ghetto the characters become invisible and so does their plight. (*The Harbour Breathes*, 8*)

Couani suggests that there are two forces impacting upon local communities. Firstly, there is the 'anglo elite' which causes 'everything [to be] swept aside and away ... submerging people like us' (*The Harbour*

---

[4] In 1988 Couani and Sneja Gunew edited a collection of experimental women's writing titled *Telling Ways*, which included multicultural writers. In the 1980s Couani's work was being taken up by multicultural theorists such as Gunew who included Couani in her 1983 and 1988 articles on multicultural writers. In 1988 Gunew published an anthology of multicultural women's writing titled *Beyond the Echo*. Although Couani's work was not represented in the anthology it was dedicated to her (along with two other women) as a 'pioneer' (of multicultural women's writing).

Breathes, 29*). Secondly they experience 'wave upon wave of americana' which 'battered [us] with information' and 'cut [us] off from our own cultures' (21*). This produces a sense of separation and atomisation:

> Through the window we stare at the separate roofs, the separate backyards, the separate fences, the separate shops, the separate street light, the separate streets, the separate factories. Separate. Separate. Separate. (*The Harbour Breathes*, 47*)

While the text of *The Harbour Breathes* to some extent mourns the transformation of immigrant communities through urbanisation, it is also a testament to the resilience and persistence of these communities, their memories and stories. Although they do not (yet) have the formal status of history, these memories and stories continue to resonate, embedded as they are within the lived fabric of everyday life:

> Everything we've ever done is busted up. Every token and sign of our activity has been smashed. Our work isn't tangible or documented but it's been done and it's taking effect. (*The Harbour Breathes*, 21*)

These memories and stories survive and 'take effect' through the urban practices of everyday life. In the interface and interchange between city and bodies, the flows and events that constitute the community are enacted. As Couani suggests, in *The Harbour Breathes*, 'the community was containing the changes' (7*) and the city itself is figured as an accommodating, bodily and mobile entity; it is old and has memories; it 'lives and breathes' (32*), it 'has feelings' (11*), it 'folds us in / opens up a space to rest' (29*). The fold is an important metaphor here for the generative relationship between body and city: 'our history shapes us / in the fold' (27*). The city is not 'just geography' (31*) but 'our lives ... softly colliding' (31*). So the bodily memories of the interface between city and people are constantly recuperated in the practices of the everyday despite their elision by the discourses of pedagogical nationalism.

Once again, Couani's narrator foregrounds the role of description in the literary enterprise of mapping the urban quotidian, insisting that 'description is my anchor' (*The Harbour Breathes*, 35*). In everyday life 'big moments ... pass by ungrasped' (44*) and it is the simple things, the 'collection[s] of objects' (48*) that are the site of our 'absorption' in the everyday:

> The vastness of the sky, the smallness of the city. The small dot on the map of the world. The seething self-absorption of this microdot. Our world – a few streets, some buildings, a couple of trees and bushes, a small group of people, some machinery, a collection of objects. (*The Harbour Breathes*, 48*)

As in her other work, first-person narration is deployed in *The Harbour Breathes*. Couani is apparently critical of this mode of narration, stating that:

> That's ancient history to me now, that personal approach to writing. Now I like to write about the things happening around me not to me. (*The Harbour Breathes*, 416*)

However, given that the piece these lines are drawn from is much concerned with the 'ancient' (and, for example, its distinction from the 'old'), it is possible to read the description 'ancient history' as a comment on the embeddedness of the rhetoric of the personalised self within literature and its persistent discursive reproduction. Couani uses the first-person narrator in various different pieces throughout *The Harbour Breathes* so in spite of her apparent ambivalence it is clear that she considers that it can still do useful literary work. I have argued that in her earlier work she constantly undermines notions of a humanist self. Even the first-person self is seen as emphatically textual rather than self-evident, unmediated or identical to itself. In this way her work foregrounds the constructedness of identity and the post-romantic idea of an unstable, fragmentary subjectivity. The first-person narrators shift even within one piece of writing as indeed they do throughout *The Harbour Breathes*, where the first-person narrator, as Scott McQuire (1989) comments, is 'never singular' (17).

Moreover in the specific detail of their lives and conversations the first-person narrators are embodied and contextualised: the site of the enactment of social relations and power asymmetries. In the insertion of the body, through description, into the text, Couani emphasises Colebrook's point that the body is not reducible to 'an intentional subjectivity': it is 'an assemblage ... of competing [racialized and gendered] affects and powers' (703). The fragmentary and partial maps of subjectivity that these interrupted, discontinuous narratives present to us, indicate the immediate, incomplete and dynamic nature of the body and the reversible nature of its relations with its urban environments in its performances of everyday life.

The Harbour Breathes received about a dozen reviews. There were the usual complaints, for example when reviewer Freda Freiberg (1990), in *Agenda*, commented that Couani's text was 'banal' *and* 'obscure' (31) – an interesting combination! Generally, however, the book met with acclaim. Scott McQuire described it as 'a remarkable and innovative experiment' (16). It received two substantial review-articles – by McQuire (1989) and Hatzimanolis (1995). Generally, many reviewers were still puzzling over the nature of Couani's project and a number were uncomfortable about the lack of a clearly delineated relationship between the visual images and the text (for example, Strauss and Raines). McQuire describes the cross-generic nature of the book most usefully, saying that it 'resists easy classification' and 'actively fashions a new textual space for itself' (17).

In her radical poetics of the urban quotidian, a poetics which foregrounds the racialized and gendered projects of nationalism, Couani's work redraws the boundaries of the field of Australian literature. In particular it interrupts the stereotyping, in the 1970s and 1980s, of multicultural writing as unmediated speech, as Gunew has argued (see

1983, 1986, 1990 and 1994). Hatzimanolis similarly suggests that Couani's writing and practice as a small publisher crucially raises issues of 'ethnic women's material and discursive access to the category "authorship" ' (91).

This stereotyping has reserved the category of aesthetics for Anglo-centric writing and relegated multicultural writing to that of sociology and history, as Gunew argues. Couani's self-reflexively literary project, as I suggest, directly intervenes in this taxonomy of Australian literature. If Couani has characterised herself as a marginalised writer (Brooks and Walker, 30–31), this marginalisation is produced both by her racialized, political and gendered 'otherness' but also by her experimentalism as a writer. I have commented upon the frequently hostile or puzzled reception of her work. Many critics and reviewers, when assessing Couani's work, admit to a certain 'difficulty' in reading it. This is without exception seen as a failing. For some, any disturbance or challenge to conventional reading habits is registered as aggressive and anti-social. For example, one reviewer, Helen Daniel (1988), of *Telling Ways* (1988), a collection of experimental women's writing which Couani edited with Sneja Gunew, regrets that 'respect for the reader' – which for her is 'a fundamental courtesy of good writing' (10) – has gone by the wayside.

It is interesting to trace in the anxiety of these remarks the disturbance Couani's work produces both within the aesthetic domain, and, by extension, within the public sphere of national memories and futures. We could characterise Couani's literary subjectivity as that of an anti-assimilationist 'non-Anglo' writer. One of the problems with the label 'non-Anglo' is, however, as Gunew (1992) suggests, its negative definition. She argues instead for imagining 'cultural difference in a non-binary manner' (1992, 45). Despite the fact that Couani herself commonly used the term, she has also made the comment that her own marginalised position is 'informed by a number of different threads, more complex than Anglo or non-Anglo' (1992, 98). There are two issues here. Firstly that there are convergences and divergences which link different racialized groups in configurations outside the narrow Anglo/non-Anglo binary. Secondly, there are cultural representations other than race which come to bear on subject- and identity-formation (for example: class, religion, generation, gender, sexual preference, region, political persuasion etc.). Perhaps one way to imagine this multiplicity of difference is in Couani's remark in *The Harbour Breathes* that Sydney is a 'middle eastern city' (16*). In this simple statement we can see that Sydney is simultaneously many different things for many different people; that it is characterised by the co-presence of a spectrum of pasts and futures. These pasts and futures of course do not exist in a state of benign harmony, however. As *The Harbour Breathes* demonstrates, the city is a site of contestation.

Anna Couani, I have suggested, is a writer whose work throughout the 1970s and 1980s, was often met with incomprehension. (Her most recent work is an ongoing serial internet novel, *The Western Horizon*). In many ways the literary and academic community during this period did not have the critical tools to evaluate her experimental poetics. During the late 1980s and 1990s there was a slow but sustained development of a more productive interest in her work, which resonated with the concerns of contemporary literary and cultural theory and with feminist theory. Issues that I have identified in this article are gendered everyday life, the body and a post-humanist, post-romantic subjectivity. These textual strategies and interests as elaborated in Couani's work, I suggest, disrupt pedagogic discourses of national homogeneity and unification. They portray the nation as a decentred, pluralistic site of competing histories.

Works Cited

Bell, Michael. *Sentimentalism, Ethics and the Culture of Feeling*. New York: Palgrave, 2000.

Blanchot, Maurice. 'Everyday Speech.' *Yale French Studies* 73 (1987): 12–20.

Brewster, Anne. Interview with Anna Couani. *Hecate* 31.1 (2005): 31–42.

——. Personal communication. 31 January 2004.

Brooks, Barbara and Anna Couani. *Leaving Queensland and The Train.* Glebe, NSW: Sea Cruise, 1983.

Brooks, David, and Brenda Walker, eds. *Poetry & Gender.* St Lucia: University of Queensland Press, 1989.

Colebrook, Claire. 'The Politics and Potential of Everyday Life.' *New Literary History* 33 (2002): 687–706.

Couani, Anna. *The Western Horizon.* 2004. Available at: seacruise.ath.cx/annacouani/westernhorizon/index.htm

——. 'Writing from a Non-Anglo Perspective.' In *Striking Chords: Multicultural Literary Interpretations.* Eds Sneja Gunew and Kateryna O. Longley. North Sydney: Allen & Unwin, 1992: 96–98.

——. 'Feminism and Publishing.' *Australian Women's Book Review* 2.2 (June 1990): 13–14.

——. 'Anna Couani: Author's Statement.' In *Poetry & Gender.* Eds. David Brooks and Brenda Walker. St Lucia: University of Queensland Press, 1989, 30–31.

——. 'Women in the Literary Small Presses.' In *Telling Ways: Australian Women's Experimental Writing.* Eds Anna Couani and Sneja Gunew. Adelaide: Australian Feminist Studies, 1988, 9–14.

——. *Italy and The Train.* Melbourne: Rigmarole, 1985.

——. *Were All Women Sex-mad? & Other Stories.* Melbourne: Rigmarole, 1982.

——. 'Anna Couani: Author's Statement.' *Australian Literary Studies* 10.2 (October 1981): 194–95.

——, and Damien White. *Island in the Sun 2: An Anthology of Recent Australian Prose.* Sydney: Sea Cruise, 1981.

——, Damien White and Tom Thompson. *Island in the Sun: An Anthology of Recent Australian Prose.* Sydney: Sea Cruise, 1980.

——. *Italy.* Melbourne: Rigmarole, 1977.

Couani, Anna and Peter Lyssiotis. *The Harbour Breathes.* East Burwood, Victoria: Masterthief Enterprises, 1989.

Daniel, Helen. 'Radical Twitches at Excellence.' *The Weekend Australian* 8–9 October 1988: 10.

Freiberg, Freda. Review of *The Harbour Breathes*, by Anna Couani. *Agenda* 10 (1990): 31.

Frow, John. *Time and Commodity Culture: Essays in Cultural Theory and Postmodernity*. Oxford: Clarendon, 1997.

Gerrish, Carolyn. Review of *The Train*, by Anna Couani. *Womanspeak* 8.1 (August–September 1983): 27.

Gunew, Sneja. 'Migrant Women Writers.' *Meanjin* 42.1 (Summer 1983): 16–26.

——. 'Ania Walwicz and Antigone Kefala: Varieties of Migrant Dreaming.' *Arena* 76 (1986): 65–80.

——. 'Home and Away: Nostalgia is Australian (Migrant) Writing.' *Island in the Stream: Myths of Place in Australian Culture*. Ed. Paul Foss. Leichhardt: Pluto, 1988, 35–46.

——. 'Denaturalizing Cultural Nationalisms: Multicultural Readings of "Australia".' *Nation and Narration*. Ed. Homi K. Bhabha. London; Routledge, 1990, 99–120.

——. *Framing Marginality*. Carlton, Victoria: Melbourne University Press, 1994.

——. Unpublished interview with Anna Couani. 2000.

——, and Kateryna O. Longley, eds. *Striking Chords: Multicultural Literary Interpretations*. North Sydney: Allen & Unwin, 1992.

Harrison-Ford, Carl. 'A Sense of Process.' Review of *Italy*, by Anna Couani. *The Sydney Morning Herald* 19 August 1978: 19.

Hatzimanolis, Efi. 'Ethnicity, in Other Words: Anna Couani's Writing.' *Southerly* 2 (Spring 1995): 91–99.

Kirkby, Joan. ' "A Woman is Watching Things": The Work of Anna Couani.' *Meanjin* 42.4 (Summer 1983): 491–98.

Massumi, Brian. *Parables of the Virtual: Movement, Affect, Sensation*. London: Duke University Press, 2002.

——. 'Too-Blue: Colour-Patch for an Expanded Empiricism.' *Cultural Studies* 14.2 (2000): 177–226.

McQuire, Scott. 'Refolding the City: Alienation at the Centre.' *The Age Monthly Review* 9.6 (September 1989): 16–18.

Rydzynski, Liliana. Review of *The Train*, by Anna Couani. *Aspect* 28 (Spring 1983): 66–68.

Stewart, Susan. *On Longing: Narratives of the Miniature, the Gigantic, the Souvenir, the Collection*. Baltimore: Johns Hopkins University Press, 1984.

Webby, Elizabeth, 'Short Fiction in the Eighties: White Anglo-Celtic Male No More?' *Meanjin* 1 (Autumn 1983): 34–41.

Weiss, Gail. *Body Images: Embodiment as Intercorporeality*. London: Routledge, 1999.

4

RE-VIEWING AND RE-SITUATING GREEK-AUSTRALIAN WOMEN'S WRITING[1]

KONSTANDINA DOUNIS

> What if ... we forgot who we are
> became lost in this absence emptied of memory
> we, the only witness of ourselves ... (Kefala 1992, 104)

My commitment to appraising what we might term *other* literatures began in 1990 when my preoccupation with concepts of identity, belonging, homeland, together with my love of literature, led me to focus on writings that emanated from *elsewhere*. Given that I am bilingual in Greek and English, Greek-Australian literature inevitably assumed a primary focus. Because first-generation writers of Greek background invariably wrote in the Greek language they were all but absent from any sort of official, literary associated discourse: book reviews, anthologies, awards, grants. Those of us who were bilingual and bicultural and who could therefore attest to the plethora of fine works being written in other languages in this country, found the following sweeping assertion in *The*

---

[1] Lovingly dedicated to the memory of my mother, Sophia Dounis (1934–2007). On the evening of the 15th of August 2007, my mother and I spoke at length over the phone as we always did. This was to be our last conversation. She died, very suddenly, in the early hours of the following morning. She was the most honourable, loving, wise and thoroughly beautiful person that I have ever met. That I was blessed with such a mother was a rare privilege and a stroke of extraordinary providence. May her memory be eternal.

Oxford History of Australian Literature (Kramer, 1981) unnervingly vacuous: 'the diversification of personal histories that we would expect to result from the influx of migrants from many countries of the world has not yet become a marked feature of Australian writing' (18).

I would suggest that the reason for this absence was not any precarious notion of perceived lack of quantity or quality, but the symbiotic relationship between underlying hegemonic structures that excluded all but Anglo-Celtic writings and the ensuing lack of structural support for literary translation into English. Having your works translated into the lingua franca of this country means that you at least have a fighting chance of entering the mainstream literary arena, thereby imperceptibly weaving some new colour and texture into Australia's literary and cultural tapestry. As Sneja Gunew (1994) was to write some years ago:

> It is not that ethnic minorities are invisible in Australian discursive formations, but that they are positioned only in certain areas: sociology, oral history, welfare legislation etc. They are consistently hailed into being as speaking subjects but not as writing subjects. (60)

In a bid to address the imbalance, to assist in the emergence of so many fine writers from the margins, several conferences were convened in the early 1990s onwards on Greek-Australian literature, each forum attracting both writers and academics from all parts of Australia.[2] Several academics came from overseas, so interested were they in this attempt at inclusion of the *other* in national discourses. Moreover, anthologies of Greek-Australian literature began to surface, two of which were bilingual in Greek and English and therefore promised the tremulous possibility of transgressing the boundaries of the Greek community (see Kanarakis

---

[2] These conferences were convened by the Modern Greek Department of Phillip Institute, Melbourne, the first being held in 1986.

1987; Spilias and Messinis 1988).[3] However, as important and well intentioned as these publications were, they raised other fundamental concerns. As a female academic it became increasingly and glaringly apparent to me that just as hegemonic structures were excluding immigrant writers in 'multicultural Australia' from participating within national literary parameters, so too were deeply entrenched patriarchal codes excluding women writers from just about everywhere. Layer upon layer of engendered marginalisation – within the wider community, within their specific ethnic community – rendered them virtually invisible.

It was in response to this fundamental concern that I convened a conference on Greek and Greek-Australian Women's Writing in 1992 (see Dounis 1994). It showcased the works of over fifty Greek-Australian women writers who travelled from all over Australia to partake and read their works. This empowering experience led my colleague Helen Nickas and me to compile the anthology *Retelling the Tale* (1994) that told the story of migration through the women's own perspective and in their own words. As editors we expressly wanted these immigrant women writers depicted as a writing subject; our passion for inclusion perennially informed by the notion that 'we never hear *her* speak, she is always spoken for; she is, in other words a palimpsest, written over with the text of other desires' (Gandhi, 181).

Helen Nickas then went on to establish Owl Publishing and the Writing the Greek Diaspora Series which continued in this vein of giving first-generation immigrant writers a voice through bilingual publications that were meticulously edited and translated within publications that were aesthetically beautiful. The 1990s were a very productive time, buffeted as they were by a socio-political climate where multicultural

---

[3] Despite their limitations where women's writings were concerned, both were ground breaking publications that imbued the multicultural dialogue of the time with a much enriched discourse.

structures were, at worst, paid lip-service to and, at best, exhilaratingly reflected through avenues that actually enhanced a multifarious cultural landscape.

Fast-forward to 2005. I begin doctoral research in the area of diasporic literatures after a self-imposed exile into the wonders of motherhood and a literal 'exile' of sorts overseas. I return to the academic arena full of passion for my subject area and a thirst to reacquaint myself with current theoretical trends and their associated societal reflections. It becomes readily apparent that the heady and nationally sanctioned multiculturalism of the 1980s and 1990s has given way to the amorphous giddiness of globalisation and the scourge of economic rationalism. Assimilation is once again aligned with patriotism, while the concept of multiculturalism is being seriously denounced as divisive and, most bizarrely, as 'un-Australian'. Greek-Australian women writers are still precariously situated within numerous margins, still inexplicably absent from current anthologies and funding for literary translations into English is all but non-existent. Carole Ferrier's (1985) poignant comment, made over twenty years ago in reference to the dearth of women's writings published at that time, came back to haunt me: 'much more needs to be done to make available lost or unpublished material ... the work of making accessible the basic material for serious study and analysis of these women writers has hardly begun ...' (5).

And so, my research into Greek-Australian women's writing stems from my unstinting belief in the imperative of what Hodge and Mishra (1991) have referred to as the 'intervention of the uncanonised' (203). Furthermore, as a means of facilitating this process, I have been singularly preoccupied with translation from Greek into English – particularly of first-generation Greek-Australian women writers who perceive keenly their exclusion from this country's collective discourse, their feelings beautifully encapsulated in surrealist prose writer Tzoumakas' (2005) terse declaration, 'I write in a dead language' (44). And so, through the *transferrings across* that the regenerative properties of translation facilitates, let's 're-view' the thematic heterogeneity of first- and second-generation Greek-Australian women writers through the power and beauty of their 'own words'.

First-generation Greek-Australian women – that is, those who came in their thousands upon thousands in response to Australia's mass migration push in the 1950s, 1960s and 1970s – worked unbelievably hard. They laboured side by side with their male compatriots in every conceivable job from the most menial and hazardous in the ubiquitous nation-building factories through to the responsibilities of running a plethora of small businesses in urban and rural areas. In her short story 'Deception', Dina Amanatides (1994) encapsulates the plight of a poverty stricken young girl living in a small Greek village who must bow to patriarchal pressures and marry a much older man who had returned momentarily to his homeland to choose a wife. She follows him to Australia and helps him run a small hotel in rural Victoria:

> All the rooms have to be swept daily, the wash basins and the toilet bowls must be left gleaming. They have a cook; they can't afford cleaners as well ... Believe it or not, she had her second child just to escape the chores and responsibilities for a week, resting in the peace and quiet of the hospital. (19)

Amanatides herself worked in numerous factories, a fact well documented in numerous poems, and most poignantly expressed when interviewed by Helen Nickas (1992):

> Without a knowledge of English, my sister and I could not hope to find anything apart from manual work in factories. That was a nightmare. Standing near those huge furnaces where the rubber was burning. Later on I worked in a stocking factory which was a breeze compared with the rubber factory. There I was even able to write poems and short stories. (191)

When Tes Lyssiotis' play 'I'll Go to Australia and Wear a Hat' was first performed in the late 1980s, it highlighted the work ethic of Greek immigrant women both through the power of the dialogue and the impact of the visual metaphor. Successive work environments were depicted ranging from that of clothing manufacturing factories through to assembly plants, the laboriousness underscored throughout by the repetitive movements and sounds emanating from the actresses and punctuated by the cacophonous wailing of the machinery.[4]

Rather than black-clad objects of derision or semiotic signposts of folkloric curiosities, first-generation Greek women emerge from these writings as strong, capable, witty and, dare I say it, attractive. Jeana Vithoulkas' prose piece 'The Artist's Daughter' (1994) is a beautifully crafted short story, funny and insightful, where preconceived formations of the aforementioned variety are progressively deconstructed. The narrator's mother takes centre stage and is depicted as opinionated, intuitive and alluring. She is writing a novel about her family's tribulations during the German occupation of Greece and attracts a wide circle of admirers. In the following passage Vithoulkas deftly weaves her way through notions of class, work ethics and the tremulous foundations of literary canonical foundations:

> Someone once compared her to Tolstoy. This was a mistake.
>
> 'Don't insult me', she said. 'He's so pompous and all those dreadful chapters in Anna Karenina where Levin is agonizing over the state of the world and his own mind just tries any reader's patience … And he has no understanding of women.' To my mother Tolstoy was a guy who wrote a book; told a story. It hadn't been drummed into her that he was a 'great' author who should be revered. Since no one had read Anna Karenina, including the poor unenlightened person who thought he was paying her a compliment, no one could argue with her.

---

[4] This as yet unpublished play was first performed at La Mama Theatre, Melbourne, in 1982.

She never finished (her novel). The truth is she never had time. Whichever poet it was that said it was mostly inspiration lied. The little perspiration required was spent over sewing machines in the sweat shops of the inner suburbs where her youth was measured by clocking cards and the time and motion methods which placed an economic value on how long she spent in the toilet. (180)

Because Greek immigrants tended to settle in Australia's major cities, one can often overlook the fact that significant numbers settled in rural areas – particularly so as a legacy of official accommodation camps such as Bonegilla, for example. Vasso Kalamaras' play *The Bread Trap* (1986) revolves around Chrysa, a young educated Greek woman who is brought out to Australia in the 1950s to be reunited with her family who had migrated several years before. Much to her dismay, life in the new country involved nothing but working endless hours on the family's tobacco farm in the 'middle of nowhere' – the insurmountable loneliness further intensified by linguistic isolation and the constrictions of culturally endemic patriarchy. Paradoxically, the only salvation comes within the very landscape that engenders her enshrouding alienation, its harsh beauty encapsulated in passages of extraordinary lyricism. Indeed, Greek-Australian women writers have written many poems inspired by the Australian bush. The omission of this 'other's gaze' from narrative threads portraying Australia's rural landscape reflects a certain tepidity in representation. The following stanzas are by Zeny Giles (2005):

Your mountains and your waterfalls
Won't fit inside my camera
And here upon this peak
encircled by immensity,
my dizzy mind can't grasp you.
Your land was made
for some great breed of giants
and while no serpent stings,

I fear you could crush me with a rock
or freeze me in your ice-blue stillness.

What comfort then to walk within your glades
beneath the canopy of filtered light
to see the green glow bright from leaves and ferns
and ragged trails of old man beard.
To feel the spongy moss on trunks and path
And drink from waterfalls that fit cupped hands. (48)

Moreover, in the bilingual picture book *Zorro, the Adventures of an Australian Terrier* (2006), Ekaterini Mpaloukas deftly establishes the interconnectedness between urban and rural immigrant dwellers through the adventures of a beloved little dog, the narrative highlighted through the landscapes of the accompanying paintings:

> Zorro is an Australian terrier. Yiota's Godmother gave Zorro to her on her sixth birthday. He was born at Yarra Junction where Yiota's Godmother runs a farm. Zorro is very playful and friendly with children. (8)

Greek immigrant women not only generated a sizeable chunk of the family income, they also single-handedly engaged in what we might term traditional women's work within the home. Apart from all the cooking and cleaning, they sewed clothes, embroidered tapestries; they perpetuated all manner of rituals associated with marriages, christenings and funerals from Greek dancing to dirges for the dead. Unsurprisingly, Greek-Australian women writers have celebrated these activities in a multifariousness of style and theme. Moreover, the most moving portraits are those of second-generation writers whose prose and poetry entail the imperative of recollection and reappraisal:

> We cooked for the inevitable feasting a week in advance ... the smell of woodsmoke laced with orangeflower water exuded by our trays of warm golden glazed koulouria ... So prolific did we become that we

established a production line to transform our narrow rolls of pliable butter-rich biscuit dough into the finished product. Double braids of dough to denote unity, circles to denote life ... The baking frenzy gave way to the dying of the eggs and the making of tarama with proper fish roe, begged from a local Greek family with access to the real thing not that pink commercial version. Finally there was the preparation of the avgolemono soup ... This was to be the basis of our breakingthefast repast on our return from church after midnight mass on Easter Saturday night. It was then that we could contest the strength of our eggs against those of others ... Having the strongest egg would seal our good fortune for the year to come. Hardly surprising that my year has always started symbolically with Easter rather than with January. (Nihas 74–75)

The night before, Mum prepares koliva, a mixture of boiled wheat, breadcrumbs, walnuts, covered by a layer of icing sugar and decorated with slivered almonds; puts the prosforo she has bought from the bakery next to her bag so as to not forget it, and writes a list of the dead. Yesterday she added the name Georgia, her oldest sister. Georgia died on Wednesday ...

I do not go into the church even though they are my dead too.

I sit in the car.

And wait ...

By eating koliva, you merge your flesh with that of your loved ones. You embrace them. Sins and all ...

Today it's hot – the church doors are open and my car window is right down.

The psalm beckons me.

And even though I am tempted for the first time to go into the church, I don't.

Yesterday while I made dinner, Mum slivered almonds and sifted the icing sugar. In a few years, I will prepare the koliva. Buy the bread. Write the list. (Tsaconas, 232–33)

The following stanzas from Angela Costi's poem entitled 'Dancing Through Mirrors' (2003) is not just a descriptive piece capturing the vitality of Greek dance – as important as such documentation is in itself lest we become 'emptied of memory' – but an extraordinary evocation of the propensity of dance to bridge nationally entrenched divides:

and as she danced
hips, lap lap lapping
a lacework of water patterns
from belly to breasts
arm pits to thighs
weaving an invite to warm lakes
for poor swimmers

she is as Greek
as I am Turkish
I accept her invitation
of hip bone and song
we dance the same history
and our seduction is fierce ...
and we always dance through mirrors
wearing ancestral father's victory grin
plucking ancient mother's eyebrows
our skin of rippling lakes
now the tosses and turns of wave
the scythe turns paddle in my hands
olive leaves are branching in her hair ... (14–15)

The tangible locus of this poem is the ongoing conflict – alternately obvious and subtle – between Greece and Turkey. The bitter rivalry between the two nations dates back to over a thousand years ago reaching its apotheosis, at least in contemporary sensibility, in the schism such as exists in modern-day Cyprus. From the palpable manifestation of this schism, 'we break one plate into two even pieces', through to the intermingling of bodies within the encircling metaphor of the dance, there is a heightened sense of the notion of borders. Ien Ang (2003) notes that borderlands 'are not the relatively free spaces where through some magical process the tension between two (or more) cultures is resolved, on the contrary, they are spaces where those tensions, formed by prevailing hierarchies and relations of power are intensified' (37). This line of tension, manifested in its geographical form in Cyprus, creates a space for itself in the conceptualisation of the 'imaginary homeland' as perceived by Greek and Turkish migrants wherever they might have settled. Within this space, the ritual of the dance – a *tsifteteli*, the shared movements of which conjoin both Greek and Turkish cultures – becomes a site of potential cohesion. This primordial common denominator, entrenched in the collective unconscious, enhances points of connection, rather than difference, Costi's sublime poetry weaving words and bodies in an erotically and electrically charged intoxicating mix.

One of the most complex themes through the prism of the diasporic experience is the experience of motherhood. The post-1950s mass migration gave rise to a plethora of women dealing with the concept of a mother who was markedly absent. I use the qualifier 'markedly' deliberately as there are certainly degrees of absence depending on the space occupied within unfolding socio-historical events. Telecommunications were meagre some fifty years ago, particularly in terms of communicating with remote villages back in Greece. The only tangible link was the written letter, the precarious fate of which was sorely tested by the comparative level of illiteracy of loved ones back home, together with the month and half it needed to reach its destination. Because of the uncertainty of this tremulous form of connection, it is no wonder that the letter attained a metaphoric spectrum that ranged from elation to the bleakness of utter despair. 'The postman brought the rain in an envelope,[5] writes Dina Amanatides

---

[5] This is one of 200 poems by Dina Amanatides that I have selected and translated from the original Greek into English. They form part of my doctoral thesis and are collated under the banner, *Dreams of Clay, Drops of Dew*. They are due to be published by Owl Press, as part of the Writing the Greek Diaspora Series, in 2011.

(2008), while Vasso Kalamaras (1977) encases the tragedy of a young child perishing in the Australian bush through the trope of the letter:

> Mother, I have lost my child! He was so full of life. I will go mad. I hear his voice; I try to avoid his tortured gaze; I weep when I think of him holding out his little hands in the void and crying out for me. Mother, oh Mother, I am grown now with children of my own, but you know how many times I used to hold out my hands to you imploringly. (17–19)

For many first-generation immigrant women finally reuniting with their mother after thirty or forty years means reacquainting themselves with a woman they barely know. In her epic poem 'Portrait of a Woman' (2003), Yota Krili paints a vivid picture of the convergence of gender, class and cultural threads, the entwining of which has served to constrict women throughout time. The final two stanzas reflect that moment of quiet resolution:

> She was 83 when I visited her.
> Her eyes were bleary but still
> she was agile and sturdy.
> She was my mother but I did not know her till then.
> She had no time to mother her girls.
> She loaded the table with fruits of her garden
> spread her woven blankets on the beds
> opened her chest and offered me her heirlooms
> some were meant to be my dowry.
> She enchanted my daughter
> with her spinning of songs and folktales
> yet was perplexed by the state of my marriage.
> I did not dare disappoint her.
>
> Finally, I had to say
> 'Mother, I don't need a man
> I am capable of supporting my child
> and living my life on my own'.

Her dim eyes gleamed.
'Good on you, my daughter!
I could never have done such a thing myself
I lived in hard times', she said wistfully ... (154)

The tragedy of the exilic condition is distilled in the horror of the moment when the mother dies without the immigrant daughter making it back in time for the last meeting; the last rites. The horror of mourning someone who is absent, of endeavouring to mourn someone whom you have never met – as was the case for the thousands of grandchildren of these grandparents 'far away' – is a social phenomenon that has been largely ignored in any sort of societal analysis of the immigrant experience. The following lines from the short story 'Snapshot' (2006) by Helen Nickas are singularly memorable, the terseness of the language creating a haunting underscore that further heightens the aching finality of it all. The writer has just given a paper at a conference in America, after which she intended going to Greece to spend some time with her mother:

Eleni, is it you?
George's voice sounded odd and remote.
I'm sorry. It's your mother. She passed away earlier today.
Silence.
Are you there, Eleni? Can you hear me? She will be buried in the morning. I've been ringing for hours but you weren't in your hotel room.
Now it was I who had an overwhelming desire to stroke my mother's forehead. It's my turn to do it, but I will not make it. I am going to miss the chance to say goodbye ...
The house is full of family and relatives, sleeping over after the funeral. I go to her room ... I lie on the mattress still warm with her body. I touch and stroke the pillow, the pillowcase with a crocheted border done by her golden hands, as people used to tell her. This is the same pillow that supported her head only the night before last, as she lay there dying. (251)

The centrality of the extended family and the relationship it renders possible between the past and the future is endemic to village life. Greek immigrant women, having lost the presence of 'all who have gone before' have focused all their energies on their offspring and on the host country that is encasing and nurturing them. One of the fascinating manifestations of this particular focus is that Greek-Australian women's writings are much less overtly nostalgic for the lost homeland than that of their male counterparts. Some of the most moving evocations of the profundity of their relationship with this 'foreign' land emerge from their pen (Bose 2007). Dina Amanatides dedicates the poem 'Traces' (2008) specifically to Glen Waverly, the Melbourne suburb that has been the home of her and her family for over thirty years:

This place sought my footsteps
this place sought my sorrows
this place know I would come
the park opposite was waiting
for me
this neighbourhood
with its deep silence
sought me out,
There is no greater joy than this.
To belong
is to exist ... (51)

Second generation women writers are invariably dealing with a mother who is very much present and whose endless hardships and many sacrifices give license to a heightened notion of expectation where their offspring is concerned. This inevitably leads to either extraordinary closeness or to the bitterness of conflict. In her short story, 'From Her Words to My Mouth' (2003), Angela Costi dexterously interweaves both states. We have here the scene where the mother pays an unexpected visit to her daughter's flat – her *lawyer* daughter, her pride and joy, the embodiment of all her hopes and dreams. Her daughter's moving out of home and insistence on choosing non-Greek boyfriends have perplexed and devastated her:

> Dina is silently appalled by Anna's flat with its cobwebbed hallway, old light-fittings, damp walls. How could Anna live in such squalor and foolishly believe it was charming? Dina knows Anna has stopped listening to her. Against her wishes, Anna left home without her blessing. She continued to see Sharif until he left her for another. Dina knew he was 'no good' from the start. Her attempts to bring Anna back home to safety, to security, to family love that would never leave her, no matter what, was not enough ... And this new one Kris, with his sharp nose and hooded eyes, looks like a devil. At least the Muslim was handsome. This German looks like he is ready to fall over at the slightest nudge from the wind. He is so skinny. Where does she find them? Under rocks? (88–89)

Just as Greek-Australian women writers have written beautiful evocations of the Australian landscape, so too have their second generation counterparts written beautifully about the Greek landscape. If the 1950s and 1960s were characterised by the 'tyranny of distance', this new millennium is plagued by what Nikos Papastergiadis (2003) has referred to as the 'tyranny of proximity' (169). One of the more fortuitous by-products is that there is a greater facility for travel back to Greece. Such visits do not merely constitute a sort of detached sojourn to the parents' homeland but entail an opportunity for the contextualisation of memory; enabling the superimposing of one's own experiences of family mythologies over the neon-bright realities of present-day landscapes. Eugenia Tsoulis (2006) highlights this in the following passage:

> I had returned many times, to pick up the pieces drifting around my memory, walking through the streets of Psillalonia, trying to find my bearings, the lemon tree in the garden, the whitewashed cottage with the red tiled roof, the yoghurt man, the horse that left the droppings we would gather for the vineyard, the hill with the paper kites flying wild above blue fields of irises. And not showing any disappointment

that nothing here had remained the same, I would drive down the hill towards the mountains of Missolongi looming like dark protective sentinels across the bay ... I drove around the streets, searching space behind one apartment block after the other, blocking the view to the sea, no vineyard close by or in the distance, my past blocked out forever. (179)

In her prose piece, 'Visiting the Island' (1994), Anna Couani paints a vivid portrait of the ancestral island Kastellorizo. Situated in precarious isolation from the plethora of other islands in the Mediterranean and just a stone's throw away from the mainland of Turkey, its strategic geographical position has ensured a turbulent and often violent history at the hands of a succession of invaders, culminating in its virtual annihilation when 'the British burned down the island' – for all the hotly contested and mythologically inspired reasons. However, the incessant array of marauders did not succeed in decimating its social fabric to the extent that mass migration and advent of globalisation, in terms of creating a 'genuinely original and authentic spot', managed to do. Into this complex narrative depicting social desolation, physical beauty and cultural formations informed by entrenched patriarchal structures, Couani interweaves her own position, beautifully encapsulating the impossibility of any vague notions of an 'objective' stance:

> the narrator (who is the writer) is no less touched by the immediate situation and no more able to achieve a distance on it than any of the other players in it. This narrator is here on the island at the time of writing – making friends, doing the washing, taking out a calculator to convert drachmas to dollars and like many others, visiting the place where the family came from. Still, after generations, stung by the events which tore the place apart. At the more personal level, the female narrator, no longer young and dewy but young enough to be expected to conform, finds herself as a tourist sitting amongst groups of men all day while the local women remain virtually unseen, at home doing the housework perhaps or holding court in private with

other women or in family groups. The narrator, deprived of female company and constantly negotiating the obstacles thrown up by the men on the passage through town. The men, like everywhere, posted like sentries at the public meeting place between cultures. (354–55)

Whereas Dina Amanatides dedicated a poem to the Melbourne suburb of Glen Waverly, Melbourne avant-garde poet Thalia dedicates the poem 'Byzantine Walls' to the northern Greek city of Thessaloniki, thus demonstrating the potential of the initially alien environment to capture their imagination and to widen the parameters of their concept of 'home'. Thalia's (1998) cognisance of the landscape of this city, eventuating as it did after a prolonged stay there, is amply reflected in the sustained metaphor of the appropriation of its hidden elements by the insightful gaze of the poet:

behind the huge wall
another city lives
the houses are small
some
two storeys high
inbetween
and in and out
narrow steep paths
curve
inbetween
small houses
some two storeys high
behind the huge wall
another city lives. (115)

I would like to bring this overview of Greek-Australian women's writing to a close by focusing briefly on Antigone Kefala, a woman for whom the metaphor of the journey has informed her own life as much as it has the unfolding cadence of her words. As Helen Nickas notes, Kefala's whole life has been lived in a state of exile entailing moving with her family as war refugees to three different countries – from Romania, to Greece, to New Zealand, and finally to Australia – and having to master two languages, Greek and English, in addition to Romanian and French which she knew as a child. (1992, 91)

As can be readily gleaned from this, Kefala became cognisant of a multiplicity of diasporas, being a child of Greek parents in another European country, and then relocating a number of times henceforth. She attended university in New Zealand and attained not only a Masters degree in Literature but also a facility with the English language that rendered it her language of choice in all her literary endeavours. In the dedication to the ground-breaking anthology *Beyond the Echo*: *Multicultural Women's Writing* (1998), editors Gunew and Mahyuddin referred to her as one of the pioneers of such writings, while Nickas offered the palpable manifestation of Kefala's multilingual persona in the form of the striking trilingual publication – in English, French and Greek – of *The Island* (2002) as part of Owl Publishing's Writing the Diaspora Series.

Derrida's assertion that 'language bears within itself the necessity of its own critique' finds tangible expression throughout this haunting novella written some twenty-five years ago (254). Consider the following passage. Melina, the protagonist, works as an assistant (during the university holiday period) to a social researcher:

> He claimed that in order to understand history, one needed a type of vision that only people placed at the crossroads could provide. That is, people who lived between cultures, who were forced to live double lives, belonging to no group, and these he called 'the people in between'. This vision, he maintained, was necessary to the alchemy of cultural understanding. (Kefala 2002, 36)

However, the sublime prospect of interlocution that this stance enhances, gives way to the vacuousness and awkwardness initiated when cultural translation is neither desired nor deemed possible. Melina has gone to check out the arrangements for a particular tutorial. She enters her lecturer's office, transgressing as she does so, the deeply embedded hegemonic structures that will not accommodate the 'other' that she so visibly embodies:

> I spoke. I could see from his face that he had not the faintest idea what I was saying, the meaning stopped somewhere mid-air between us, he incredulous that he will ever understand me, I incredulous that he will ever understand me. He was busy swallowing thin mouthfuls of vinegar, watching me with preoccupied eyes, rubbing his hands as if drying them of sand, trying to get rid of it. I could see in his whole attitude the immense surprise of being confronted, here in his own room, at the University, by something as foreign as myself. The implied extravagance of my voice, the rapid nervousness of my movements, my eyes that looked too directly at him. He made social concessions outwardly, but inwardly he kept repeating to himself – why the hell do I have to put up with this in my everyday life, one is not safe anywhere these days. (Kefala 2002, 60–62)

The whole unfortunate incident inspired Melina to declare to her aunt later on that 'the nature of the understatement … was more miraculous and more subtle than the Pindaric Ode, and I had already given up hope that I would ever master it' (Kefala 2002, 60–62). Indeed, Kefala's tone oscillates between a pathos generated through deep affinity with the plight of her fellow immigrants, and a penchant for irony rendered possible through the detachment of standing outside the host society's margins. In *Alexia, A Tale of Two Cultures* (1984), Kefala explores cultural/linguistic difference and the ensuing misconceptions through the eyes of a recently arrived young girl in the immediate post-war period. Well-meaning teacher Miss Prudence has invited a group of students to lunch, completely oblivious as to the complex 'transferrings across' of words, the cyclical nature of translation from one code to another, the collective effect of which is to render obsolete the notion of fixed meanings:

> The table was covered with a white starched tablecloth, and they all sat down in silence. Miss Prudence at the head of the table, looking at them with her blue eyes and smiling as if they were all the bearers of glad tidings. Then she served them roast beef, mashed potatoes, which were very white and sparkled in the light, and boiled peas with sauce, and as she passed them one by one to Mavis, to Andrea, to Basia, to Alexia, she asked them: 'Are you Happy?'
>
> Alexia immediately went into a panic. For she felt happy to be an Enormous Word, a word full of flamboyant colours, which only people who had reached an ecstatic state had a right to use. She saw it as the 'apotheosis' so to speak, of a series of events, which as far as she could see lay totally outside her life.
>
> The more she thought about it the more confused she became. Did Miss Prudence mean:
>
> Was she happy eating her mashed potatoes?
> Being in her house with the grandfather clock chiming?
> Happy living on the Island?
>
> There she was, with the salt-cellar in her hand which she had been asked to pass on to Mary, not knowing what to say, getting more and more confused between Happiness and Salt ... (Kefala 1984, 40)

In *Modernity as Exile* (1993), Papastergiadis' examination of this epoch's essential 'unlocatability' of the moment of departure and arrival – 'when did one truly leave ... was it in a dream, with a rumour, on a wish, or in a ship ... as for the arrival, is it the place of destination or some way between destiny and return?' (6) – resonates in much of Kefala's creative output. In her prose she meanders constantly around such notions. Melina, in *The Island,* is beseeched by her university friends to sing one of the 'old songs' from her country. She obliges, all the while her thoughts racing around the 'roads of forgetfulness that went deeper and deeper, taking away the mind's landscape, and the signs, and the return journey an unmapped dream' (2002: 166). All of these thoughts further elucidated in numerous poems:

> In dreams begins the journey they would say
> moving the candle in the darkened room
> that smelt of cherry jam and basil.
> I watched their shadows moving on the walls
> straining to hear the corners creaking in the dark
> afraid of the black night that fell outside … (Kefala 1992, 13)

I would like to round off this consideration of Antigone Kefala's work with a quote that I have always immensely liked. It warms my heart because it presents a snapshot of our mothers and our aunts as we, the second-generation daughters, remembered them as being and not as some media stereotype portrays them. These courageous women, who migrated here in the 1950s and 1960s, worked extremely hard both at work and at home. They also had innate style and their dexterity at the sewing machine meant that on the countless Saturday evening and Sunday outings they always looked beautiful.

> I was in high spirits. Professor Stevens had liked the essay, minus A, full of complimentary remarks in the margins. I could see in Dinos' face that I was beautiful tonight. I felt well in Aunt Niki's black velvet coat, an adventurous woman going out for the evening with a man. I moved down the aisle between the seats and laughed. Beautiful and foreign I could feel it in their eyes. Dinos followed, full of solicitude, as if escorting a celebrity. (Kefala 2002, 148)

Greek-Australian women's writing can be readily situated within Australian literary parameters. All the writings reviewed above were written in this country either directly into English or were translated into the English language. The duality of perspective that so much of this literature entails finds its historical precedent in Australian literary trends dating back to the 1800s; the immigrant experiences that inevitably inform the thematic preoccupations are deeply embedded in Australia's socio-historical fabric (see 'Fellowship of Australian Writers 1942'; Clark et al. 1979).

However, when 're-situating' these writings within this new millennium, it becomes apparent that they are informed by another dimension and in *The Turbulence of Migration* (2000) Papastergiadis succinctly articulates it when he notes that 'the twin processes of globalisation and migration have shifted the question of cultural identity from the margins to the centre of contemporary debates' (5). As delineated throughout the discussion of the writers' works above, this mysteriously configured phenomenon of globalisation has certainly shifted preconceived notions of space, place and borders. Lines of demarcation between centre and periphery have at very least been blurred.

Given that cultural translation has attained significant theoretical positioning in terms of its propensity to facilitate cross-cultural understanding and a deeper level of affinity, I would argue that literary (as opposed to literal) translation merits the centre stage spotlight as the process that includes the entire spectrum of cultural and linguistic transference. Moreover, if one of the features of globalisation is that the 'structures of the local are increasingly formed by elements and ideas from distant sources' (Papastergiadis 2000, 6), then it must be said that immigrants have always lived a global mentality. Postwar immigrants' lives were informed by notions of others' lives lived elsewhere, the letters, photographs and memories forming the collective signifier.

If one of the feared negative by-products of globalisation is the oft-cited 'McDonaldisation' of culture through the processes of homogenisation, then surely bringing to light the heterogeneity of a country's cultural and linguistic fabric is one of the most effective antidotes to it. Within the sphere of Australian letters, a canon of literature that actually reflects this diversity would highlight the exciting prospect of a multi-textured jigsaw puzzle as opposed to the monotonous and predictable joining of the dots.

I began this paper with a dedication to my beloved mother's memory. My mother, together with my father, migrated to Australia fifty-two years ago and many of the thematic preoccupations outlined throughout this paper are crystallised in her life. I, too, am a writer and would like to bring this paper to a close with the poem, 'For My Mother' (1994), that I wrote for her some years ago:

They say I look like you
when you were young
but they are just being kind.
You had an aura of still beauty
about you
as if the colours of the loom
where you laboured
had found personification of form
in you.

You had a seriousness of purpose
as you sewed for endless hours
to educate brothers and sisters
younger than you
then later, on foreign shores,
endless hours spent
in factories, in shops, at home
encircling husband and two little girls
within the intangible spark
of your glow.

But most of all
you had a gentleness of spirit
that had to learn very early

the salient logic of accepting one's fate
with dignity.

When they say I resemble you
I smile and wait

for the natural powers
of regeneration
to transmit your wisdom
through me. (278)

Works Cited

Amanatides, Dina. 'Deception.' In *Retelling the Tale*. Eds Helen Nickas and Konstandina Dounis. Melbourne: Owl Publishing, 1994, 16–20.

Ang, Ien. 'Cultural Translation in a Globalised World.' In *Complex Entanglements: Art, Globalisation and Cultural Difference*. Ed. Nikos Papastergiadis. London: Rivers Osram, 2003, 30–41.

Bose, Brinda. 'Mixing Memory and Desire: The (Dis)location of Nostalgia in Diasporic Indian Cinema'. Unpublished paper presented at a La Trobe University English Research Seminar, 31 May 2007.

Clark, A., J. Fletcher, and R. Marsden, eds. *Between Two Worlds*. Sydney: Wentworth, 1979.

Costi, Angela. *Dinted Halos*. Melbourne: Hit & Miss Publications, 2003.

Couani, Anna. 'Visiting the Island.' In *Retelling the Tale*. Eds Helen Nickas and Konstandina Dounis. Melbourne: Owl Publishing, 1994, 253–56.

Derrida, Jacques. *Writing and Difference*. London: Routledge, 1978.

Dounis, Konstandina, ed. *Greek Women Writers from Sapfo to Sappho*. Melbourne: RMIT, 1994.

Fellowship of Australian Writers. *Australian Writers Speak*. Sydney: Angus & Robertson, 1942.

Ferrier, Carole, ed. *Gender, Politics and Fiction*. St Lucia: University of Queensland Press, 1985.

Gandhi, Leela. 'Women and India.' In *Reflected Light: La Trobe Essays*. Eds Peter Beilharz and Robert Manne. Melbourne: Black Inc., 2006, 179–80.

Giles, Zeny. *Blackbutt Honey*. Dangar, NSW: Koel Koel, 2005.

Gunew, Sneja, and Jan Muhyuddin, eds. *Beyond the Echo: Multicultural Women's Writing*. St Lucia: University of Queensland Press, 1988.

Gunew, Sneja. *Framing Marginality*. Melbourne: Melbourne University Press, 1994.

Hodge, Bob, and Vijay Mishra. *Dark Side of the Dream*. Sydney: Allen & Unwin, 1991.

Kalamaras, Vasso. *The Bread Trap*. Melbourne: Elikia, 1986.

——. *Other Earth*. Freemantle: Fremantle Arts Centre Press, 1977.

Kanarakis, George, ed. *Greek Voices in Australia*. Sydney: Australian National University Press, 1987.

Kefala, Antigone. *The Island*. Melbourne: Owl Publishing, 2002.

——. *Absence*. Sydney: Hale & Iremonger, 1992.

——. *Alexia: A Tale of Two Cultures*. Sydney: John Ferguson, 1984.

Kramer, Leonie, ed. *The Oxford History of Australian Literature*. Melbourne: Oxford University Press, 1981.

Krili, Yota. *Triptych*. Melbourne: Owl Publishing, 2003.

Mpaloukas, Ekaterini. *Zorro: The Adventures of an Australian Terrier*. Melbourne: Pisces Publishing, 2006.

Nickas, Helen. *Mothers from the Edge*. Melbourne: Owl Publishing, 2006.

——. *Migrant Daughters*. Melbourne: Owl Publishing, 1992.

Nickas, Helen, and Konstandina Dounis, eds. *Retelling the Tale*. Melbourne: Owl Publishing, 1994.

Papastergiadis, Nikos, ed. *Complex Entanglements: Art, Globalisation and Cultural Difference*. London: Rivers Osram, 2003.

——. *The Turbulence of Migration*. Cambridge: Polity, 2000.

——. *Modernity as Exile*. Manchester: Manchester University Press, 1993.

Spilias, Arthur, and Stavros Messinis, eds. *Reflections*. Melbourne: Elikia Books, 1988.

Thalia. *New and Selected Poems*. Melbourne: Collective Effort, 1998.

Tsoulis, Eugenia. 'A Place called Melitsa.' In *Mothers from the Edge*. Ed. Helen Nickas. Melbourne: Owl Publishing, 2006, 171–82.

Tzoumacas, Dimitris. *Merry Sydney*. Melbourne: Owl Publishing, 2005.

Vithoulkas, Jeana. 'The Artist's Daughter.' In *Retelling the Tale*. Eds Helen Nickas and Konstandina Dounis. Melbourne: Owl Publishing, 1994, 178–84.

5

DOGBOYS AND LOST THINGS; OR ANCHORING A FLOATING SIGNIFIER: RACE AND CRITICAL MULTICULTURALISM IN SHAUN TAN'S *THE LOST THING* AND RANULFO CONCON'S *NIRVANA'S CHILDREN*[1]

DEBRA DUDEK

In Sneja Gunew's 2004 book on multiculturalism, *Haunted Nations: The Colonial Dimensions of Multiculturalisms*, she persistently refers to the term *multiculturalism* as a floating signifier. While this notion of a floating signifier is helpful because it acknowledges different ways in which multiculturalism functions in specific contexts, it may be unhelpful when it floats so much as to lose any signification. While I identify myself as a postmodernist and, therefore, regularly resist universalist terminology, I find myself in a peculiar position of wanting to put limits on the term *multiculturalism*.[2] If multiculturalism can mean

---

[1] I presented an early version of this article to the English Departments at the University of Calgary and the University of Winnipeg in July 2005; I thank my colleagues who attended these talks for their generous support and helpful suggestions. This was first published in *Ariel* 37.4 (October 2006): 1–20, and is reproduced with kind permission of the ARIEL Board of Governors, University of Calgary, Calgary, Alberta.
[2] This impulse originated because I wanted to have limits for my Australian Research Council-funded research project 'Building Cultural Citizenry:

anything, then why is it important to analyse children's literature through the lens of multiculturalism, I wonder.

My response to this question about the importance of analysing children's literature via multiculturalism stems from Stuart Hall's (2001) assertion that with the rise of multiculturalism comes the rise of racism:

> it is worth identifying with one of the most difficult things to comprehend nowadays about this society – the absolute coincidence of multiculturalism and racism. Far from being the opposite ends of a pole so that one can trade the rise of one against the decline of the other, it seems to be absolutely dead central to society that both multiculturalism and racism are increasing at one and the same time. (48–49)

While Hall speaks about British society, this dynamic is not unique to Britain, if, in fact, this claim is valid. But the *link* between race and multiculturalism is important for the purposes of this essay. I believe it is crucial to understand how *race* anchors multiculturalism in order to fight against *racism*.

In *Race: The Floating Signifier* (1996), Hall defines race as a socio-historical or cultural, not a biological, category, and I employ his definition in this article. Hall, following Appiah, emphasises that the idea of race he deconstructs is not an anthropological and biological imperative based on skin, hair, and bone but is rather a way of reading the body as text, and, in this case, as racialized text. He calls race a discursive category, a system of classifying difference, and he states that race works like a language. Hall believes that one of the most difficult, urgent and important tasks is 'to live with difference without eating the other'. What matters to Hall, and what I am engaged with in this essay, is articulating a system of meaning by which difference is made intelligible. I believe that critical multiculturalism, which I define as a version of

---

Multiculturalism and Children's Literature', which I am working on with Dr Clare Bradford and Dr Wenche Ommundsen.

multiculturalism that is self-reflexive insofar as it examines how race underpins culture within narratives of multiculturalism, can be such a system of meaning, a system which allows one to recognise and to include racial difference into culture rather than to promote a multiculturalism that privileges homogeneity under a rhetoric of multicultural difference.

By reading children's literature via critical multiculturalism readers will be able to flesh out ideologies of race that are being advocated and will, in turn, have a better understanding of the racial dynamics from which the literature stems. In the first part of this article, I argue for a critical multiculturalism that acknowledges and makes visible how race underpins multiculturalism. In the next section, I chart the field of multiculturalism and Australian children's literature and argue for the inclusion of critical multiculturalism as another aspect of this field. In the final part of this paper, I put this theory to work by analysing Shaun Tan's picture book *The Lost Thing* (2000) and Ranulfo Concon's young adult novel *Nirvana's Children* (2001), which, I argue, are cautionary tales that bring to the surface the dangers – dangers of exclusion and erasure, for instance – inherent in a multicultural society that fails to embody racialized others into a society in ways that neither erase difference nor default to a multiculturalism of tolerance.

Defining Multiculturalism

The first general usage of the term *multicultural* began in Canada in the late 1950s. The term *multiculturalism* was first used in the Canadian *Preliminary Report of the Commission on Bilingualism and Biculturalism*, which was published in 1965, and Australian multiculturalism borrows much from the Canadian version. In general terms, multiculturalism is put forth as policy in order to recognise officially the diverse ethnic groups living within state borders and to provide support for the cultural differences of these groups (Stratton and Ang, 128). Thus we see governments, including the Australian federal government, using some version of the phrase 'united in diversity' in order to call attention to how diverse ethnic groups can still unite under the banner of nationalism.

In his 'Introduction: Multicultural Conditions', David Theo Goldberg (1994) states, 'Broadly conceived, multiculturalism is critical of and resistant to the necessarily reductive imperatives of monocultural assimilation' (7), and this definition is one to which I shall return in my analysis of *The Lost Thing*. Many authors, however, are inclined to distinguish between various kinds of multiculturalisms rather than to define it in the singular. Ien Ang, Jacqueline Lo, Jon Stratton, and Ghassan Hage for example, draw attention to the distinction between Australian government-sanctioned policies of multiculturalism and 'on-the-streets' or everyday multiculturalism of the people, without universalising either of these versions. It is useful to have the term *multiculturalism* move between these distinctions because both of these usages attempt to understand and to account for racialized cultural diversity, which is specifically where multiculturalism needs to be mobilised. In multicultural discourse, culture is already anchored to race. In other words, in a racist culture, culture is racialized.

Of course, the everyday 'on-the-streets' version of multiculturalism is very different from the Disneyland version of friendship and tolerance that hegemonic constructions of multiculturalism present. In his book *White Nation: Fantasies of White Supremacy in a Multicultural Society* (1998), Ghassan Hage argues that multiculturalism in Australia works only as a model in which the White nationalist controls the racialized other. In other words, as long as the so-called ethnic other obeys the rules of the non-racialized status quo, then multiculturalism works. Hage demonstrates how tolerance fades when there is a perceived danger of the racialized other changing the fabric of (White) Australian life and identity. In this paper, I shall demonstrate how critical multiculturalism exposes these workings of everyday multiculturalism as they are represented in *The Lost Thing* and *Nirvana's Children*.

It is important to acknowledge that multiculturalism was named and sanctioned by the government in response to diverse groups of migrants immigrating to Australia and therefore, does not, in the first instance, include Indigenous peoples, who generally and rightly resist being categorised under this term.[3] Multiculturalism was not created to acknowledge the diverse First Nations within nation-state borders. Indeed, with the collapse of immigration and Indigenous affairs into a single portfolio in Australia, namely the Department of Immigration and Multicultural and Indigenous Affairs (DIMIA), both migrants and Aboriginal peoples are in danger of being homogenised under the middle term of the portfolio, *multicultural*.[4] Multiculturalism needs to be revised, so that it does not subsume radically diverse groups under a single heading in order to deny services and benefits to everyone who is of non-Anglo-Celtic background.[5] This stance does not aim to dismiss Indigenous peoples' very real concerns about becoming another 'ethnic

---

[3] In Canada and Australia at least, many Indigenous peoples do not want Indigenous issues to be subsumed under the category of multiculturalism because multiculturalism is largely understood to be concerned with migrant issues (see Stratton and Ang 1994). In his introduction to the special issue of *Continuum* titled 'Critical Multiculturalism' in which Stratton and Ang's article appears, Tom O'Regan (1994) states, 'The inclusion of indigenous issues under the multicultural rubric is one reason for calling the issue "Critical Multiculturalism" rather than simply "multiculturalism" ' (1).

[4] In the time between writing this article and having it go to press, the Australian federal government has shifted DIMIA to DIMA, the Department of Immigration and Multicultural Affairs, and most recently to DIAC, the Department of Immigration and Citizenship. Indigenous Affairs are now in the newly formed Families, Community Services and Indigenous Affairs portfolio.

[5] In 'Not Just Another Multicultural Story', Jon Stratton (2000) analyses a process by which some British migrants assert that British culture is distinct from Australian culture and should, therefore, should be treated like other migrant groups in Australia.

minority'; instead, I suggest that the underlying category of multiculturalism needs to shift from ethnicity to race.

I want to return here to the discussion with which I opened this paper in order to anchor more firmly the floating signifier *multiculturalism* to the floating signifier *race*. In Chapter Two of *Haunted Nations* titled 'Colonial Hauntings: The Colonial Seeds of Multiculturalism', Gunew claims in at least four places that multiculturalism serves as a floating signifier: 'a kind of floating signifier which gains both meaning and strategic capabilities only in a specific context' (2004, 28); 'there *is no inherent content* in such floating signifiers as "postcolonialism" or "multiculturalism" ' (2004, 34; italics mine); 'these floating signifiers ("multicultural," "Australian" etc.) *are attached to implicit assumptions* concerning the nature of European modernity and civilization' (2004, 35; italics mine); and 'While both multiculturalism and postcolonialism have indeed been recognized as floating signifiers, there is necessary work to be done in looking at their interactions and mutual exclusions in settler colonies' (2004, 39). I would like to reiterate my argument here by stating that I do not disagree with the notion of multiculturalism as a floating signifier, but I do want to go further with this claim in order to clarify what I believe needs to be acknowledged within this concept.

I do, however, disagree with Gunew's statement that 'there is no inherent content in such floating signifiers as "multicultural" '. I would like to interrogate Gunew's distinction and the potential contradiction between her claims that while there 'is no inherent content' in the floating signifier *multiculturalism*, it is 'attached to implicit assumptions'. I contend that the concept of race is both inherent content and one of the implicit assumptions located in the term *multicultural*. The content inherent in multiculturalism contains a narrative about living united in a nation-state within which resides peoples of many races. The implicit assumptions attached to multiculturalism – assumptions about European modernity and civilisation, which Gunew does not clarify – stand for a progress and history that claims one must leave behind a past in order to move into a new developed future, a future in which all people respect each other's differences.

Gunew does claim that multiculturalism needs to be more proactive against racism, and it is this point that merges with my thesis: in order for multiculturalism to be more proactive against racism, critics need to be attentive to how race underpins multiculturalism. Gunew comes close to this conclusion by way of postcolonialism. She states, 'colonialism, as the mechanism of postcolonialism, structures multiculturalism [which] tends to be reserved for what are perceived (implicitly and explicitly) as racialized interactions within the boundaries of nation states' (2004, 37). Interestingly, her discussion about multiculturalism as a floating signifier takes place around this claim. The 'inherent content', the 'implicit assumptions', and the perceived structures of multiculturalism are, I argue, precisely these 'racialized interactions'.

Multiculturalism and Race

In 1994, Jon Stratton and Ien Ang published their article 'Multicultural Imagined Communities: Cultural Difference and National Identity in Australia and the USA'. They end their article with a discussion of the crucial part that the category of race plays in discussions of multiculturalism. They state,

> in Australia multiculturalism has thrived through an eclipse of race into the more flexible concept of ethnicity. In both cases then, the discourse of race exposes the fact that the idea of an unfractured and unified national imagined community is an impossible fiction … the category of race should be seen as the symbolic marker of unabsorbable cultural difference, the range of heterogeneous cultural differences which cannot be harmonised into multiculturalism's conservative vision of unity-in-diversity. To seize on multiculturalism's more radical potential is to give up the ideal of national unity itself

without doing away with the promise of a flexible, porous, and open-ended national culture. (155–56)

My argument pivots on this idea of a radical critical multiculturalism but takes this idea in a different direction; instead of focusing on the notion of an 'open-ended national culture', I highlight the necessity of a racial turn in the discourses of multiculturalism, a turn that does not turn away from the ways in which race should visibly and vocally inform multiculturalism.

This need for a racial turn has been expressed recently in at least two places. In *Overland* (2005), Tseen Khoo and Som Sengmany review the 'Dialogues Across Cultures' conference held in Melbourne 11–14 November 2004. They articulate the slippage between culture and race when they say, 'It is in this climate of alleged equality for all, and the promotion of multicultural (multiracial?) societies as a "natural" good, that the boundaries of "nation," already ill-fitting, become ever more stretched and split' (58). While this bracketing of race may be a nod towards how race informs culture, in addition, I read it as an acknowledgement of the need to racialise multiculturalism. Later in the review, they speak to the difficult negotiations that happen between Aboriginal and migrant communities. They draw upon Ann Curthoys' (2000) metaphor of the 'uneasy conversation' to characterise the relationship between Aboriginal and migrant communities.

The second place in which this racial turn has been articulated is at a one-day symposium 'Locating Asian-Australian Cultures', which took place at Monash University in Melbourne on 28 June 2005. In the symposium's keynote address, Jacqueline Lo contextualised Asian-Australian studies by talking about how multiculturalism informs the area of Asian-Australian studies. Employing Gayatri Chakravorty Spivak's terminology, Lo discussed the need to employ race as 'strategic essentialism' within discourses of multiculturalism. She argued that the sublimation of race in multiculturalism does not allow critics and writers to deal with racism, which is a point that brings my argument back to Stuart Hall's claim that with the rise of multiculturalism comes a rise of racism.

Multiculturalism and Children's Literature

Over the past fifteen years, critics working in the field of Australian children's literature have developed arguments about the connections between multiculturalism and children's literature. In 'Advocating Multiculturalism: Migrants in Australian Children's Literature after 1972', John Stephens (1990) argues that Australian children's literature shifted towards an ideology of multiculturalism in keeping with the educational and political ethos of the 1970s in Australia (180). Stephens claims that the version of multiculturalism present in Australian books written for children during this time promotes an 'acceptance of difference and heterogeneity' (180) but does not offer a radical examination of multiculturalism per se. He attributes this lack of radical engagement with multicultural issues to three factors: most authors are members of the Anglo-Celtic Australian majority, most narratives are focalised through this majority voice, and themes of migration and culture are subordinated to themes of personal development. One of the ways in which multiculturalism is represented is that the cultural minority enriches and engages with the majority group with little representation of minority groups engaging with each other (181).

Stephens returns to the topic of multiculturalism and children's literature in his article 'Multiculturalism in Recent Australian Children's Fiction: (Re-)constructing Selves Through Personal and National Histories' (1996). He suggests that Australian children's literature has responded to multiculturalism by representing 'inexplicit expressions of nostalgia' on the one hand, and by promoting a multicultural ideology on the other hand (1). This article deals primarily with the second trend and argues that in novels for children explicitly depicting so-called multicultural issues the construction of a character's individual subjectivity is ... inextricable from the character's sense of cultural affiliation and intercultural positioning. As a consequence, development of a personal identity functions as an analogy for a national development of multicultural awareness and agency. (4)

This analogy, however, results in an uncritical promotion of a multicultural ideology that advocates for an engagement with cultural difference – without acknowledging any of the potential difficulties of this encounter – in order to promote the growth of the self beyond her/his own cultural limitations (17).

In 'Cultural Solipsism, National Identities and the Discourse of Multiculturalism in Australian Picture Books' (1997), Robyn McCallum denotes the 1970s as a turning point for the development of Australian picture books. She marks three main shifts: the move towards equal signification between visual and verbal text; the move towards texts that represent Australian nationalism; and, in the 1980s and 1990s, a move towards representing Australian society as multicultural (103). This multiculturalism fluctuates, however, between token representation via an Anglo-Celtic perspective and a seemingly realistic representation that normalises multiculturalism as a part of everyday life (110). Through a reading of Jenny Wagner's *The Bunyip of Berkeley's Creek* (1973), McCallum examines how subjectivity is formed in relation to another and argues that *The Bunyip of Berkeley's Creek* suggests that this subjectivity can only be realised when the other is like oneself, which suggests an ideology of homogeneity at odds with the heterogeneity of multiculturalism (113).

In 'Continuity, Fissure, or Dysfunction? From Settler Society to Multicultural Society in Australian Fiction', John Stephens (2000) revisits his earlier arguments about how children's literature represents a movement from settler to multicultural society and argues that this transition 'was not the smooth continuity imagined in the early 1990s' (56). In this article, he argues that an ideology of multiculturalism is fractured and critiqued by narratives of social alienation and dysfunction. He analyses two late 1990s young adult narratives, Allan Baillie's *Secrets of Walden Rising* and Matt Zurbo's *Idiot Pride* (1997), and demonstrates how these two novels depict an emerging multiculturalism and offer a critique of the fiction that represents multiculturalism as a static and fully formed entity (68).

In 'Messages from the Inside? Multiculturalism in Contemporary Australian Children's Literature', Sharyn Pearce (2003) summarises Stephens' earlier work as outlining two stages of multicultural progression in writing for children, which she claims still hold, and offers a third stage. According to Pearce, Australian multiculturalism has been represented in children's literature as inherent to Australian society historically, as a move from intercultural to multicultural subjectivity, and as background to the foregrounded plot. In other words, Pearce's third stage of multicultural representation is a multiculturalism that is 'incidental rather than pivotal' to both plot and character development (245), which she summarises by stating, 'ethnicity is not a marker of cultural difference, but an accepted part of Australian life' (246).

My purpose for outlining the above arguments is to situate my analysis of *The Lost Thing* and *Nirvana's Children* within these discussions about multiculturalism and to offer yet another stage to this multicultural progression. This fourth stage, I argue, is a stage of critical multiculturalism, which can be read as the radical examination of multiculturalism to which Stephens (1990) alludes. In this fourth stage, texts can be read as scrutinising and criticising Australian multiculturalism, revealing that ethnicity and race *are* markers of cultural difference, *even though* they may be part of Australian life. Readers are positioned to see how characters that are marked as racially different are alienated because they are viewed by other characters as 'not like me' and therefore not Australian. Although the prevailing ideology of multiculturalism purports an acceptance of difference, reading these two texts via critical multiculturalism reveals that this ideology is really business as usual and this business is the creation of a homogenous Australian culture.

The Lost Thing

One might argue that Shaun Tan's picture book *The Lost Thing* is a story about any marginalised subject who is rendered invisible. I suggest, however, that the lost thing itself can be fruitfully read as a racialized subject, who challenges and makes visible some of the ways in which people and institutions cannot embody the racialized other into the unified (read homogenised) body politic. The basic narrative of the book is that a young boy, whose primary pastime is collecting and categorising bottle caps, finds the so-called lost thing on the beach 'a few summers ago'. The boy reads the lost thing as lost, or as other, because its huge, red, tentacled machine-body is visually unlike any other being known to the boy. After trying, without success, to determine to whom the lost thing belongs, the boy takes the lost thing to his artist friend Pete's place, who explains that some things do not 'belong to anyone' but are 'just plain lost'. From Pete's place, the boy brings the lost thing home, but the boy's parents do not see the lost thing until the boy brings their attention to it. After hiding the lost thing in the back shed, the boy sees an advertisement in the paper from the Federal Department of Odds and Ends, which advertises 'pigeon holes' to file away 'Objects Without Names', 'Troublesome Artifacts of Unknown Origin', and 'Things That Just Don't Belong'. The boy takes the lost thing into the city and attempts to find a place for the lost thing via bureaucratic channels. A custodian redirects the boy and the lost thing away from this bureaucratic place of 'forgetting, leaving behind, smoothing over' and towards Utopia. The boy leaves the lost thing in this Utopia and returns to his dystopic world of symmetry, uniformity, classification, and straight lines.[6]

---

[6] For a reading of *The Lost Thing* as a critical dystopia, see Dudek 2005.

The text announces its engagement with discourses of race before the story begins, although one might argue that the story neither begins nor ends, but performs itself from front cover to back cover. I shall rephrase then: the text announces its engagement with race before the boy begins telling his story about finding the lost thing. The inside front and back covers depict a collection of seventy-seven bottle caps spaced equidistant in eleven by seven rows. The sepia-toned background contains sketches of scenes from the book, so the visual text is basically summarised on the opening and closing pages of the book. Each bottle cap is unique insofar as the top of each bottle cap is decorated with an image, a mathematical equation, a word or some words, and other excerpts presumably from engineering and physics textbooks.

Each bottle cap has a reference inside the book, and one of these caps in particular both utters and refers to racialized discourses in the body of the book. The text in its entirety has been fragmented to fit on the top of one bottle cap, so the quotation that appears reads,

> Onsidering
> y be *like*, it is
> e words *like* and
> ing dissimilar,
> visibly unlike,
> On the (The Lost Thing)

This truncated quotation italicises and therein highlights a central theme in the book: the negotiation between sameness and visible difference. The ambiguity of the quotation also suggests that to be similar, to be like, is to be liked and to be dissimilar is to be visibly different and unlike, or unliked.

While visible difference does not necessarily point towards racial difference at this point, the reference becomes more clear as one progresses through the text due to the sheer accumulation of signifiers for race. On the publication information page, the title of the book is constructed as a version of a passport with the word 'LOST' formed out of fingerprints and overlaid with a stamp from Immigration and Ethnic Affairs, which claims that the traveller departed from Perth, Australia. On every page from here onwards – except for the two pages on which the boy and the lost thing encounter the monoliths of bureaucracy, which I argue leave no space for different voices – there are pieces of paper in the collaged background that contain fragments of Chinese characters, which I read as counter-hegemonic utterances that speak alongside the visual and written text to provide another level of racialized discourse.[7]

The lost thing first appears on a beachscape stretching along the base of what may once have been escarpment but which now most resembles the side of a large ship on top of which sits the city. It is unclear whether the lost thing has emerged off the ship that is the escarpment or from the water towards which it faces. That the boy 'finds' the lost thing on the beach situates the encounter as one between centre and margin, between host and migrant. Given Australia's history of asylum seekers arriving by boat on the shores (if they are lucky), it is not a stretch to read the beached position of the lost thing as a migrant newly arrived to this place. That the boy characterises the lost thing as having 'a really weird look about it' and 'looking out of place' (*The Lost Thing*) strengthens the connection between the lost thing as a visible minority in a place not its own.

---

[7] Each page, except for the one page that represents the newspaper advertisements and the two pages that represent Utopia, uses as the background a collage of 'Dad's old physics and engineering textbooks' (*The Lost Thing*) and other objects, such as stamps and passport fragments, which is overlaid with the visual painted text and the narrator's hand written text. Each page, then, contains three texts: the narrator's story unfolds in sentences printed on lined notebook paper seemingly cut and pasted on top of the background collage; the collage of physics and engineering texts underlie and supplement the paintings especially; and the paintings themselves are richly textured, detailed depictions of a machinistic, industrialised city-scape.

Tan more explicitly signals the book's engagement with and representation of discourses of homogeneity with the inclusion of a sign in the bottom right corner of this image, whose heading reads, 'HOMOGENEOUS EQUATIONS'. The sign, however, only exemplifies what is obvious in the rest of the painting. The rectangular-shaped people on the beach stand alone with only their shadows for company, and the rectangles repeat themselves in lampposts, signs, and buildings, so people are barely distinct as human forms. This flattened, sepia-toned landscape is a homogeneous equation wherein people = buildings = signs = lampposts in both shape and colour, except for the bright red lost thing, whose rounded bulk and brightness stand out and catch the boy's eye.

On the following page, 'MISCELLANEOUS DIFFEREN-TIATION' replaces homogeneity – indicated explicitly by one of the underlying collage clippings – which occurs once the boy starts talking through gestures and playing with the lost thing. This replacement of homogeneity of distance by a differentiation of proximity characterises a move from stranger to guest, from alien other to potential friend, which is made explicit by the boy's statement, 'It was quite friendly though, once I started talking to it' (*The Lost Thing*). To push this idea even further, I suggest that this move from homogeneity to differentiation is an analogy that signifies a move from a monocultural to a multicultural imperative, to recall Goldberg's conception of multiculturalism. It is also significant that the boy is the only person who seems to notice the lost thing, which demonstrates the extent to which mainstream ideology operates to erase, or at least not to see, radical difference. The story as a whole is the child narrator's recollection of a time when he could still see and identify difference and not reject someone on the basis of this difference.

The extent to which the child has been raised in this environment that does not acknowledge difference becomes even more apparent when the boy brings the lost thing home. The boy's narrative states, 'My parents didn't really notice it at first' (*The Lost Thing*), but the accompanying visual text shows the lost thing squished and bulging into the lounge

111

room where the boy and his parents gather. To the reader, it is impossible not to see the lost thing, which exemplifies the extent to which the parents have internalised the inability to see difference. When the boy does finally point the lost thing out to his parents, his mother shrieks, 'Its feet are filthy!' and his father warns, 'It could have all kinds of strange diseases' (*The Lost Thing*). The parents' utterances clarify how the body is the site of difference. Furthermore, their next words, which they utter together, 'Take it back to where you found it' expresses their control over the lost thing's body (*The Lost Thing*). The parents look at the lost thing and express fear that it will infest their home, but they do not express any doubts about their rights to send it back.

The Lost Thing is firmly situated within a fourth stage of multicultural children's literature because it critically engages with multiculturalism by demonstrating how the narrator internalises mainstream ideologies of race and multiculturalism, which subsume race under the signifier 'culture' in order render invisible those beings whose physical markers cannot be absorbed as cultural difference, to restate Ang and Stratton's argument. This process of internalising ideologies of race happens via public and private discourses, including how the city and the family are constructed and function. In effect, the boy cannot exist or conceive of an outside to this ideology, even when it opens to him in the shape of an alternative utopian space. Tan, however, warns against this limited way of seeing and understanding one's surroundings by constructing a text that makes it impossible for the reader to engage with it in only one way.

Nirvana's Children

Both *Nirvana's Children* and *The Lost Thing* criticise the family home as a site of alienation and where racist ideology is manifested. In *Nirvana's Children* this ideology is presented via a discourse of 'polite' multiculturalism, but the narrator's scathing unspoken responses demonstrate to the reader the extent of the discourse's racist underpinnings, which cast the racial other into the role of ethnic curiosity. As with *The Lost Thing*, *Nirvana's Children* demonstrates Stephens' argument that narratives of social alienation and dysfunction fracture narratives unified around multicultural issues, but I argue that the representation of multicultural issues in both these texts goes further than fracturing multiculturalism; they offer a critique of multiculturalism.

Unlike in *The Lost Thing* in which the racialized other does not speak (the lost thing made 'a small sad noise' and 'an approving sort of noise' only), in *Nirvana's Children*, the narrative is focalised through Napoleon Taal, who rants, in street-talk and abbreviations, more than he speaks. On the first page of the novel, Napoleon informs the reader of his age (fifteen), his ethnicity ('born in the Philippines & transported to Oz'), his family situation (nuclear: mother, father, brother, sister), and immediately launches into his first diatribe against adults in general and teachers in particular, who are training students to become adults: 'I hate Adults. Adults are evil, cruel, hypocritical, shallow, boring, braindead, fat, ugly, money-effing, nauseating fascist oink-oinks! ... [who] worship power, play the game, kiss arse, backstab, consume, DESTROY' (*Nirvana's Children*, 3). Indeed, section one of the novel is entitled 'Dogboy', a name that his girlfriend Sammie calls him throughout the remaining sections of the novel as an expression of love, because Napoleon initially believed that his dog was his mother because 'Mum = love + caring + guidance + affection + protection. Thus, dog = Mum' (*Nirvana's Children*, 4). By the end of section one, readers understand the extent to which Napoleon is estranged from his mother and beaten by his father, which leads him to run away from home.

In addition to demonstrating Stephens' argument, *Nirvana's Children* also can be read via Pearce's argument that a third stage of multicultural-ism represented in children's literature is a multiculturalism that is incidental rather than pivotal. That Napoleon was born in the Philippines, that he has a Korean friend named Song, that his friend

Gazza has a Chinese girlfriend, that he lives on the street with a diverse group of children – whose names are 'like a United Nations rollcall' (*Nirvana's Children*, 57) – including Tracey, an Aboriginal Australian, and Soo, who is South Korean, that an Italian baker gives him a free apple turnover, that he tries to join an Indian family for dinner, all can be read as a representation of multicultural Sydney, while the main plot and characterisation focuses on a general critique of a world adults have created and how children are the hope for a better future.

To read *Nirvana's Children* only for a multiculturalism fractured by dysfunction or as a backdrop would be to miss the novel's criticism of how everyday multiculturalism is performed and specifically performed within the family home, which constructs racial difference as a difference that places the object of its interpellation as outsider. The most overt expression of this critique takes place when Napoleon has dinner with Christine (his sometimes ex-girlfriend) and her family. I shall quote this rather lengthy passage in its entirety in order to show Napoleon's internal and external dialogue, which demonstrates the extent to which he internalises and anticipates ideologies around racial difference in this Australian multicultural society. Christine is 'a sweet young resplendent blonde Aussie. Her home is a … typical Aussie home – boring, bland, & the booze bar enshrined in the corner' (*Nirvana's Children*, 14). When he goes there for dinner they

> have Aussie food, bland roast beef with bland vegies. Where's the rice? Where's the soy sauce? No wonder Australians are white. They're so devoid of spice & oomph. I sit quietly & wait for ethnic questions about my country & stuff. To remind me that I'm not Aussie & they are. It finally comes.
>
> 'I suppose', sez the Cow, 'that your meals are very different from ours?'
>
> Yep, we're cannibals, we eat human beings like you.
>
> Yep, our meals have actually got taste & flavour in them.

'Yes, we have our Filipino dishes. But we eat Western half the time. Except we always have rice with our roasts'.

'I've never tasted Filipino food', she moos, then munches on some greens. 'You should bring some over some day'.

'Yes, sure'. I'll bring boiled missionary.

The Bull butts in with his facts. 'Filipino food would be influenced by Spanish cuisine, wouldn't it? The Philippines was a Spanish Colony for five hundred years. So I would gather that it would have a lot of tomato-based foods'.

'Yes'.

'Paella, for instance. They have that in the Philippines'.

'Yes'. Zzzzzzzzzz.

I've had enough of this. I pull out a zapper & zap him & the cow. Now I can eat my bland meal in peace. I dollop their blood on the food to give it some taste. Yummy just like tomato sauce. (*Nirvana's Children*, 21)

Napoleon's criticism of typical Australians, their homes, and their food, immediately establishes that he does not identify himself as an Australian, even as he anticipates questions about his ethnic background, which will make obvious that he is not like them. One can read this denial of himself as an Australian via his anticipation of the questions to come: he has obviously heard the questions before and has been interpellated by them. That he has internalised yet resists ideologies around race, which separate (White) Australians from ethnic others, manifests itself as sarcastic rhetoric in which he dismisses Australianness, even as he is attracted to it in the figure of Christine. The questions themselves and Napoleon's silent and spoken responses reveal the racial bias within the ethnic designation, which goes back to the etymological root of *ethnic* meaning the heathen in the nation (*OED*). On the surface, questions about food may seem innocent and polite, but Napoleon's responses demonstrate how his body is being read as a racialized text, complete with the assumptions, spoken as facts, about history and savagery made by the 'non-ethnic' inquisitors. To Christine's parents, it is not out of order, in fact it is their right, to make assumptions and to ask questions about Napoleon's cultural practices, which are always already anchored to their reading of him as racialized other.

Conclusion

The Lost Thing and *Nirvana's Children* are examples of a fourth stage of multicultural children's literature, which I call a stage of critical multiculturalism. Both these narratives speak back to and warn against a 'unity in diversity' version of multiculturalism that works only as long as radical difference, and especially racial difference, can be transformed into or controlled by the figure of the (White) nationalist. Within studies of children's multicultural literature and multicultural literature generally, I believe that it is imperative to acknowledge how race anchors multiculturalism in order to shift discourses of multiculturalism from cultural difference to racial difference and therein to work against racism. If multiculturalism is to work as a system for analysing, in this case, children's literature in Australia, in order to challenge and to critique a hegemonic multiculturalism that seeks to homogenise peoples residing within Australian borders (and when it fails to exclude them from being recognised as Australian), then critics must put to work critical multiculturalism as a reading and writing strategy in order to examine and to contest how race anchors culture in multicultural discourses in their current manifestations.

Works Cited

Baillie, Allan. *Secrets of Walden Rising*. Ringwood, Victoria: Viking, 1996.

Canada. Royal Commission on Bilingualism and Biculturalism. *Report of the Royal Commission on Bilingualism and Biculturalism*. Ottawa: Queen's Printer, 1967.

Concon, Ranulfo. *Nirvana's Children*. Brisbane: University of Queensland Press, 2001.

Curthoys, Ann. 'An Uneasy Conversation: the Multicultural and the Indigenous.' In *Race, colour and identity in Australia and New Zealand*. Eds. John Docker and Gerhard Fischer. Sydney: UNSW Press, 2000, 21–36.

Dudek, Debra. 'Desiring Perception: Finding Utopian Impulses in Shaun Tan's *The Lost Thing*.' *Papers* 15.2 (November 2005): 58–66.

Goldberg, David Theo. *Multiculturalism: A Critical Reader*. Boston: Blackwell, 1994.

Gunew, Sneja. *Haunted Nations: the Colonial Dimensions of Multiculturalisms*. London: Routledge, 2004.

——. *Framing Marginality: Multicultural Literary Studies*. Ringwood, Victoria: Penguin, 1994.

Hage, Ghassan. *White Nation: Fantasies of White Supremacy in a Multicultural Society*. Sydney: Pluto, 1998.

Hall, Stuart. 'Modernity and Difference: Interview with Sarat Maharaj.' *Annotations* 6 (2001): 36–56.

——. *Race: The Floating Signifier*. Video. Prod. and Dir. Sut Jhally. The Media Foundation, 1996.

Khoo, Tseen, and Som Sengmany. 'Dialogues Across Cultures.' *Overland* 179 (Winter 2005): 58–59.

Lo, Jacqueline. 'Disciplining Studies: Projections and Introjections.' Locating Asian-Australian Cultures: A One-day Symposium Focusing on Research in Asian-Australian Cultures and Cultural Production. Monash University, Melbourne. 28 June 2005.

McCallum, Robyn. 'Cultural Solipsism, National Identities and the Discourse of Multiculturalism in Australian Picture Books.' *Ariel* 28.1 (1997): 101–16.

O'Regan, Tom. 'Introducing Critical Multiculturalism.' *Continuum* 8.2 (1994): 1–3.

Pearce, Sharyn. 'Messages from the Inside? Multiculturalism in Contemporary Australian Children's Literature.' *The Lion and the Unicorn* 27.2 (2003): 235–50.

Stephens, John. 'Continuity, Fissure, or Dysfunction? From Settler Society to Multicultural Society in Australian Fiction.' In *Voices of the Other: Children's Literature and the Postcolonial Context*. Ed. Roderick McGillis. New York: Garland, 2000, 55–70.

——. 'Multiculturalism in Recent Australian Children's Fiction: (Re-)constructing Selves Through Personal and National Histories.' In *Other Worlds, Other Lives*. Vol. 3. Eds. Myrna Machet, Sandra Olen, and Thomas van der Walt. Pretoria: University of South Africa, 1996, 1–19.

——. 'Advocating Multiculturalism: Migrants in Australian Children's Literature after 1972.' *Children's Literature Association Quarterly* 15.4 (1990): 180–85.

Stratton, Jon. 'Not Just Another Multicultural Story.' *Journal of Australian Studies* 66 (2000): 23–47.

Stratton, Jon, and Ien Ang. 'Multicultural Imagined Communities: Cultural Difference and National Identity in Australia and the USA.' *Continuum* 8.2 (1994): 124–58.

Tan, Shaun. *The Lost Thing*. South Melbourne, Victoria: Lothian, 2000.

Wagner, Jenny. *The Bunyip of Berkeley's Creek*. 1973. Illus. Ron Brooks. Ringwood, Victoria: Penguin, 1975.

Zurbo, Matt. *Idiot Pride*. Ringwood, Victoria: Penguin, 1997.

6

A READING OF *THE MYRTLE TREE* BY JAD EL HAGE[1]

NIJMEH HAJJAR

When I spoke to Jad a week ago, I told him I had mixed feelings about *The Myrtle Tree*. I couldn't explain why. I have known Jad as a writer of short stories, a novelist, a poet, and of course, above all a friend. I have always loved his creative writings. *The Myrtle Tree?* I couldn't make up my mind, until I began writing for tonight's launch.

I began reading it immediately when I received the copy Jad had sent to me. It was last January, I was on a short trip to Lebanon to visit my family and publish a book in Beirut. After she had survived a most destructive war in July, Beirut was again 'on a demon's palm', *'akaff 'afreet* as we say in Arabic. Strikes, demonstrations, blockades, boycott, clashes! In short, it was very tense, a ticking bomb! People didn't know what was going on. Many didn't know what to do. Those who could afford it just packed and left. Some were happy at least their children were away! Somewhere in the vast world! Far away from them, no matter! As long as they were away from everything that was happening in Lebanon. After

---

[1] Jad El-Hage is a poet, novelist and playwright who was born in Beirut in 1946. In 1985 he emigrated to Australia. He has published a novel, short stories, poetry, and radio and stage plays in Arabic. He has written two novels in English: *The Last Migration: A Novel of Diaspora and Love* (2002) and *The Myrtle Tree* (2007). This piece was written for the launch of *The Myrtle Tree* in Sydney, 12 March 2007.

years of senseless conflicts, people had hoped the war had finished with no return. They resumed the reconstruction. They began building again! They had dreams of love and life. But now, all they could see was shattered hopes. It was very sad really! I could actually read the sadness in people's eyes. How could I read a 'novel of love and dreams in war-torn Lebanon'? Again?! I said to myself. I too once had a dream in Lebanon. I've lived the war. I know it all!

But *The Myrtle Tree* has its roots deep into Lebanon's soil. And if you were from this country you couldn't help but hope. The first leaf Jad borrows from the novelist and poet, Laurence Durelle: 'It had come so softly towards us over the waters; this war … But as yet it had not broken. Only the rumour of it gripped the heart with conflicting hopes and fears' (*The Myrtle Tree*, 5). This opening appealed to me. Just before leaving to Lebanon, I had submitted a paper for a book on 'hope'. I am interested in 'hope' in the Arabic novel, more specifically the dynamics of fear and hope in the Lebanese feminist Hanan al-Shaykh's *Story of Zahra* (1995), a story of a woman's resistance to power, set against the background of the civil war in Lebanon.

With the title in hot red against black and grey background, a feature *The Myrtle Tree* has inherited from her nineteen-year-old Arabic mother *al-Akhdar wal-Yabis (The Green and the Dry)*, the cover design may inspire a gloomy ambience of war and death. But *The Myrtle Tree* lends itself to a more hopeful reading. This is the story of a young man fearing the spread of civil war, which had started in Beirut six months ago, and hoping for his small village, Wahdeh, to continue life as normal. His life dream is to work the olive grove and revive his father's olive press. Adam has hoped that his pacifist approach could defeat those blowing the trumpets of war. What was he to do with the officer Murshed Effendi who came to preach war? Interesting this name of 'Murshed'! An Arabic word that means advisor and guide to the right way!

> 'The more I listened to Murshed the wider the gap between us opened', says Adam. 'What I see beneath his strategy of 'defence' was burning the green and the dry, firing cannons at fleeing olive trees. Shall I take him on a tour of the old olive press, Father? Pretend to be showing him a small piece of recent history and then casually, very casually, tell him about you, about your devotion to Ghandi and your conviction – which became my conviction – that non-violence can defeat a whole empire?' (*The Myrtle Tree*, 17)

Adam is the central character and the principal narrator of the novel. *The Myrtle Tree* is actually his life story narrated by his own self, and complemented mainly through the letters, diary and journal of his next-door neighbour and junior pupil, Faour. I like this technique of narrating from different perspectives. It gives some sense of immediacy, accuracy and realism. Arab novelists have used it with a certain degree of success, and let's remember, Jad is first an Arab novelist.

Does the author identify with any of his characters? This shouldn't concern us. But I could sense some sympathy with Adam and with Faour, the aspiring young writer whose journal provides the only record of events and impressions for five out of the novel's thirty-nine chapters.

I am not going to tell you much about Adam. This would be the third narrative, and in the third person. You would rather see for yourself what the 'I' says, and how his junior twin, Faour, sees him. To me this Adam, son of Awad, as he is often referred to in the village, is too *ādamī* (in Arabic that is a good person, a true and genuine human being). I find this young humanist-educated villager too idealistic in the context of his time and place. He is too idealistic in his pacifism and his hope, in his love and life. Most idealistic of all is his love of the land and stubbornness to stay in the country. Here is one of his conversations with his wife Yousra:

> 'If war is coming to our doorstep, we're out of here, I'm not going to waste my time fretting and begging a living in my own country. I'd rather clean toilets somewhere else that still has peace and dignity'.

Yousra spoke slowly but with carved precision. Like someone reading a will.

I was stunned. Staying in Wahdeh was the challenge we'd long ago chosen. We were a rare species: young, educated professionals who'd opted out of city life. We had sealed our love beneath the vaults of the olive press we'd vowed to revive. But one look at my wife's face told me she was dead serious. It was obvious she'd been fermenting this brew of thoughts to herself for a while. Sure we both objected to the war, but we had never considered leaving the country. (*The Myrtle Tree*, 39)

Adam may be too idealistic, but he is not unreal. Reading *The Myrtle Tree* I couldn't resist making parallels between Adam and a person very close to me: my own brother. After finishing his medical studies and specialisation in Europe, and despite all the risks, he returned to Lebanon and stayed there to serve his country, in his own way, and safeguard the land we all loved but had to leave for one reason or another. He's perhaps one of the best surgeons of his generation in Lebanon. Although he has dual Lebanese-French citizenship, and was offered several professional opportunities outside Lebanon, he refused to leave the country. Jad met him recently. I wish he could see him tending the olive trees! See how he sprays them with water so they don't break under the heavy snow! See how he speaks and sings to the trees, and how he teaches his small children to cherish and love them as he does.

My brother is full of hope, not unlike Adam. And he's still holding on, we don't know for how long. For Adam, things don't look too bright. He had to exit Wahdeh for a safer place, with his two friends, the young lovers Faour and Sana. But something happened and their 'exit had become flight'. In Adam's words, '[their] hopeful expectations had disappeared' (*The Myrtle Tree*, 286). Did his hope completely vanish?

In my opinion, despite the tragedies of *The Myrtle Tree*, Jad's narrative permeates a powerful sense of hope. This can also be said about his other work in English, *The Last Migration: A Novel of Diaspora and Love* (2002), and about his Arabic writings in general. In *The Myrtle Tree*, the author's hope is so strong that the conflict between hope and despair, and hope and fear, lingers on after the end of the novel. Or perhaps there is no 'end' in *The Myrtle Tree*?!

Adam's closing words in the last chapter read:

> Faour aimed straight at the roadblock that had suddenly appeared. The oak tree engulfed us. Then a huge wave rose and swallowed the great oak. The boat behind my eyes capsized and drowned in the wide and endless light. (*The Myrtle Tree*, 286)

What happened? Did they die? The author doesn't tell. In the Epilogue, a paragraph-length section added at the end of the novel, Adam, his father, his uncle, his grandmother, and Sana, are sitting 'by the myrtle tree', all doing what they loved most. So, where is the 'myrtle tree'? Here is how the Epilogue closes:

> Then from within the big light comes Sana with a clay pitcher and gives it to me. 'You must be thirsty', she says. 'Yes', I say, and look around.
>
> 'Where are the boys?'
> 'Playing'.
> 'Faour?'
> 'Writing', Sana says, and sits down with us to eat. (*The Myrtle Tree*, 287)

I couldn't dismiss the symbolism in the Epilogue. To me, the end of *The Myrtle Tree* is just another beginning. Could it be a new story of love, creativity and hope? Could it be another *The Myrtle Tree* in the making?

But why *The Myrtle Tree*? And why not? – I hear you say. In the Penguin *Dictionary of Symbols* (2005) we find, 'As symbols of life constantly developing and ever rising to the Heavens', trees 'serve to symbolize the cyclical character of cosmic development in death and regeneration' (1026). I could see now why in the Epilogue they all met by the myrtle tree, father passing olive to his son, and woman quenching man's thirst. But I'm still puzzled – why 'myrtle'? I am not questioning the author's choice, but rather interested in his intention. I'm not fully convinced by Roland Barthes' 'death of the author' theory. And I find it more interesting when reading a text to consider both the reader's reception and the author's intention.

Frankly, the first time I heard about Jad's *The Myrtle Tree*, I wondered, what did 'myrtle' mean? In Lebanon, I grew up on the land. It should have come to me naturally. But English is not my first language. Learning it as an adult in Australia meant that I needed to work harder on my flora and fauna vocabulary! I turned down the dictionary, my best friend, stubbornly insisting that I should be able to guess the meaning of the word 'myrtle' from the context. It so happens that while reading the novel in Lebanon, I ate *hinblass* berries, direct from the tree for the first time in more than twenty years. It didn't occur to me that myrtle is actually *hinblass*. I even phoned my sister in Sydney to tell her. We have always longed for *hinblass*, which we loved in Lebanon, but rarely found in Australia.

So as a reader alone, I couldn't re-create the symbolic meaning of the myrtle tree. Nor could I guess why of all the trees he mentions in the text, more frequently the author has chosen the 'myrtle tree'. Why for example, doesn't Adam leave his father's pail and stick in the shade of the oak tree? Didn't his father carve that stick out of oak? Why not the almond tree, if his precious daughter loved almonds so much? And why not the olive tree, his most cherished tree and the focal point of his own lifetime dream?!

For those of you who haven't seen it, myrtle or *hinblass*, is an evergreen shrub with aromatic foliage and white flowers bearing purple-black ovoid berries, which turn yellow-green when ripe. It's common to eat *hinblass* berries in Lebanon (well at least the Lebanon I grew up in!), but it's an exotic delicacy for many Lebanese in Australia. Of course, I don't think this is enough to interpret the symbolism in Jad's *The Myrtle Tree*, especially as in the context of this novel it is compelling to compare the myrtle shrub to the evergreen olive tree, as a symbol of continuity, and a symbol of peace and reconciliation.

But this is the author's novel, and he wants it to be *The Myrtle Tree*. And if I go on about it, it is to emphasise the role of the reader in the creation of the text. I hope you as readers have other keys to the mystery of *The Myrtle Tree*. Or perhaps the author himself wants it to remain a mystery, what makes his text a creative work of art.

I could say a lot about Jad's new work. But there is no room tonight. So I'd like to briefly comment on two more issues that are central in *The Myrtle Tree*: women and language. Both are equally close to my heart, and each deserves a study in its own right. But this is just a launch!

Women of *The Myrtle Tree* appear in a positive image. Their presence is no doubt stronger here than in much Arab male literature. Basically all the female characters in this novel are depicted as better humans than most men, certainly better than all the warlords! Despite their positive contribution, the author decides to absent the women from the scene. How and why? I'll leave it to the readers to discover for themselves. I personally find very interesting the interrelatedness of the meanings of 'masculinity' and 'femininity' in *The Myrtle Tree*, and how these meanings interconnect with such concepts as war and peace, reason and insanity, love and hatred, life and death, fear and courage, and hope and despair.

I loved *The Myrtle Tree*. But I still have mixed feelings about it. Remember? Reading Jad in Arabic, I could see him behind the words. Well Jad, while reading your beautiful *The Myrtle Tree* I was taken by an inexplicable feeling of joy and sadness. I could speak with your birds and sing your *'ataba* and *mijana*. But I felt like doing all this in our beautiful Arabic tongue. I felt sad. Because I fear that after *The Myrtle Tree* you might decide not to write Arabic novels. I hope this is not the case. I congratulate you on your new English *riwaya*, and hope to see her twin sister in Arabic soon.

Enjoy reading!

Works Cited

al-Shaykh, Hanan. *Story of Zahra*. Trans. Peter Ford. New York: Anchor, 1995.

Chevalier, Jean, and Alain Gheerbrant. *Penguin Dictionary of Symbols*. Trans. John Buchanan-Brown. Toronto: Penguin, 2005.

El Hage, Jad. *The Myrtle Tree*. London: Banipal Books, 2007.

——. *The Last Migration: A Novel of Diaspora and Love*. Melbourne: Panache, 2002.

7

RE-ENVISIONING THE JAPANESE: *THE GODDESS OF 1967* AND *JAPANESE STORY*

DENNIS HASKELL

Australian identity was once clearly defined in terms of the bush, the battlers, the diggers, mateship, down-to-earth egalitarianism and larrikin disrespect for authority, hard physical work and a refusal to whinge about it – all the characteristics of the Australian legend. Many factors, including the growth of feminism, of Indigenous awareness and of a large middle class, of immigration and a consequent socio-political policy of multiculturalism, and the impact of globalisation and postmodernism, have made that Australian mythology seem dated to the point of quaintness in a remarkably short time. However, national mythologies transmute rather than change abruptly and disappear; that the Australian legend still has some force is shown in many ways: the annually increasing popularity of ANZAC Day, the legend's use in the Opening Ceremony at the Sydney Olympic Games, the nature of talk on popular television football (i.e. Australian Rules) programs, and the former and current Prime Ministers' recourse to it in numerous speeches and interviews and in the reporting of the 2010 Queensland floods.

One key aspect of the revaluation of Australian identity in the last thirty years has been a reconsideration of Australia's relationships with Asia. This paper takes up this issue in relation to Japan, for many years Australia's largest economic trading partner, through examination of two Australian films, *The Goddess of 1967* (2000) and *Japanese Story* (2004).

Each film examines gender and cross-cultural interactions through the development of an initially improbable romantic relationship between an Australian woman and a Japanese man during a trip from the city into the outback; each film begins with the Japanese man, *The Goddess of 1967* in Tokyo itself, and each moves from cultural opposition towards greater cultural understanding through sexuality; each is more a character study than a plot-driven film, although each can be seen as an odd version of the road movie; both films are concerned thematically with the arbitrariness of death, and both flirt with melodrama; despite their predominantly outback settings, both have a contemporary 'feel', partly through a relationship between humans and technology which is so central that it is almost taken for granted. Interestingly, each film is made by a woman director, with a central female actor who won a Best Actress award (Rose Byrne and Toni Collette respectively), and a central male actor in his first feature film (Rikiya Kirokawa and Gotaro Tsunashima); in both films music is prominent, as is spectacular cinematography.

Each film begins by emphasising the gulf between the central characters' cultures in ways that have nothing to do with the Second World War, once the key point of contact between the two countries. *Japanese Story* includes one scene in which an older Australian refers to the war, about two-thirds of the way through the film, but his comments mean little to the Australian and Japanese central characters, who were not born then. The scene is disconnected from the rest of the film and has no consequence in it, as if pointing to the contemporary irrelevance of the issue. By this stage, through adversity in the outback an empathy has developed between the two central characters and at the end of the older man's comments, the Australian woman gives the young Japanese man a look of reassurance; they are separated from an older Australia rather than from each other. By showing the initial gulf between their cultures at least partially overcome in the context of new possibilities provided by the Australian landscape, *Japanese Story* and *The Goddess of*

1967 are both concerned with national mythologies that inform the personalities of the central characters. In re-envisioning the Japanese, these films re-envision Australians, contributing to the issue of nation-building so prominent in both countries in the contemporary period. While Australia through immigration and increased geographical awareness has become more Asianised, Japan has become more Westernised. Although the two countries are commonly seen in contrast, they have more in common than is often realised. Both are modern, affluent, highly technologised, island nations participating in an international economy. Both have ageing societies, falling birth rates, with consequent economic and social pressures, and both have changing conceptions of sexuality, family and gender roles; both have intricate relations of the present to their histories, with a complex interplay of tradition and postmodernity. Roger Buckley in his study, *Japan Today* (1998), notes that 'the subject of Japanese identity is one dear to the hearts of many Japanese' (156) but he declares that Japan 'can be rebuked for not breaking out of its chrysalis to approach the rest of the world except largely on the economic level' (157). Buckley observes that 'Japan's post-war advances have given many the opportunity to visit other nations' but these visits frequently are restricted in time and 'in groups on Japanese carriers' so that 'a sense of difference and separateness is still at the heart of the Japanese identity' (161). By contrast, Ross Terrill (2000), an Australian expatriate resident in America, believes that while 'all nationalities have their flaws, self-doubts and blind spots ... on the whole Australians are very confident of their identity', to the point that they are 'little dependent for their belief in themselves as Australians on political leadership' or 'media pontificating' (299). Nevertheless, Prime Minister John Howard showed great skill in making use of Australia's propensity for insularity from time to time in his handling of the One Nation and refugee issues, or in his complaints about some actions being 'un-Australian'. This is the context in which these films are to be seen.

Clearly the more imaginatively titled of the two films is *The Goddess of 1967*. The film's opening sequence is of screaming through a tunnel and then on something like a roller-coaster in hazy blue light, then the words typed onto a computer screen, 'I want to buy a Goddess.' The early sequences feature silence and music; the only dialogue appears on the computer screen – all in this blue light. It is a colour the film associates with the entirely constructed world of Tokyo – humanly made but mechanised and dehumanised: we do not see the fingers that do the typing. It is a world that is in every sense material, with apparently no spiritual element. The fingers belong to the central Japanese man, who later describes living in Tokyo as 'like living in Mars'. He is described by the director, Clara Law, as 'a disconnected person, like a lot of us modern people' (Millard 2001), and the goddess he wants to buy is in Australia. It is not a divine woman but a Pygmalion car: a 1967 Citroën DS – in its French pronunciation *Dé-es*, homophonically known as a *Déesse*, a Goddess. The fetishistic notion is reinforced by the film's quoting Roland Barthes' 'It is obvious that the new Citroën has fallen from the sky' (Barthes, 169).[1]

It is a good indication of the film's Tarantino-like tone that the car is in the possession of a young blind woman because her aunt and uncle who offered it for sale on the internet are dead, killed in a murder-suicide, and she takes the Japanese man, just arrived from Tokyo, to see her aunt's blood and her uncle's brains still splattered on the walls and ceiling. When he asks, 'Can I see it?', she asks in return, 'The body?', and he replies, a little uncertainly, 'The car.' This Pythonesque grande guignol is juxtaposed with the seriousness of her blindness and of the situation of her young niece whom she has 'inherited' and is looking after. This is just

---

[1] Barthes (1957) continues, 'The "Goddess" has all the characteristics … of one of those objects descended from another universe', having begun his essay, 'I believe that the car is today an almost exact equivalent of the great Gothic cathedrals' (169–71; translation mine).

one of a number of contrasts; his fascination with the car – he cries with joy when he sits behind the wheel – is contrasted with her blind apathy to it, as is his formal politeness with her Australian casualness. The latter is a feature of both films and marks a key difference between the depictions of Japanese and Australian cultures.

What the two characters do have in common is a certain weirdness and a sense of alienation from everything, not only each other. Before he arrives in Australia we see the menagerie of snakes he keeps in his Tokyo apartment and his feeding them mice; this is as close to nature as Tokyo gets but the eerie blue lighting makes even the snakes seem unnatural. She abandons her young niece, and when she and the Japanese man go driving she fires a gun at a car that inexplicably tries to run them off the road. The driving sequences at this stage in the film are clearly 'shot' in an unrealistic way, and this scene seems an imitation of a B-grade movie cliché. This is one of many times when the film challenges its audience to take it seriously. Another comes in a flashback when a buffoon ocker character, a bush tent boxer who is in many ways well meaning, nevertheless tries to rape her, only to find that she is wearing a chastity belt! Afterwards he is filled with remorse, and drives around looking for her – is this sequence comic or serious? – but the sequence ends with our seeing her asleep under a tree, unaccountably partly dressed, and surrounded by apparently protective dingoes. The image cuts to red light and information about the 1967 Citroën's having enabled General de Gaulle to survive an assassination attempt.

We then cut to her in the car with the Japanese man driving. She in fact has him driving for five days to Lightning Ridge, although neither he nor we know this until much later. It turns out that the Japanese man is on the run from the law, for computer fraud, a fraud he enacted only after a friend was killed in a car accident just after they have had a noodle-eating contest. In the film at times we see her obsessively eating, like a crazed animal; when, after feeling him all over as an equivalent of sight, and then licking and nuzzling him, all in dark light half-way to x-ray depiction, she says, 'You're an unhappy human being', she could be describing herself – or in fact the central Australian woman and Japanese man in *Japanese Story*. Although Law has said that she dislikes 'stories which are cause and effect. As if there is a reason to everything and you can explain everything' (Millard 2001), many of the film's problems come from it turning into a different film from the one I have been describing, with Freudian explanations of the blind woman's erraticness and moments of frenzy as due to the experience of childhood sexual abuse by her father-grandfather. Flashbacks show that, in reaction to the murder of his wife, her Irish grandfather retreated from society and denied its rules, sexually abused his daughter, who retreated into religion before suiciding in a self-lit purgatorial fire, and then sexually abused his blind granddaughter. Now the blind woman is intent on revenge, which is the undeclared purpose of her journey into the outback. Stumbling through his underground mine, she finds her father-grandfather crazed and Alzheimerish. Near his Miss Havisham-like dining table, complete with dead rats and wine glasses, the Japanese man, who has declared his love for her, watches apprehensively. When she drops the gun, love has triumphed over hate, and the film ends with the two central characters, now come together, driving the Citroën through the bush with her hands covering his eyes so that he drives blind down a dirt road.

Japanese Story is a more realistic and more straightforward film, and more readily accords with the Australian legend, at least in its early stages. While a blind woman who alternates between an unreal calm and frenzy hardly seems an Australian type, Toni Collette's Sandy Edwards is a drover's wife for the computer age. A geologist and software engineer, she is familiar with the bush and has the masculine strength and battler qualities of the bushman. However, hard-smoking, irritable and quick to anger, she is alienated from her own life. 'Even when you're here you're not really here', her friend Jane tells her. Forceful and direct, the Japanese man, Hiromitsu Tachibana, finds her 'very loud and aggressive'. He is accustomed to female subservience. He is stiffly formal, indirect, frightened by the country and its overwhelming space, at home with endless corporate statistics, formal enough that he will not go to the toilet in the bush, and always determined to maintain face. However, even when he's here he's not here. Hiromitsu – mercifully the characters in this film have names – has his own burdens which eventually are purged through his sexual relationship with Sandy and his greater – it could hardly be lesser – understanding of the Australian bush which together teach him much about himself. In truth he is a cultural stereotype, and a dated one at that, before his change to warm smiles as he throws away the map. This film also breaks in two, at its moment of greatest happiness turning to grief. As he comes to understand himself through utterly un-Japanese experience in the Pilbara, she gains greater understanding – it could hardly be lesser – of herself and of Japanese culture through him. This understanding deepens when she meets his wife back in the city, in tragic circumstances. Sandy shares with his wife a relationship with him and a deep sense of loss, both powerfully revealing what can fairly be called a common humanity, made all the more poignant by its being recognised only by them. Both the Japanese and Australians around them are friendly but functional, and unaware of the dimensions of what they are witnessing. Slow, formal, repetitive but beautiful Japanese music plays recurrently in the deeply emotional scenes. *Japanese Story* gains in emotional depth as it goes along whereas *Goddess* empties it out through its compulsive Freudian explanations.

Graeme Turner in his seminal study of Australian narrative in literature and film, *National Fictions* (1986), argues that Australian narrative is characteristically seen as pitting the country against the city in what is 'essentially a Romantic opposition between Society and Nature, an opposition which is resolved in favour of the search for some harmony with Nature', a search which 'the hostility, vastness, indifference or cruelty' of Australian nature makes 'fruitless' (25). In this characteristic Australian mythology, 'compensations lie in the assertion of a unique natural beauty, in the discovery of a certain spirituality in communion with the land, or in the mastery of the stoical, pioneering virtues of endurance and acceptance' (Turner, 28). Turner sees all this as ultimately negating 'the value of individual action' and legitimating 'powerlessness and subjection' in nature or in society (9–10).

Some basic facts about these films show that Australia has moved on from this myth. In both *The Goddess of 1967* and *Japanese Story* Australian identity is unfolded partly through comparison with Japanese identity; both films are clearly much more concerned with Australia than with Japan, where they tread on uncertain ground. However, the very presence of the Japanese men show the impact of globalisation, one in Australia to buy a French car sold on the internet and one because of his father's company's investment in the Australian mining industry. We are not in a world of innocence or of Australian isolation. In each case it is the Japanese man rather than the Australian woman who is deeply affected by the bush, and technology is as prominent as landscape; the Australian woman is deeply affected by her relationship with him, which reveals depths of humanity and vulnerability she was unaware of. There is in this something deeper than mateship, and a breaking through the barriers of Australian scepticism. The journey into the outback is a journey into the heart of darkness but also a journey into the heart of brightness. Endurance and acceptance are required, but not in the Lawsonian way that Turner has in mind. In the case of *Goddess* the protagonist's power is shown through her not acting, not killing 'the fucking bastard' when she could. In *Japanese Story* a kind of power is realised in the protagonist's being awakened into a capacity for empathy, including with members of a foreign culture. Both films move from types to individuality, and end with something more than fruitlessness and pessimism, in *Japanese Story* despite the film's tragic ending. Sandy, alone at the airport with her sense of loss, is less alone than when eating baked beans for dinner in her apartment with Jane observing her, or when storming about her office or arguing with her mother.

The Goddess of 1967 and *Japanese Story* are set in the heartland of the Australian legend but play variations on it that show how much Australia has changed. Graeme Turner argues that Australian narrative in fact 'has the Australian protagonist responding to a secularised and alienated environment by admitting the withdrawal of meaning and value, but without inventing a replacement for which he may accept responsibility' (9). At the end of *Japanese Story* Sandy, unfairly to herself, declares 'It was my fault. My responsibility', and both films portray central female characters who overcome alienation and thereby discover meaning and value. Ross Terrill, in his conclusion to *The Australians*, argues that 'socioculturally, Australia in the last quarter of the 20th century engaged in a complex transition: it tried to solidify a national identity and also leapt to cosmopolitanism' (317). These are films which exemplify that process, portraying complex, internationalised situations in which Chips Rafferty would be stoning crows and pretty much lost.

Works Cited

Barthes, Roland. *Mythologies*. Paris: Éditions du Seuil, 1957.

Buckley, Roger. *Japan Today*. 3rd ed. Cambridge: Cambridge University Press, 1998.

Japanese Story. Dir. Sue Brooks. Prod. Sue Maslin. Samuel Goldwyn Films, 2004.

Millard, Kathryn. 'An Interview with Clara Law.' *Senses of Cinema* 13 (April–May 2001). 2 March 2009 www.sensesofcinema.com/contents/01/13/law.html

Terrill, Ross. *The Australians: The Way We Live Now*. 2nd ed. Sydney: Doubleday, 2000.

The Goddess of 1967. Dir. Clara Law. Prod. Eddie Ling-Ching Fong. Palace Films, 2000.

Turner, Graeme. *National Fictions: Literature, Film and the Construction of Australian Narrative.* Sydney: Allen & Unwin, 1986.

8

LOCATING INDO-AUSTRALIAN FICTION IN MULTICULTURAL AUSTRALIA

SISSY HELFF

The acclaimed Bangladeshi-Australian author Adib Khan writes in the essay 'Trends in Australian Fiction' (2002) that in the last two decades or so, 'the universe in Australian fiction has begun to creak open, but not without protests and frenetic writing about the perceived threats to mainstream culture' (1). What Khan obviously refers to is a shift in Australia's literary landscape, namely from a mainly white Anglo-Celtic writing tradition and imagery towards a more multicultural one, including Aboriginal, and increasingly, Asian voices. According to Khan the 'acceleration in the proliferation of cross-cultural voices in fiction' emphasises 'the diversity that reflects the type of society that Australia is' (3). This development, however, also triggers never-ending agonising debates over the intrinsic cultural merits and the original materiality of Australian literature (see Khan 2002 and Ommundsen 1999). Against this backdrop generic terms such as 'multicultural literature' or 'migrant writing' are popularised in literary and culturally studies, terms that underline the need to do justice to the local and the global dimensions of Australian literature. While this new awareness is a giant stride towards an urgently needed redefinition of Australian literature, the terminology carries several problems, as Graham Huggan (2007) notes:

> 'Migrant writing' implies impermanence, as if migrant writers had no proper place in Australia; it also invites a treatment of the literature in

terms of an applied but thoroughly unprofessional sociology, as the distillation of a homogenized 'migrant situation' in which one writer's experience, transparently mirrored in his/her writing, is made to stand in metonymically for all ... 'Multicultural literature' avoids some of these problems, only to substitute others of its own making. The term 'multicultural' is theoretically more inclusive than 'migrant' or 'ethnic', but it still has the ring of alterity to it. It implies a primary relationship to the nation, albeit a highly complicated one, that potentially underestimates the equally complex transnational networks in which both the writers and the writing are enmeshed. It reinforces the dominance of English, either by assuming the centrality of English-language writing or by performing ... a homogenizing act that levels out differences between cultural groupings. (115)

In keeping with Huggan's critique concerning 'multicultural literature' and the term's underlying homogenisation, I believe that 'migrant literature', on the contrary, especially when referring to work by authors of the first migrant generation, does not sound too inept. Nonetheless, the term seems somewhat inopportune if used when analysing artefacts by writers of the second or even third generation. In such diasporic contexts, the term 'transcultural literature' is probably most significant (for a discussion, see Mycak 2004 and Helff 2008). It goes without saying that there are obvious connections between these terms and concepts emphasising hyphenated identities. As might be expected from the title of this essay, I emphasise the importance of plural and fluid cultural concepts when talking about mainstream culture and national identity (for a discussion of hyphenated identities, see Caglar 1997). In line with Aihwa Ong (1996) and Thomas Hammar (1985), I believe that modern diasporic communities not only mediate transnational governance but also national identity.[1] It is in this context of

---

[1] In the last fifteen years or so a new research agenda within Australian social science developed, which aimed to research dimensions of Indian-Australian cultural interaction (see Awasthi and Chandra 1994; Clarke, Peach, and Vertovec

1990; Faria 2001; as well as Waddell and Vernon 1987). In the context of Indian migrancy it is interesting to note that many Indian migrants considered the journey an issue of life and death. Not only because for some desperate souls staying would cause further suffering and probably even death, but also because for many boarding the ship and crossing the Kala Pani, the black waters, meant a loss of cultural identity. Besides the fear of diseases and inhumane living conditions, the most serious problem was that at sea it was difficult, if not impossible, to observe the dietary restrictions that accompany each caste. Breaking the diet meant contamination and impurity, which, in turn, caused the individual to lose their caste status and thus a part of their identity. Indian immigrants on their way to their new working places were regarded as outcasts in India. Interestingly enough, in particular, the group of indentured labourers had been unwittingly simplified by equating their ports of departure with their regional origin. This mistake, which has often been repeated by historians, is not surprising given that the Indians referred to themselves in the same incorrect manner (for a detailed study on the consequences of migration movements for Indian indentured labourers, see Ebr.-Vally 2001). The confusion over the immigrants' origin might explain why many migrants of ostensibly Bengali heritage spoke Hindi, even though most inhabitants of Bengal speak Bengali. As a consequence of the poor education Indian indentured labourers experienced, only few Indian-Australian writers emerged from that first wave of Indian-Australian contact. However, just a few decades later, during the partition phase, a second wave of immigrants, mainly consisting of Anglo-Indians, left the Indian subcontinent in search for a better life somewhere else in the world. Despite being British citizens deciding to settle in Australia in large numbers, they were still subsumed under the rubric 'Indian' Nationals in the Census. In the 1970s a third major wave hit Australia, when well-educated, young Indians joined the global brain-drain and were welcomed not only in Australia but in many metropolitan centres all over the world. Due to a constantly growing and well-educated Indian middle-class, Australia has increasingly become, next to Switzerland, one of the favourite travel destinations for cosmopolitan Indians in recent years. Thus not only the Indian perspective on Australia has changed but a new self-esteem and self-confidence among Indian-Australians might be observed. This self-confidence is evident in the way Indian-Australians eloquently tell about their lives, or to put it this way, have started only recently to perceive their lives worth talking and writing about. Interestingly enough, next to more traditional ways of diaspora that ideas of transnational identities and flexible citizenship provide a basis for the international acceptance of multiple national bonds between people and homes without being necessarily dismissive of debates about national identity.[2] Seeing Australian mainstream culture and national identity through a transcultural lens might open up new avenues of coming to terms with the complex category of national literature.

The Indo-Australian Author And The Literary Scene

> Literature produced by South Asian Diaspora in Australia is still largely uncharted territory as far as textual criticism is concerned ... Only some critical articles have been published by prominent critics ... who have explored the seminal accounts of the lives of South Asian migrants in Australia like Mena Abdullah and Ray Mathew's *The Time of the Peacock* (1965), Yasmin Gooneratne's *A Change of Skies* (1991); Chandani Lokugé's *If the Moon Smiled* (2000) and *Turtle Nest* (2003); Christopher Cyrill's *The Ganges and Its Tributaries* (1993); Adib Khan's *Seasonal Adjustments* (1994), *Solitude of Illusions* (1997), and *Spiral Road* (2007); Suneeta Peres da Costa's *Homework* (1999); and Shalini Akhil's *The Bollywood Beauty* (2005). (Sarwal and Sarwal, lxv–lxvi)

Pondering over this quotation it becomes clear that Indo-Australian writing is still readily comprehensible and the research on critical texts dealing with Indo-Australian literature is as yet not too time consuming (for a conceptualisation of Indian studies in Australia as well as

---

storytelling the emerging stories gradually employ more digital media formats. Such technological developments not only represent a new self-esteem of the Indian-Australian or South Asian-Australian community, it furthermore presents a social reality of modern migratory practices.

[2] For a discussion of the constructions of Indian dual citizenship against the background of the Indian dual citizenship legislation of 2003 and the 2003 Pravasi Bharatiya Divas (Overseas India Day) campaign, see Dickinson and Bailey 2007.

discussions of selected Indo-Australian novels, see Bennett 2006 and Sharrad 2009). This observation might well explain why most critical studies decide to work with categories subsuming Pakistani, Sri Lankan, Bangladeshi as well as Malaysian, Chinese and Japanese literature under the very label of Asian-Australian writing. Nevertheless, such homogenisation is misleading and becomes problematic when it emerges from nationalistic and racist assumptions. It makes one wonder why literary and cultural criticism often misses the chance to point to these problematic dimensions of constructed homogeneity (for a discussion related to this problem, see Alexander 2007). The Danish critic Lars Jensen (2000) remarks that the term Asian-Australian literature, as it is used in literary and academic circles alike, reflects the blurred status of South-Asian, South-East Asian and East-Asian literature in Australian debates. This 'chaotic' labelling practice, of course, is telling, since it signals a longstanding cultural ignorance:

> Australians have been asked to make a decisive ideological shift in their thinking, away from the colonialist frame that has traditionally informed their perceptions of Asia to a post-colonial outlook which challenges the racist assumptions of cultural dominance and superiority. Yet most of their attempts to revise their thinking have at best been clumsy, with the new practices of representation failing to make a decisive break from the residual racist expressions that had rendered Asians as a homogenised mass, socially inept and culturally inferior. (Rizvi, 173)

According to Fazal Rizvi (1996), this unwillingness to differentiate between different cultural communities can be read as a 'silent' claim to white Australian cultural dominance and superiority.[3] In the context of

---

[3] Nevertheless, in the last few years a new critical awareness of Indo-Australian identity, or better, identities can be witnessed. Thus, a number of conferences, magazines and virtual communities in cyberspace have emerged all of which are exclusively dedicated to either Indo-Australian or South Asian-Australian topics.

cultural production in general and literature in particular such homogenisation further suggests a clear hierarchy of 'literary worthiness'. In the article 'Nice Work if You Can Get it' (1991), the Australian broadcaster-cum-writer Robert Dessaix states, for example, that

> the reason so much migrant writing is marginalised is that ... it's often not very good – and for obvious reasons: the author's English simply doesn't allow him or her to produce meaning at the same number of levels – to intersect with the same number of other texts and contexts as a native speaker's. (23)

Dessaix's statement is unconvincing because, as Adib Khan rightly states, '[it] does not contend with the fact that there are large numbers of migrant Australians with a background of the British colonial experience that has commonly entailed an education in which English has been the medium of instruction' (5). In light of more recent developments, namely the 2008 winning of the Man Booker Prize by the Indian-born Australian author Aravind Adiga, Dessaix's generalisation turns into nothing but a narrow remark (for a discussion of Dessaix's essay, see Ommundsen 1999). Following this train of thought, one starts wondering if an author has to live in Australia at all to be considered an Australian writer. Likewise, readers might question whether Australian writing needs to be inevitably identifiably Australian in order to be considered Australian literature. Graham Huggan proposes that 'it seems reasonable to expect that an Australian passport should be the minimum requirement for eligibility as an Australian writer' (11). However, there are always exceptions to rules especially in the case of dual or flexible citizenship. The Australian twice Booker-Prize winner Peter Carey epitomises such an exception. Carey, who left Australia for the United States where he lives today with his family, also located some of his writing outside the

---

See the following Australian Indian portal sites: indians.australians.com, www.indiandownunder.com.au, www.aboutus.org/Ozedesi.com, www.indiainfo.com.au, www.indiaoz.com.au, www.indiatoday.com.au.

Antipodes. Yet, without doubt Carey, often considered a poster child of Australian culture, would leave an enormous gap in Australia's literary landscape if he was suddenly considered American (for a discussion on Australianness and authorship, see Huggan, 1–14). Thus Peter Carey's case in many ways challenges the invisible national boundary within literary and cultural criticism and somehow makes the Australian literary scene (and here I include in addition to writers and publishers, editors, reviewers and academics) rethink and probably even open up to more ambivalent vistas of what publically may be considered Australian. By transferring these ideas to the Indo-Australian diasporic literary scene, this essay seeks to answer the question to what extent Indo-Australian writing should be considered part of Australian literature. My argument will evolve around a close reading of Suneeta Peres da Costa's literary debut *Homework* (1999) and Bem Le Hunte's second novel *There, Where the Pepper Grows* (2005).

The two novels vividly demonstrate how modern life is evoked in contemporary Indo-Australian fiction by covering a huge time period, namely from the 1930s to the present-day, and taking the reader to such diverse places as Poland, India and Australia. By mapping this particularly broad spatio-temporal fictional frame, we circumvent artificially maintained national borders within Australian imagination. The two novels demonstrate how authors seek to locate their writing within an Australian imagination. Peres da Costa's approach to multicultural Australia and Indo-Australian life is presented through a sense of immediacy, she directly negotiates multicultural Australian life on the plot level by asking her narrator-protagonist to position herself within society. Le Hunte's, by contrast, chooses the opposite in handling multicultural Australia, which is evident in an intense extra-literary representation through which the author directly presents her original reflections on multicultural Australia. These reflections are mirrored in the book's overall structure and come alive in the well-thought-out usage of paratextual elements, that is to say in the added materials and interviews as well as in the novel's elaborated acknowledgments.

Two Different Ways of Imagining Multicultural Australia

In her 1999 novelistic debut *Homework* the Australian author Suneeta Peres da Costa tells us about the predicaments of growing up in an immigrant family in contemporary multicultural Australia. Mina Pereira, the unreliable child narrator, experiences the many faces of integration not only in her everyday school life but also at home, in her family's various attempts at homemaking in Australia. Homemaking for the parents becomes synonymous with experiences of loss and homelessness. Against this background Mina tries to recollect her and her family's past in order to create her own Australian world – a world that consists of multiple stories. It is the story of her unhappy and mad mother, who has never overcome her own refugee experiences (*Homework*, 123–49). As a consequence the mother steals food and stores it in old suitcases under her bed. And it is the story of her father, who works for the Department of Immigration and Ethnic Affairs while seeing himself as a freedom fighter, who is not willing to accept that his homeland Goa is no longer under Portuguese rule. He even transfers his political struggle to Australia, always claiming Goa's independence from India.[4] To complicate the already complex life of Mina even further, the girl is 'blessed' with a genius sister 'who simply knows too much' (79), whereas Mina has to cope with a physical disability, which, from an Indian perspective, always indicates the work of karmic intervention. Her physical deformity, two antennae on her head, cannot be removed because they are rooted in her

---

[4] Mina describes her father's political actions as follows: 'Dad was still devising a plan to reconquer his homeland [Goa]. And it wasn't just the Sikhs from whom he took his lead; he borrowed anthems from the Tamil Tigers of Elam, the Inkartha Freedom Fighters; the Basques and the Sinn Fein were separatists whose aspirations and minor histories my father reconstituted into private education' (*Homework*, 155).

brain and to Mina's hard luck they even start growing during her adolescence. Mina's feelers, however, are visible indicators of her 'otherness'. Hence, her tentacles mark her as an outsider not only in Australian society but also disconnect her from her mother's love. It is because of Mina's longing for this love that she eventually starts to invent alternative worlds.

With these themes, the novel weaves a dense narrative web of family experiences and childhood memories that portray the life of a young Australian who experiences otherness as a part of her daily negotiations of the self, while questioning both the traditional values of diasporic Indian communities in Australia as well as the commonplace norms presented by official representatives of multicultural Australia. The emerging imaginary home becomes Mina's site of reconciliation as well as a fabricated net of memories and funnily unreliable stories that generates the narrative drive within the novel. This narrative drive is supplemented by intertextual devices such as vibrant references to Lewis Carroll's children's classic *Alice in Wonderland* (1865).

> Now I felt I was down the Rabbit Hole, dwarfed by a huge grandfather clock, giant-sized oak dining chairs, a huge scroll of a rug … I felt I may have been hallucinating, had, like Alice, perchance drunk some strange elixir and this was its potent side effect. (55)

References to the world of Indian myths such as the story of Kali, the Indian goddess of destruction, are also included:

> She [Mina reflecting on her sister's friend Jacinta] was no suitor, no charmer, she, an incarnation of Kali, goddess of destruction, wreaking havoc on our lives and then dancing barefoot on the violated sacrificed corpses. (94)

It is the variety of cultural signifiers, dramatising rhythms and language modes that generates the protagonist-narrator's rich and vivid transcultural narrative style. Such stylistic novelty is characterised by the

145

emergence of new cultural forms which are, as John McLeod (2001) reminds us, 'simultaneously autochthonic yet emerge out of a colonial legacy' (93). Mina's narration is constantly playing with fantastic elements thus the text suggests that the construction of history, memory and truth features prominently within her act of storytelling. When the protagonist-narrator's parents finally die in a fire accident, Mina gets rid of her tentacles, too:

> I ran crying and tearing those rotted knobs from my scalp. Gone for good my umbilical cord to the world! Gone my chrysalis! My antennae ripped forever from my skull, I finally knew while I ran what it was to feel the blood that might previously have surged to those organs flowing in predictable patterns only through my veins. (254)

This plot development marks Mina's awakening and suggests that Mina has grown into a young independent woman who realises that her longing for her mother's love, implying an ultimate protection from the world, is rooted in nothing but an illusion:

> It was a vigil maintained in vain, for we begin at a time beyond the womb, a disjunct moment; and we love after having survived the unnameable and unmasterable miseries of the past. And on and on each one of us arrives and advances, flying with her face forever gazing at the nebulous sometimes hideous and occasionally divine shapes of the history from whose thigh she sadly slides. (259)

Having lost her parents, who represented her 'Indian heritage' and the general postcolonial legacy of her family, Mina starts creating a space for negotiating and inventing her Australian self. In an efficient combination of various storylines, the haunted pasts live on and interact with the protagonist's presents and compose a transcultural narrative space where the postcolonial past comes alive in the protagonist's multicultural present. *Homework* thus not only provides a new perspective on the discourses of postcolonial and transcultural literature by adding a fictionalised transcultural perspective of Indian-Australian women, it also enriches the literary landscape by adding a distinctive Indo-Australian aesthetic. Accordingly, this aesthetics represents modern transcultural lifeworlds of Indian-Australians and their postcolonial legacy. Seen in this light, the intellectual enterprise of postcolonialism, indeed, has become an integral part of modern transcultural life in transforming societies. Interestingly enough, *Homework* represents its particular multicultural background by staging modern worlds and transcultural lifestyles not as readily available spaces but rather as spheres of constant negotiation. The novel's unreliable stories hence not only emerge from and combine different cultural traditions, they also highlight the novel's struggle with its own transcultural and multicultural contents (for a more detailed discussion of the genre of the transcultural novel, see Helff 2008).

In contrast to Suneeta Peres da Costa's *bildungsroman* the second book under scrutiny *There, Where the Pepper Grows* by the Indian-born Australian novelist Bem Le Hunte only loosely connects to the Antipodes at first sight. Yet, as the author notes in an interview, the impulse to write the novel, was strongly connected to a severely felt disapproval of Australian politics in the early years of the new millennium. It was in this atmosphere of disillusionment that she 'wanted to write about refugees' as she 'was saddened by Australia's stance to mandatory detention' (*There, Where the Pepper Grows*, 6). Transplanting her critique and her piercing unease to a different time and place, Le Hunte chooses Kolkata, formerly known as Calcutta, as the novel's main fictional setting since to her the city always appeared to be 'the refugee capital of the world' (6).[5] This partly explains why the Australian landscape and people feature only a little in the novel's plot, whereas the Antipodes are very much present in the book's paratext. Le Hunte writes:

---

[5] For a discussion of the representation of refugees in Australian life writing see Helff 2007.

147

There, Where the Pepper Grows also goes into historical detail on the lives of Calcutta's Jewish community, who are as exotic as you'll get. Known as 'Baghdadi Jews', they originally made their way from places like Iraq to settle in Calcutta. These Jews never dressed like Indians and mostly identified with the British. (When) India was given her independence, they were confronted with a crisis of identity and questioned their sense of belonging. A massive exodus ensued, and what was once a flourishing Jewish community of around 5,000, has now dwindled to around fifty elderly Jewish stalwarts who won't leave Calcutta – either because they're too old, their loved ones are buried there, or they have never been tempted elsewhere. Interestingly, around thirty per cent of Calcutta's Jewish population came to Australia, and I know several of them who now live at Bondi Beach![6]

The author consciously turns to the life story of Olek, her father-in-law, whom Le Hunte never had the chance to meet in person (this is also stated in the novel's acknowledgments, see *There, Where the Pepper Grows*, 359). Yet, through recollecting and eventually writing down the story, Le Hunte's novel becomes part of her husband's family history, a new chapter in a familiar 'storybook' which has been told over and over again. In this light the novel serves as a sort of case history of the many hitherto untold stories of Sydney's Jewish community who settled in Bondi during the Second World War after having escaped Nazi occupation and Holocaust (at this time Australia witnessed a high influx of Eastern European Jews coming from countries such as Poland, Russia, Hungary, Czechoslovakia and also Germany[7]).

Bem Le Hunte's novel pursues reconciliation by travelling down memory lane and telling parts of her husband's family history. It is through storytelling that memories are exchanged and translated into

---

[6] Le Hunte (n.d.), Author Notes: *There, Where the Pepper Grows* [Online] Available: bemlehunte.com/bemlehunte/Pepper%3B_Authors_notes.html [Accessed 3 May 2011].

[7] For a discussion of Jewish writers in Australia see Jacobowitz 2009.

words, sentences and stories. Such an *exchange of memories*, to use Ricoeur's wording (1996), and the ability to piece together 'the splintered shards of memories' (5–6) are crucial for peaceful interpersonal relationships and help build foundations of modern multicultural societies. This process of recollection is, indeed, significant to reconciliation and healing. This might explain why Le Hunte chose to tell this seemingly private story. In a way it represents her plea for a more tolerant and humane society.

The novel, as such, could be described as a jigsaw of different historical characters and incidents whose tales unfold against a canvas of invented stories. As already said, Le Hunte's father-in-law Olek was a Holocaust survivor who escaped a Nazi transit camp in Poland. He lived during the war with Polish partisans. This 'real-life episode' is the starting point to the narrator-protagonist Benjamin Rahabi's fictional journey which is marked by an extended stopover in Kolkata. The city eventually becomes a home to him and his family for many years before he and his wife Rivka finally follow their children to the United States. However, besides these mnemonic moments, Le Hunte strongly emphasises the fictional quality of Benjamin's story. Another interesting 'real life connection' is the historical figure of the Japanese diplomat Chiune Sugihra, 'a kind of Japanese Schindler' who, as Le Hunte states, rescued 'up to 10,000 Jews during the war by providing visas for entry into Japan. When the Japanese Government found out that there were hundreds of people going to this man at their embassy in Kovno, he was relocated and later lost his job' (7–8). A historical incident worth mentioning is the story about the *Asama Maru*, a boat fully packed with Polish Jewish refugees. This tale also feeds into the novel's storyline, since 'this boat', as Le Hunt states, 'was on its way to Palestine from Japan, when it stopped in the Bay of Bengal with engine failure' (6). It is no coincidence that Benjamin experiences similar problems during his flight. Accordingly an engine failure makes the narrator-protagonist stop in the world's refugee capital, Kolkata.

I will start this story on a boat ... I am a younger man, and I travel with a group of Polish Jewish refugees ... We don't have much to take ashore ... I have a prayer shawl I was given by a man in Singapore, where our boat, the *Asama Maru*, stopped on its way here. We are told that we must disembark here in Calcutta and find our own accommodation, as our boat has engine failure ... We are too exhausted to try to convince some kindly Bengali gentleman of our plight. However, the Jews in the city – they will understand. We can rely on shared sentiments, shared ancestors and common knowledge of our duties. There is no doubt about it – we have to find some of our own people. (2–3)

After having set foot on Indian soil, it does not take long until Benjamin manages to contact members of Kolkata's Jewish community who eventually offer him and his family shelter. Le Hunte emphasises this human gesture by placing some of Benjamin's horrifying memory sequences telling of his former fight for survival in Poland next to his new life in Kolkata's Jewish community where he experiences intimate moments of what Jacques Derrida (2000) so astutely called 'unconditional hospitality'.[8] The interplay of such diverse textual realities generates an intense narrativisation of anxiety, betrayal and the rampant malformation of humanity as experienced in times of totalitarianism. However, the novel also suggests that the shared experience of Jewish persecution evokes a powerful imagination of solidarity, belonging and community. 'Our ancestors shared the same exodus, the same revelations and the same promises, so these people must understand in principle what it feels like to be persecuted' (15). Le Hunte's characters call on the globally spread imagined community of the Jewish diaspora in order to find redemption. Consequently, it is Kolkata's Jewish diasporic

---

[8] Such an act of hospitality, as Derrida has astutely argued, requires a delicate balance in which a host, the *hospes*, is in power to receive and host strangers in such a way that neither 'the alterity (*hostis*) of the stranger nor the power (potential) of the host is annulled by the hospitality' (Caputo, 110).

community which offers the new arrivals, the homeless, hospitality and a new place of belonging.

> It seems as if, somewhere, somehow, a little piece of Polish Jewry is manifesting here in a synagogue in Calcutta. In spite of all odds, it has survived and transported itself across the world, and we feel at home for a moment, showing our fellow worshippers something of ourselves, our former lives. This is the way we have done things for many, many years, since the tribes were parted. Really, the exchange is truly beautiful, and I am beginning to feel hopeful that there is some way we can return the extraordinary generosity of our hosts. (16)

However, Benjamin's new home once again reveals to be nothing but another pit stop on a much longer journey. Placing such individual experiences in a much broader framework, Jon Stratton (1997) reflects on these experiences of 'unbelonging' and the century-old lack of a national home as follows:

> The crucial Jewish experience of modernity was the lack of a national home. This lack made the nationalizing peoples of Europe suspicious of Jews; they were seen as a nation without land, suggesting that they would not assimilate into the national population and be loyal to the country in which they lived, but rather give their allegiance to the Jewish nation spread, as the Jews were, across almost all the new nation-states of Europe. (305)

This observation is also reflected in Le Hunte's novel, especially in the episodes which deal with Benjamin's adolescence and his parents' experiences of discrimination against Jews in Poland before the outbreak of the war. This becomes very explicit in a talk between his parents:

> 'Now that Poland is a nation' she [Benjamin's mother] said, 'we must be careful, for every nation needs an enemy. The Germans are no longer our enemies. Nor the Austrians nor the Hungarians. The enemies of the Poles have gone, so they will have to find some new ones. Believe me, no nation is possible without enemies. We don't

151

know what we're fighting for unless we know what we're fighting against. They're going mad outside with patriotism. It's dangerous for Jews, Salomon.' (181)[9]

Sadly enough, Benjamin's mother's premonition of what the future holds in store turns out to be true and it soon gets worse for Jews in Poland. Benjamin becomes even more aware of this lack of national home when he has to live through the days of war in Poland and India. While Poland during Nazi occupation was a death zone for all Jews, India in times of independence and the subsequent partition of the subcontinent was also not an easy place to live. After the British had left the subcontinent life became extremely hard for the Jewish community. As a result many Jews continued their journeys towards either Palestine, the United States or Australia. Le Hunte fictionalises this new wave of Jewish migrancy from India to other parts of the world and sends many of her novel's characters to different shores. In the wake of this new movement many of Benjamin's friends decide to leave India in the hope for a peaceful and better life somewhere else. Australia, as a country of plenty, is mentioned by Benjamin's friend Aaron Isaacs who together with his wife and son Ezekiel have also decided to leave Kolkata.

> 'Where are you going', I ask, knowing that we will not follow … 'Israel or Australia', Aaron says. 'We are having difficulties proving that we're not Indians for the Australian government, but if permission comes through, Australia will be our first choice.' Then he continues: 'There'll be better opportunities. Who knows how long the jobs will stay open here for minorities?' (324)

Interestingly enough throughout the novel Australia remains an unreal and somewhat distant imaginary place which seems to be merely a projection surface for an apparently 'European dream' of a faraway exotic

---

[9] For further references to this lack of a national home which marks a 'Jewish condition' and the consequences, see also chapters 3, 20 and 21.

land and a relaxed lifestyle. This is epitomised in Benjamin's brief representation of his friends' new lives in Australia:

> Letters also arrive from Aaron, Farha and family who keep inviting us to go and live with them in Australia. They are doing extremely well in Sydney, living in a place called Bondi Beach, which makes me think of palm trees and monkeys throwing coconuts at each other. One of these days we will go and visit them and eat coconuts together on their Bondi Beach, but will we stay? I don't think it's possible. Aaron has found a good job in shipping, and Ezekiel writes long letters telling Daniel about mountains that are blue and heroes who save people from drowning in the sea; stories about picnics on beaches and people lying in rows to get suntans. (331)

This quotation is interesting for several reasons: firstly it evokes Australia as an easy place to live in with its warm climate, beautiful beaches and thrilling surf and, furthermore, a great deal of promising leisure activities. This clichéd, brightly polished image of Australia produces a relative distance between the reader and the world's smallest continent. It is this artistically established distance which puzzles the reader in light of Le Hunte's originally stated concern about the ill-treatment of refugees in Australia. So what are we supposed to do with Le Hunte's representation of Australia? Probably, Le Hunte wanted to put a distance between her narrative and the still sore spot in Australia's recent migration history. Accordingly, some may argue that *There, Where the Pepper Grows* is an Australian novel which structurally refuses to be fully inscribed in Australia's history. Others, however, may regard the novel as Indian diasporic writing with a strong focus on the partition. Read in this light the novel becomes a site of remembrance and forgiveness both on an individual and collective level. To engage with individual and collective memory is certainly central to *There, Where the Pepper Grows*, and yet there is more than meets the eye. Through the novel's intertwined representation of plot and paratext the book's structure opens up a new narrative space which to some degree repeats on a narrative level the dialectical relationship between the diaspora and the nation-state (for a discussion, see Axel 2002). Following this train of thought, Peres da Costa's *Homework* and Le Hunte's *There, Where the Pepper Grows* are engaging in a writing project of an Australian history in the making.[10] Driven by diverse agendas both books use different narrative strategies (in terms of literary immediacy) to approach multicultural Australia; yet their vivid negotiation of history and Australia's multicultural society presents profoundly narrated dimensions of Australian multicultural and transcultural reality.

Works Cited

Alexander, Vera. 'Beyond Centre and Margin: Representations of Australia in South Asian Immigrant Writings.' In *Australia – Making Space Meaningful*. Eds. Gerd Dose and Britta Kuhlenbeck. Tübingen: Stauffenburg, 2007, 153–74.

Axel, Brain Keith. 'The Diasporic Imaginary.' *Public Culture* 12.2 (2002): 411–28.

Awasthi, S. O., and Ashoka Chandra. 'Migration from India to Australia.' *Asian and Pacific Migration Journal* 3 (1994): 393–409.

Bennett, Bruce. 'Glimpses of India.' *Homing In: Essays on Australian Literature and Selfhood*. Perth: API Network, 2006, 101–10.

Caglar, Ayse S. 'Hyphenated Identities and the Limits of "Culture".' In *The Politics of Multiculturalism in the New Europe: Racism, Identity, and Community*. Eds. Tariq Modood and Pnina Werbner. Houndmills, Basingstoke: Palgrave Macmillan, 1997, 169–85.

Carroll, Lewis. *Alice in Wonderland. Completed Stories and Poems of Lewis Carroll*. 1865. New York: Geddes and Grosset, 2002.

---

[10] One should keep in mind that Peres da Costa has already left Australia again for the United States and thus writes with a greater physical distance about multicultural Australia.

Clarke, Colin, Ceri Peach, and Steven Vertovec, eds. *South Asians Overseas: Migration and Ethnicity*. Cambridge: Cambridge University Press, 1990.

Derrida, Jacques. *Of Hospitality*: *Anne Dufourmantelle Invites Jacques Derrida to Respond*. Trans. Rachel Bowlby. Stanford: Stanford University Press, 2000.

Dessaix, Robert. 'Nice Work if You Can Get it.' *Australian Book Review* 128 (February–March 1991): 22–28.

Caputo, John D., ed. *Deconstruction in a Nutshell: A Conversation with Jacques Derrida*. New York: Fordham University Press, 1997.

Dickinson, Jen, and Adrian J. Bailey. '(Re)membering Diaspora: Uneven Geographies of Indian Dual Citizenship.' *Political Geography* 26.7 (2007): 757–74.

Ebr.-Vally, Rehana. *Kala Pani: Caste and Colour in South Africa*. Cape Town: Kwela, 2001.

Faria, Ana Ivete. 'The Future of Indian Ethnicity in Australia – An Educational and Cultural Perspective.' *International Education Journal* 2.4 (2001). [accessed 14 January 2011] ehlt.flinders.edu.au/education/iej/articles/v2n4/FARIA/BEGIN.HTM

Hammar, Thomas. 'Dual Citizenship and Political Integration.' *International Migration Review* (1985): 438–50.

Helff, Sissy. 'Shifting Perspectives: The Transcultural Novel.' In *Transcultural English Studies: Theories, Fictions, Realities*. Eds Frank Schulze-Engler and Sissy Helff. Amsterdam: Rodopi, 2008, 75–89.

——. 'Children in Detention: Juvenile Authors Recollect Refugee Stories.' *Rethinking Multiculturalism: Cultural Diversity in Contemporary Texts for Children*. Spec. issue of *Papers: Explorations into Children's Literature* 17.1–2 (2007): 67–74.

Huggan, Graham. *Australian Literature: Postcolonialism, Racism, Transnationalism*. Oxford: Oxford University Press, 2007.

Hunte, Bem Le. *There, Where the Pepper Grows*. Sydney: Harper Collins, 2005.

Jacobowitz, Susan. 'Under the Southern Skies: Jewish Writers in Australia.' In *Reading Down Under: Australian Literary Studies Reader*. Eds. Amit Sarwal and Reema Sarwal. New Delhi: SSS Publications, 2009, 283–94.

Jensen, Lars. 'From European Satellite to Asian Backwater?' *Australian Studies: Contemporary Issues in Australian Literature*. Ed. David Callahan. London: Frank Cass, 2002, 133–52.

Khan, Adib. 'Trends in Australian Fiction.' *Kosmopolis* 2 (2002). Centre de Cultura Contemporània de Barcelona. 10 January 2008 www.cccb.org/rcs_multimedia/Adib_Khan-eng.pdf

McLeod, John. *Beginning Postcolonialism*. Manchester: Manchester University Press, 2000.

Mycak, Sonia. 'Transculturality in Australian Literature: Multicultural Writing Practices and Communities.' *Multiculturalism in Australian Literature*. Spec. issue of *Journal of Australasian Studies* 1 (2004): 59–66.

Ommundsen, Wenche. 'In Backlash Country: Revisiting the Multicultural Literature Debate in the Wake of Pauline Hanson' in *Australian Nationalism Reconsidered*. Ed. Adi Wimmer. Trier: Stauffenburg, 1999, 223–33.

Ong, Aihwa. *Flexible Citizenship: The Cultural Logics of Transnationality*. Durham: Duke University Press, 1996.

Peres, da Costa Suneeta. *Homework*. London: Bloomsbury, 1999.

——. 'Reflections on a New Ethos for Europe.' 1995. *Paul Ricoeur: The Hermeneutics of Action*. Ed. Richard Kearney. London: Sage, 1996, 3–13.

Rizvi, Fazal. 'Racism, Reorientation and the Cultural Politics of Asia-Australia Relations.' In *The Teeth Are Smiling: The Persistence of Racism in Multicultural Australia*. Eds. Ellie Vasta and Stephen Castles. Sydney: Allen & Unwin, 1996, 173–88.

Sarwal, Amit, and Reema Sarwal. 'Reading Down Under: Australian Literary Studies and India.' Introduction. In *Reading Down Under:*

Australian Literary Studies Reader. Eds. Amit Sarwal and Reema Sarwal. New Delhi: SSS Publications, 2009, lix–lxxv.

Sharrad, Paul. 'Convicts, Call Centres and Cochin Kangaroos: South Asian Globalizing of the Australian Imagination.' In *Reading Down Under: Australian Literary Studies Reader.* Eds. Amit Sarwal and Reema Sarwal. New Delhi: SSS Publications, 2009, 571–82.

Stratton, Jon. '(Dis)placing the Jews: Historicizing the Idea of Diaspora.' *Diaspora* 6.3 (1997): 301–29.

Waddell, Charles E., and Glenn M. Vernon. 'Ethnic Identity and National Identification: The Social Construction of Commitment of Indian Immigrants to Australia.' *Studies in Third World Societies* 39 (1987): 13–23.

9

WRITING CHINESE DIASPORA: AFTER THE 'WHITE AUSTRALIA POLICY'[1]

DEBORAH L. MADSEN

Chinese-Australian literature constitutes a barely recognised sub-category within the nationalist paradigm of 'Australian literature'. Of all reference works, Elizabeth Webby's *Cambridge Companion to Australian Literature* (2000) was the first one to mention Chinese-Australian literary production and even that takes the form of a brief paragraph devoted to Brian Castro in the chapter concerning contemporary Australian fiction. Recently, works by Chinese-Australian writers including Castro and Ouyang Yu were also included in *Macquarie PEN Anthology of Australian Literature* edited by Nicholas Jose et al. (2009). This is not to suggest that Chinese-Australian literature has been entirely neglected. Individual authors, such as Brian Castro, have attracted critical attention. And over the course of the past decade essay collections, such as Wenche Ommundsen's *Bastard Moon* (2001), have created an intellectual space for the discussion of Chinese-Australian literature. More common, however, has been the strategy of including Chinese Australia under the more general rubric of Asian Australia. Works like Tseen Khoo's study, *Banana Bending: Asian-Australian and Asian-Canadian Literatures* (2003) and *Alter/Asians: Asian-Australian Identities in Art, Media and*

---

[1] First published in *Reading Down Under: Australian Literary Studies Reader* edited by Amit Sarwal and Reema Sarwal (New Delhi: SSS Publications 2009, 263–70).

Popular Culture (2000) edited by Ien Ang and others, place Chinese cultural production within the larger context of Asian-Australian culture and thus give a greater critical mass to the field. However, this contextualisation can come at the cost of attention to the specifics of Chinese culture in Australia. An alternative strategy, one pursued by Tseen Khoo in the essay collection edited with Kam Louie, *Culture, Identity, Commodity: Diasporic Chinese Literatures in English* (2005), is the placing of Chinese-Australian literature in the context of global Chinese diasporic literature. This move has the advantage of maintaining a focus on the Chinese ethnic dimension of Chinese-Australian literature, though again the specific context of Chinese historical experience in Australia is minimised by this approach. The opportunity to compare the experience of Chinese communities in Canada, the United States, South-East Asia, and elsewhere, with those in Australia can prove to be very productive. For example, shared historical experiences of exclusion can be highlighted. In this way the *1901 Immigration (Restriction) Act*, commonly known as the White Australia policy, which reserved immigration to Australia for Europeans only, can be brought into relation with the Chinese Exclusion Acts that were enforced in the United States and Canada throughout the early twentieth century.

In this critical field, Anglophone Chinese-Australian literature remains under-acknowledged as a distinct form of expression. The causes of this relative invisibility can be traced historically to the slow emergence of an Anglophone Chinese community of artists in the later part of the twentieth century and specifically after the reform of the *1901 Act*, which brought to an end the era of the White Australia policy. As critics like Ien Ang (2001) have noted, the 1901 Act coincided with the creation of the Australian Commonwealth and consequently anti-Asian prejudice has been a defining characteristic of Australian national identity. This accounts in part for the erasure of writers of Chinese descent from the national literary canon. The Whitlam government, elected in 1972, reformed the criteria for immigration to Australia and a 'race-free' quota system was introduced. Also at this time, the official recognition of the People's Republic of China, and acceptance of refugee immigrants fleeing the Vietnam conflict, contributed to large-scale Asian migration. While acknowledging that the Chinese community of Australia is of long historical standing, this essay focuses upon the emergence of a significant body of Chinese-Australian literature following the end of the White Australia policy. This post-1975 period is characterised by several waves of migration. Chinese immigrants came to Australia from other parts of the South-East Asian diaspora: from Indonesia, Malaysia, Singapore and Hong Kong, for example; later, after the events of Tiananmen Square, a further wave of immigrants entered Australia or, in the case of Chinese students studying in Australia who became involuntary migrants, remained in Australia. These very different migrations have served to complicate the history of the Chinese-Australian community. Dating from the goldrush period of the nineteenth century (1850s), the older migrant communities were overwhelmingly Cantonese speaking and it was this culture of coastal southern China that shaped the formation of urban Chinatowns in the major Australian cities. Later migrants were not necessarily Cantonese-speaking, rather they might speak Hokkien or Mandarin, or various other regional dialects. The difference between migrating from the Chinese mainland or from another point in the global overseas Chinese diaspora added another significant point of difference. Mapping the impact of these differences upon Chinese-Australian literary production, while attending to points of convergence that allow us to speak of a coherent body of work that would constitute modern Anglophone 'Chinese-Australian Literature', is the aim of this essay.

Beth Yahp represents in important respects this post-1975 generation of Chinese-Australian writers. She was born in Malaysia in 1964, of Chinese-Thai background, and migrated with her family to Australia in 1984. In 1998 she moved to Paris and now she divides her time among Sydney, Kuala Lumpur and Paris. Beth Yahp's heritage requires us to ask how we should determine who counts as a Chinese-Australian writer. She was not born in Australia; and she spends more time living outside than in Australia. Her best known work, the novel *The Crocodile Fury* (1992), does not refer to the experience of being Chinese-Australian, though it won her several prestigious Australian literary awards. Technically, it is a highly accomplished work, representing a fusion of oral narrative and a cyclical, repetitive symbolic structure. The formal nature of the novel reflects the anti-colonial theme: much of the action takes place in and around the convent which acts as a power of 'civilisation' that sets out to oppress, Christianise and Europeanise the 'natives'. Yahp refuses to produce a linear narrative that might replicate this process of producing or reproducing oppressive meaning systems. The narrative tells the story of three generations of Malaysian women: the unnamed first-person narrator, her mother and grandmother. The form of the novel aims to memorialise their suffering but in the context of vengeance rather than victimhood. Imagery of crocodiles and metaphors of angry ghosts carry this thematic freight, in a text that deploys techniques of magical realism to represent the quest for vengeance by both the living and the dead. Yahp offers a critique of colonialism that is fundamentally ontological, by contrasting colonising and native worldviews.

Another important recent Chinese-Australian text that uses symbolic technique in order to pose ontological questions is Lau Siew Mei's novel *Playing Madame Mao* (2000). Mei migrated to Australia from Singapore in 1994 and now lives in Brisbane. In her narrative, which offers a reappraisal of Mao's widow, the appearance of a mythical underwater mirror-world of vengeful spirits stresses the same kind of ontological uncertainty that is thematised by Yahp's use of the Malaysian *pontiak* figure. Lau's novel is structured around the symbolism of mirroring, as the actress-protagonist finds her own identity becoming increasingly indistinguishable from that of the woman she is performing: Mao's third wife, Chiang Ching. The idea of life as a performance gives rise to a novel in which illusion undermines our understanding of history, mythology and reality.

The play 'Chinese Take-Away' (1997) by Anna Yen similarly explores the effect on the individual psyche of the pressure of migration, in this case from Hong Kong to Sydney. The autobiographical drama concerns the circumstances, both historical and emotional, that led Anna's mother to commit suicide. The play documents this woman's gradual loss of sanity as her disappointed ambitions are replaced with a life of drudgery, exclusion and isolation. Yen uses techniques of dance and of movement to transform the theatrical space into various geographical and historical spaces: the China where her grandmother was sold as a child slave; the Hong Kong family that her mother left behind; the restaurant in which her father lived out so much of his own life of drudgery. The combined pressures of Chinese patriarchy and Australian racism break down her mother's sense of self as a sovereign human subject as she begins to lose even the fundamental distinction between human and animal. Finally, the frustrations culminate in a deadly act of violence against a disappearing self, leaving the daughter, Anna, to make sense of her mother's disintegration and attempt to find a way to forgive all the actors in this tragic drama.

The undermining of the ontological line between sanity and insanity, self and other, real and unreal, is explored by another Singapore-born Chinese-Australian writer, Simone Lazaroo. Her two novels, *The Australian Fiancé* (2000) and *The World Waiting to Be Made* (1994) explore intercultural relations between the Eurasian community of Singapore and Anglo-Australia. *The Australian Fiancé* is set in 1949, during the time when the White Australia policy was in full force, and tells of a young Eurasian woman who travels to Australia to be married. However, she has been brutalised as a 'comfort woman' during the Japanese occupation of Singapore and she struggles to reconstruct a viable sense of self through this history and in the context of endemic anti-Asian racism in Australia. Indicative of this history, the young woman remains unnamed throughout the novel. In Australia, the combined effects of patriarchy and racism render life unbearable and the fiancée finally returns to Singapore. *The World Waiting to Be Made* takes a more ironic approach to the story of the migrant Dias family, as they move from Singapore to Australia. The contrast between suburban Perth and Malacca provides a context for self-discovery for the young female protagonist, as she struggles to find a way to belong in a society dominated by Australia's beach/surf-culture and finally returns to her birthplace, Singapore.

The difficulty yet inevitability of 'Australianisation' and Chinese-Australian cultural hybridisation is addressed by the Malaysian-born writer Hsu Ming Teo in her two novels: *Love and Vertigo* (2000) and *Behind the Moon* (2005). *Love and Vertigo* concerns the return to Asia from Australia as a consequence of the death of the protagonist's mother. Much of the narrative concerns the history of Pandora, the mother, as her daughter Grace tries to deal with her own problems of migrant identity. The novel presents a story of multiple migrations: from Singapore to Malaysia to Sydney. In this way, Teo captures a sense of global Chinese diaspora that is common to many Chinese-Australian texts. The originary ethnic 'home' of the Lim family is a China now so distant in the family's history that it is never mentioned in the narrative. The narrative captures the complexity of the Chinese diasporic experience by tracing this family history through several generations. Hsu-Ming Teo's second novel is also in some respects a family history but focused upon life in suburban Sydney for three adolescents: Justin Cheong who is Singapore-born, middle class and gay; the Vietnamese-American girl Tien Ho, who arrives in Australia as a refugee; and Anglo-Australian Nigel 'Gibbo' Gibson. They meet in school, and vow to remain lifelong friends. However, they become estranged by the tensions generated by Justin's homosexuality, and by Gibbo's feelings of insecurity because he sees himself as insufficiently 'multicultural' to truly belong in contemporary Australian society, the way that Justin and Tien seem to do. Through the network of family relationships and friendships Teo explores the cultural conflicts between Anglo- and Asian-Australians and also the conflicts among Asian immigrant groups in Australia.

One of the more controversial Chinese-Australian writers, Lillian Ng, also uses the interplay between personal and historical narratives in her fiction. Her first novel, *Silver Sister* (1994), dramatises the multiple migrations characteristic of Chinese-Australian diasporic experience in this period, and Ng's own personal experience. She was born in Singapore, grew up in Hong Kong, Singapore and the United Kingdom, before migrating to Australia in 1972. *Silver Sister*, set during the Second World War in China and South-East Asia, reveals the ways in which history shapes the migratory routes and cultural identities available to an individual at any given moment. Ng's second novel presents a similar view, focusing as it does upon a Chinese student stranded in Sydney in the aftermath of the 1989 Tiananmen Square disturbances. *Swallowing Clouds* (1997) is structured by a parallel between the contemporary experience of the protagonist Syn and the ancient story of a woman drowned in a pig's basket as punishment for adultery. Syn is characterised as a modern reincarnation of the executed woman in her relationship with her boss, the married butcher Zhu. This controversial novel, which dwells explicitly on the details of their sexual relationship, has been condemned by critics like Tseen Khoo (2000) as an orientalising representation of Asian women as passive, acquiescent and sexually available.

Recent writers like Hsu-Ming Teo, Simone Lazaroo and Lau Siew Mei all grew up in Australia. However, there is a significant group of writers, sometimes referred to as the Tiananmen generation, who are recent direct migrants from the Chinese mainland, like Lillian Ng's fictional character Syn. Fang Xiangshu's autobiographical narrative, *East Wind, West Wind* (1992), for example, describes the many difficulties confronted by a Chinese dissident who seeks to settle in Australia. Many of the interviewees in Sang Ye's *The Year the Dragon Came* (1996) are post-Tiananmen migrants who express their disappointment and anger in the face of Australia's residual anti-Asian racism.

Perhaps the best known of these 'angry' Chinese-Australians is the poet and fiction writer Ouyang Yu, whose themes centre on anger, exile and the question of literary voice. Yu was born in 1955 in Huangzhou, China and arrived in Australia in 1991. He is the editor of *Otherland*, Australia's only Chinese-language literary journal. Yu's writing, *Moon Over Melbourne and Other Poems* (1995), speaks of the 'between worlds' condition of failure to belong as either Chinese or Australian in terms of language, culture, history and identity. The poem 'Alien' proclaims:

> I stand on this land
> that does not belong to me
> that does not belong to them either. (*Moon Over Melbourne*, 28)

This failure to belong is explored in terms of gaze and voice: the racist gaze and its deliberate absence is the subject of the poem 'Ways of Not Seeing' where he documents various forms of (not) seeing that reinforce his status as a (barely) tolerated outsider:

> One way of not seeing is remote control
> that senses your approaching and looks away well in advance
> another way of not seeing is staring into your eyes
> and right through until s/he sees someone behind you. (*Moon Over Melbourne*, 81)

As Yu observes this process of not-seeing, it eventually promotes a similarly selective vision in the 'foreigner' who will learn to look back with a dehumanising gaze, as if 'they' were 'a tree, a blade of grass, a kangaroo or anything' (*Moon Over Melbourne* 81). The 'between worlds' condition is described in the poem 'Seeing Double':

> wherever you go
> china follows you

like a shadow
its ancientness
recast in australia. (*Moon Over Melbourne* 36)

Cultural translation is a necessary but painful condition of migrant life in Australia. However, this continual process of interpretation and translation is endlessly confusing, threatening the loss of self and of identity, rather than the acquisition of additional cultural 'selves':

you can't help but
translate everything back and forth so many times
that it becomes unrecognisably
fascinating as a doubled, tripled, multiple double. (*Moon Over Melbourne*, 36)

The idea of cultural hybridity marks the work of a number of contemporary cosmopolitan Chinese-Australian writers: notably, Tom Cho (previously known as Natasha Cho) and, the most prominent of recent Chinese-Australian writers, Brian Castro. Not only does Cho experiment with the possibilities for hybrid ethnic and racial identities, he also plays with gender in unsettling ways. In the short story 'Speaking English' (2003), published in the webzine *CornerFold Magazine*, Cho juxtaposes pop cultural references in a comic and ironic fashion. The story begins with the narrator's confession that speaking English became much easier once she adopted the habit of substituting for unknown words or phrases either the name of a celebrity or a string like 'yada yada yada'. This gives rise to a series of comic juxtapositions between a 'home' or ethnic origin thought of in 'traditional' terms, and the contemporary Australian 'here', which is characterised by a pantheon of popular movie and television icons. Gender switching, by having a female narrative voice identify as Ricardo Montalban, the American actor best known as the unctuous host of the eponymous 'Fantasy Island' in the US television series of the late 1970s, meets racial cross-dressing in a narrative that posits the possibility of encountering a Chinese Heather Locklear or

Hispanic Martha Stewart. In another story, 'Dinner with My Grandmother' (2005), Cho plays with some of the typical features of canonical Anglophone Chinese diasporic fiction, of the kind inspired by the Chinese-American writer, Amy Tan. The story begins with a description of the grandmother's house as a scene of stereotypically 'Chinese' culture. However, this comfortably familiar description of the grandmother figure is quickly destroyed by the introduction of an outrageously incongruous detail:

> She has traditional Chinese costumes, genuine jade jewellery from China, Chinese posters, corpses of real Chinese people that she stole from cemeteries in Beijing, and more. (Cho, 35)

The stereotype of the diasporic Chinese woman is held up to ridicule: from her 'authentic' Chinese artefacts, to her inability to speak Chinese (so she speaks French malapropisms instead), and the absurd story of patriarchal oppression that compels the grandmother to go by the ridiculous name (Joe Lobarto) that her husband demands she use. Cho has taken the commodified elements of fiction by writers like Amy Tan as the object of his scathing irony. Cho's is a narrative voice securely embedded in both Chinese and Australian cultural worlds. Tom Cho performs a hybrid cultural production of 'Chinese-Australianness', where there is no authentic point of origin, only a hybrid and multicultural present.

The best known of all contemporary Asian-Australian writers is Brian Castro, whose work systematically deconstructs the notion of an 'authentic' Chinese cultural heritage. Castro was born in 1950 and, symbolically, at sea in transit between Macao and Hong Kong; he came to Australia in 1961. His works have won all of the major Australian literary awards and he is the only Chinese-Australian writer to have been accorded recognition in published histories of Australian Literature. His novels include *Birds of Passage* (1983), *Pomeroy* (1991), *Double-Wolf* (1991), *After China* (1992), *Stepper* (1997), and the fictionalised autobiography *Shanghai Dancing* (2003). He is also the author of an acclaimed collection of literary essays, *Looking for Estrellita* (1999). In the essay 'Writing Asia', hybridity is represented as his Australian heritage, but his Australian experience is of a society resistant to cultural and ethnic difference. He also describes his personal subjection to the imposition of difference or foreignness. In the essay 'Memoirs of a Displaced Person', in *Looking for Estrellita*, he considers this external imposition of 'Chineseness':

> What did it mean to look Chinese? I hadn't thought about it before until it was pointed out to me ... I became, from that moment of being named a 'Chink', defensive, anxious, unsure. Which leads me to a generalisation – a legacy and a habit – that most Chinese people in Australia, no matter how clannish or Westernised, become outsiders at some stage, because for once they have to take account of themselves – something that is alien and foreign to their nature and culture. Forced to think about notions of national identity, many become evasive and cautious; for such notions disrupt the essential harmony of their being, their unstated family philosophy. Besides, the idea of a national identity is a gross simplification, often confusing racial type with a crude definition of culture. (Castro, 43–44)

Certainly, simplified national identity is eschewed in Castro's fiction. Australia is described as a position from which he is able to speak as shown in Castro's 1994 address to the Fourth Conference of Australian Studies at Guangzhou: 'I live permanently now in Australia', he says, 'but j'avance masque. I go forward still, with a mask on my face' ('Heterotopias: Writing and Location', 181). In a 2002 interview, Castro rejects the kind of historical project that characterises the work of contemporaries such as Hsu-Ming Teo and Lillian Ng. His writing shares a commitment to the kind of unstable, multifaceted, and empowering cultural personae explored by writers like Beth Yahp, Lau Siew Mei, and Tom Cho.

Castro's 2005 novel, *The Garden Book*, returns to themes explored in his first and most 'Chinese' novel, *Birds of Passage*, where the protagonist seeks a sense of self from a past that is mediated by writing. In *The Garden Book* a librarian, Norman Shih, reconstructs from various written clues the life, and particularly the romantic life, of Swan Hay, who was born Shuang He, the daughter of a country schoolteacher. Underlying the narrative is the question: what is the nature of the relationship between these two? *Birds of Passage* juxtaposes two stories: the historical narrative of Lo Yun Shan, a 'sojourner' of the 1850s goldrush, and the modern narrative of Seamus O'Young, an Australian-born Chinese. Seamus, an orphan with no roots, encounters Shan through a sheaf of decaying letters and comes to suspect that Shan, who possibly left a child behind upon his return to China, may be his ancestor. Seamus describes living in exile in the land of his birth. It is Seamus' experience of living with no secure sense of identity or history, of living perpetually in transition, and facing the challenge of creating his own sense of self that is the focus of the novel and, indeed, of Castro's positioning as a multicultural writer in Australia.

Australian multiculturalism historically emerged as a response to the limited numbers of Northern Europeans coming to Australia after the major post-Second World War migrations. In need of people to sustain the nation's economic critical mass, immigration regulations were relaxed to permit migrants from Southern Europe, notably those of Italian and Greek heritage, to enter the country. Only when this source of immigration threatened to dry up did the historic attempt to keep Australia 'white' and 'Anglo-Celtic' finally come to an end. Only in 1975 with the end of the White Australia policy did the notion of Australia as a multicultural nation enter the public discourse. Despite the presence of Chinese immigrants and Chinese-Australian communities since the time of the goldrush, it was only after 1975 that a generation of writers of Chinese heritage began to emerge as they found not only a literary voice with which to speak out about Australia's history of anti-Chinese prejudice and aggression but also a colonial history, a philosophical problematic, and a national future about which and towards which to write. Brian Castro, Tom Cho, and Beth Yahp are among a generation of Chinese-Australian writers who have transformed Australian multicultural writing into the most lively and innovative field within contemporary Australian literary production.

Works Cited

Ang, Ien. *On Not Speaking Chinese: Living Between Asia and the West.* New York: Routledge, 2001.

Ang, Ien, Sharon Chalmers, Lisa Law, and Mandy Thomas eds. *Alter/Asians: Asian-Australian Identities in Art, Media and Popular Culture.* Sydney: Pluto, 2000.

Barker, Karen. 'Theory as Fireworks: An Interview with Brian Castro.' *Australian Literary Studies* 20.3 (2002): 241–48.

Castro, Brian. *The Garden Book.* Artarmon, NSW: Giramondo, 2005.

——. *Shanghai Dancing.* Artarmon, NSW: Giramondo, 2003.

——. *Looking for Estrellita.* St Lucia: University of Queensland Press, 1999.

——. *Stepper.* Milsons Point, NSW: Random House, 1997.

——. 'Heterotopias: Writing and Location.' *Australian Literary Studies* 17.2 (1995): 178–82.

——. *Drift.* Port Melbourne, Victoria: W. Heinemann, 1994.

——. *After China.* Sydney: Allen & Unwin, 1992.

——. *Double-Wolf.* Sydney: Allen & Unwin, 1991.

——. *Pomeroy.* Sydney: Allen & Unwin, 1990.

——. *Birds of Passage.* Sydney: George Allen & Unwin, 1983.

Chinese Take-Away. Script. Anna Yen. Dir. and Prod. Mitzi Goldman. SBS, 2003.

Cho, Natasha. 'Learning English.' *CornerFold Magazine* 4 (2003). 15 September 2005. In *West of the West*. Eds. S. Brook, Natasha Cho, and B. M. Janssen. Melbourne: Common Ground, 2005, 50.

Cho, Tom. 'Dinner with My Grandmother.' *The New Quarterly* 99 (2005): 35–36. 15 September 2005. www.diadic.com/Tom/fset_fiction.htm

Jose, Nicholas, et al., eds. *Macquarie PEN Anthology of Australian Literature*, Crows Nest, NSW: Allen & Unwin, 2009.

Khoo, Tseen-Ling. *Banana Bending: Asian-Australian and Asian-Canadian Literatures*. Montreal: McGill-Queen's University Press, 2003.

——. 'Selling Sexotica: Oriental Grunge and Suburbia in Lillian Ng's *Swallowing Clouds*.' In *Journal of Australian Studies* 65 (2000): 164–72.

Khoo, Tseen-Ling, and Kam Louie, eds. *Culture, Identity, Commodity: Diasporic Chinese Literatures in English*. Montreal: McGill-Queen's University Press, 2005.

Lazaroo, Simone. *The Australian Fiancé*. Sydney: Picador, 2000.

——. *The World Waiting to be Made*. Fremantle, WA: Fremantle Arts Centre Press, 1994.

Mei, Lau Siew. *Playing Madame Mao*. Chichester: Summersdale, 2000.

Ng, Lillian. *Swallowing Clouds*. Hopewell, New Jersey: Ecco, 1997.

——. *Silver Sister*. Port Melbourne: Mandarin, 1994.

Ommundsen, Wenche, ed. *Bastard Moon: Essays on Chinese-Australian Writing*. Spec. issue of *Otherland Literary Journal* 7 (2001).

——. 'Birds of Passage? The New Generation of Chinese-Australian Writers.' In *Alter/Asians: Asian-Australian Identities in Art, Media and Popular Culture*. Eds. Ien Ang, Sharon Chalmers, Lisa Law, and Mandy Thomas. Sydney: Pluto, 2000. 89–106.

Teo, Hsu-Ming. *Behind the Moon*. St Leonards, NSW: Allen & Unwin, 2005.

——. *Love and Vertigo*. St Leonards, NSW: Allen & Unwin, 2000.

Webby, Elizabeth, ed. *Cambridge Companion to Australian Literature*. Cambridge: Cambridge University Press, 2000.

Xiangshu, Fang, and Trevor Hay. *East Wind, West Wind*. Ringwood, Victoria: Penguin, 1992.

Yahp, Beth. *The Crocodile Fury*. Sydney: Angus & Robertson, 1992.

Ye, Sang. *The Year the Dragon Came*. St Lucia: University of Queensland Press, 1996.

Yen, Anna. 'Chinese Take-Away.' Dir. Therese Collie. Music. Charlie Chan. Brisbane, 1997.

Yu, Ouyang. *Moon Over Melbourne and Other Poems*. Melbourne: Papyrus, 1995.

10

SLOVENIAN MIGRANT LITERATURE IN AUSTRALIA: AN OVERVIEW WITH A READING OF THE WORK OF JOŽE ŽOHAR

IGOR MAVER

The first Slovenians came to Australia in the 1850s and 1860s, working on Austrian warships on their journeys around the world, since Slovenia, like most of the other Central European countries, was part of the Habsburg and the later Austro-Hungarian Empire. They did not decide to settle there, despite the alluring sensational news of the goldrush in Victoria. In the period between the two world wars, some 10,000 Slovenians migrated to Australia. They were mostly people from the Primorje (the Slovenian Adriatic Littoral) region, which after the Great War became part of Italy. They wanted to avoid the strong Italianising process in the area, and also find a better life, since the economic situation was extremely difficult because of the Great Depression. The main reasons for the migration of Slovenians to Australia after the Second World War were, however, the changes in the socio-political system of the then socialist Yugoslavia Slovenian territory, as well as the increasingly difficult economic situation in the country which had resulted from rapid industrialisation and de-agrarisation. The number of Slovenian migrants living in Australia today is around 25,000, although with the second generation of migrants included, it may be as high as 30,000. Since the 1970s the massive immigration stream has vanished and even some return migration has occurred. Slovenian migrants have established a number of associations/clubs in all the major cities, they have their churches and newspapers, they broadcast on multicultural radio and, most importantly, they can learn the Slovenian language at the elementary and secondary level.[1]

The literary creativity of Slovenian migrants in Australia started soon after the biggest influx of migration to Australia at the beginning of the 1950s. It was then that the publication of the journal *Misli* [Thoughts] started (1952), where along with the discussion of religious issues and life among the migrants, the Slovenian Catholic priests first tried their hand at writing literary pieces – Rev. Klavdij Okorn and Rev. Bernard Ambrožič. Later laypersons started publishing their works in the journal, among them Neva Rudolf and Ivan Burnik-Legiša. Rudolf lived in Australia only a couple of years; however, with her collection of poems *Južni Križ* [The Southern Cross] (1958) and the collection of sketches, *Avstralske Črtice* [Australian Sketches] (1958), though not published on Australian ground, she was one of the first literary authors among the Slovenians living in Australia. With the publication of the migrant magazine *Vestnik* [The Bulletin] in that period literary creativity received a new impetus and a new possibility of getting migrant literature published emerged. Ivan Burnik-Legiša, despite his numerous collections of verse, has drawn critical attention only in the last two decades with his collections *Jesensko Listje* [Autumn Leaves] (1991), *Za Pest Drobiža* [For a Handful of Coins] (1993), *Hrepenenje in Sanje* [Yearning and Dreams] (1995), and *Klic k Bogu: Pesmi* [The Call of God: Poems] (2008). In the poems he recollects his youth at home in Slovenia; it seems he has never come to accept the new Australian environment as his very own, while, clearly estranged, he does not feel at home in Slovenia either.

The first book in the Slovenian language to be published in Australia was the collection of poems by Bert Pribac, *Bronasti Tolkač* [The Bronze Knocker] (1962). Among his numerous publications, the collections *V*

---

[1] See the Slovenian-Australian Network, www.glasslovenije.com.au.

Kljunu Golobice [In the Beak of a Dove] (1973) and *Prozorni Ljudje* [Transparent People] (1991) have to be mentioned, and more recently *Kiss Me Koštabona = Poljubi me, Koštabona: Ljubezenske Pesmi in Baladice* [Kiss Me Koštabona: Love Poems and Short Ballads] (2003) and *Tam daleč pod Južnim križem* [Far Away under the Southern Cross] (2010) which indicate that Pribac with his substantial quality literary output ranks along with Jože Žohar and Pavla Gruden among the very best Slovenian migrant poets in Australia (see Maver 1994). In 2000 the second edition of his first collection *Bronasti Tolkač* with some additional poems was published in Slovenia in Koper, the Northern part of the Istrian peninsula. In these the poet, both a Slovenian Istrian and an Australian, symbolically (and literally) returns to Slovenia, although he remains split between the two countries,

> neither in this nor in the other homeland
> fully anchored,
> yet frozen in the love of both … (Pribac, *Bronasti Tolkač*, 199; my translation)

Pribac can be placed high among Slovenian poets writing in Australia. It is true that his early work is characterised by a somewhat baroque language, coupled with the typical migrant nostalgia and longing for home. However, he quickly outgrew this early apprentice stage to mature into a subtle impressionist poet of his native Slovenian Istria along the Adriatic Sea and his 'new' second homeland, Australia. He can for this reason also be called a poet of two homelands, who feels at home here in Slovenia and in Australia; who uses in his verse images taken from both lands and whose poetry transcends the borders of space and time to address generally valid issues. Pribac, who has now permanently moved back to Slovenia, has also written a number of essays on the literary productivity of Slovenian migrants in Australia and was instrumental in bringing to publication various recent translations from Australian verse into Slovenian (see Pribac 2003).

Together with Jože Žohar, Danijela Hliš and Jože Čuješ, Bert Pribac was a co-founder of SALUK (1983), the Slovenian-Australia Literary and Cultural Circle, which was founded as a natural outgrowth of the literary magazine *Svobodni Razgovori* (see Suša 1996 and 1999). This magazine, established in 1982 by the energetic editor Pavla Gruden, was a natural Slovenian literary response to *Naš List*, a literary journal of Yugoslav migrant writers in Australia and New Zealand. SALUK gathered most literary Slovenians in Australia, but its foremost merit was that it brought its exponents during the 1980s into close contact with their Slovenian counterparts, resulting in numerous publications of Slovenian migrant authors in Slovenia and several organised reading tours. There were three major literary anthologies published during that time by SIM, the Slovenian Emigrant Association from Ljubljana, which featured fictional and verse works by the authors gathered in SALUK: *Zbornik Avstralskih Slovencev* (1985; An Anthology of Australian Slovenians), *Zbornik Avstralskih Slovencev* (1988; An Anthology of Australian Slovenians), and *Lipa Šumi med Evkalipti* (1990; The Lime-tree Rustles among the Eucalypts).

Pavla Gruden, along with her important work as editor, published a number of poems both in English and Slovenian. Her poetic strength can especially be seen in her collection of haiku verse *Snubljenje Duha* (1994; Courting the Mind). She reveals herself as a subtle poet of this originally Japanese epigrammatic verse, which helps her to depict her migrant experience in Australia (see Jurak 1997). Australia is no longer conceived as a foreign land but rather as a *terra felix*, which may offer migrants refuge, showing them the way out of the controversies of the modern world:

Softly the Southern Cross
Shows the way to the shipwrecked –
The Earth is all turned upside down. (Gruden, *Snubljenje Duha*, 53;
my translation)

Her contemplative stance and *carpe diem* approach speak in favour of a harmony between Nature and Man. Pavla Gruden's recent book of verse published in Slovenia is titled *Ljubezen pod Džakarando* [Love under the Jacaranda Tree] (2002).

The group of migrant poets include the interesting but little published poet Peter Košak – *Iskanje* [Search] (1982), *Ko Misel Sreča Misel* [When a Thought Meets Another Thought] (2006), Marjan Štravs – *Pesmi iz Pradavnine* [Poems from Ancient Times] (1993), Ivan Žigon, Danica Petrič, Ivan Lapuh, Ciril Setničar, Caroline Tomašič, Ivan Kobal, Draga Gelt, Marcela Bole, Rev. Tone Gorjup, and others. Jože Žohar deserves special attention, for he belongs among the best of Slovenian poets in Australia. His collection of verse *Aurora Australis* (1990) was the first book by a Slovenian migrant from Australia to be published in Slovenia, and its thematic and stylistic experimentation and innovations received a very positive critical response (Maver 1992). In 1995 he published his second collection in Slovenia, *Veku Bukev* [To the Crying of Beeches], and in 2004 his third collection *Obiranje Limon* [Lemon-picking] was published. For a detailed analysis of Žohar's work, see the second part of this paper.

As regards Slovenian migrant poetry written in English and sometimes bilingually, the poetry and prose of Danijela Hliš comes first to mind. She represents the first-generation of migrants who write in English, with, for example, Michelle Leber and the deceased Irena Birsa-Škofic, as members of the second generation of Australians born to Slovenian parents. These writers are no longer preoccupied with such typical migrant themes as nostalgia for home or the problems of migrants trying to establish themselves in a linguistically and culturally different environment, for they take as themes existential issues, urban impressions and the like, though tainted with the typical Slovenian melancholy. Bilingualism fits into the framework of the Australian policy of multiculturalism and has thus changed the conditions of literary creativity, especially since the 1980s (Maver 1999, 305–17). Hliš writes her sketches and poems mostly in the two languages. With her perfect command of English as a literary medium of expression, she is the first author of Slovenian origin who has managed to enter Australian multicultural anthologies and even a secondary school reader for Australian schools, with her bilingual verse collection *Whisper/Šepetanje* (1991) and the collection in English *Hideaway Serenade* (1996). Poems in the latter book show her migrant experience as essentially ambivalent: she describes the Slovenia she had left behind not only nostalgically but also bitterly, and, on the other hand, she seems to have accepted Australia as the new homeland with which she emotionally identifies not only in the poems but also in the short stories, essays and sketches.

Apart from poetry a great number of short prose or documentary writings have appeared in Australia and Slovenia: Rev. Bernard Ambrožič, Marijan Peršič – *Per Aspera ad Astra* (2001), Draga Gelt, Stanka Gregorič, Danica Petrič, Ivanka Sluga-Škof, Pavla Gruden, Danijela Hliš, Ivan Žigon, Lojze Košorok, Aleksandra Ceferin, and many others. From among the longer prose works, the book by Ivan Kobal written in English as *Men Who Built the Snowy* (1982) appeared first, published later in the Slovenian language as *Možje s Snowyja* (1993). This essentially memoiristic work is based on the author's personal experience working on the construction of the Snowy Mountains hydro-electric system in the during 1954–58 in which many migrants participated, including Slovenians. The book is a documentary testimony of this project, which according to Kobal, brought migrants of various nationalities together to work in a harmonious union to build the new Australia.

Cilka Žagar is probably the best-known migrant fiction author, for two of her published novels were received very favourably: *Barbara* (1995) and *Magdalena med Črnimi Opali* [Magdalena among Black Opals] (2000). She published the book *Goodbye Riverbank* (2000) in Australia, describing various life stories of Australian Aborigines who she knows well from her work and life among the opal seekers at Lightning

Ridge; she also wrote about Aborigines in the book *Growing Up Walgett* (1990). Žagar's novel *Barbara*, written originally in English and then translated into Slovenian, presents a chronicle of the Slovenian migrant community in Australia, from the construction of the Snowy Mountains Hydro-Electric Scheme to the current problems of the community. Through the eyes of the protagonist Barbara and her family in the fictitious town of Linden, one receives an insight into the sad and even cruel but also happy moments in the lives of Slovenian migrants living under the Southern Cross. Her novel *Magdalena med Črnimi Opali* is about a split personality, the double ego of a single migrant (Magda-Lena) and develops into a saga of a migrant family. While Magda takes care of the family, Lena looks back and tries to find ways to return to the past, when she was loved and she herself loved and still nourished the hope of a better future. Magdalena, two aspects of a personality, dualistically set asunder between the search for the material and the spiritual aspect of life, constantly seeks a perfect love that would provide safety and spiritual meaning as opposed to material things.

Ivanka Sluga-Škof, author of many articles, published in 1999 a memoir on her childhood in Slovenia and her life and cultural work among the Slovenians in Australia. Among the younger generation of writers Katarina Mahnič should be mentioned. She has for some years now been editing the journal *Misli* and has already received important recognition of her writing published in Slovenia. She now lives in Slovenia again, where she also acts as a translator of Australian literature into the Slovenian language. In 2000 a book was published by Ivan Lapuh – *Potok Treh Izvirov* [The Brook of Three Sources] (2000), containing mostly sketches, some poems and a few aphorisms. Two more books should be mentioned in the context of Slovenian migrant literature, although they are written in English. *The Second Landing* (1993) by Victoria Zabukovec, who is not of Slovenian origin, is an historical, memoiristic and part-documentary book based on the experiences of her Slovenian husband. Janko Majnik in his memoir *Diary of a Submariner*

(1996) describes his experience of the Second World War as a Yugoslav submariner, when, not wanting to be captured by the Germans he, together with the crew, defected to the allies and via Egypt eventually migrated to Australia (Maver 1999, 75–84).

The Poetry of Jože Žohar

Born in 1945, Jože Žohar has been living in Australia since 1968. As a contemporary Slovenian migrant poet, Žohar experiments with the potential of the Slovenian language and constantly tries to expand the borders of his world and language through linguistic self-awareness by transcending traditional poetic aesthetics. Žohar's verse written in Slovenian is characterised by linguistic experimentation using palindromes, alliterations, vocal colouring, puns, homonyms and ornamental adjectives, as well as lexical and syntactic play – for Žohar, as a migrant in an English-speaking environment, is interested in testing the very borders of Slovenian poetic (linguistic) expression. Experimentation is central to contemporary Slovenian 'poetology' and to Žohar it in a way signifies even more: his personal freedom.

He could also be described as a migrant poet from the Prekmurje region, for *genius loci* is of great importance in his verse: the Prekmurje region on the one hand (the plain and the hills of the Goričko region in Slovenia bordering with Hungary and Austria), and the arid bush of Australia on the other. Žohar constantly moves between the two locales and identifies with each of them in his poems. The fact that the poet writes about his Prekmurje experience is significant, because this experience is like the region itself, close to the archetypal, elementary folk tradition, and the typical melancholic, mostly flat Prekmurje landscape may be seen as the landscape of the mind. In all three collections of his poetry, the specific geographical environment is strongly present and it appears in a dual relationship: on the one side the poet's native Prekmurje and Goričko, and on the other the Australian desert landscape. He wishes to be at the same time 'one in two, be there and be here', something he considers a special yet agitating privilege.

Jože Žohar migrated to Australia in 1968 and published several of his poems in the Slovenian press as well as the migrant press in Australia. But it was only in 1990 that his first collection of poems in Slovenian, *Aurora Australis*, appeared in Slovenia, which became an independent European country in 1991 after the dissolution of the former Yugoslavia. In an interview Žohar made it clear that he did not approve of the division between a physical and a spiritual migration, for 'a physically displaced Slovenian is at the same time also a spiritually displaced Slovenian'. He chose exile primarily for social-economic and not for political reasons, unlike many of the Slovenian migrants who left immediately after the Second World War to go to Argentina, Canada and Australia. He describes his situation thus:

> To spend half of my life in a country that is so terribly remote and different from my mother country, to overcome all the migrant traumas and problems, to try to integrate into the foreignness and probably to live with homesickness, is to be an Australian, and still, especially to be a Slovenian. All of this must influence a migrant to make his world alive in quite a different manner. (Žohar 1990b)

In his verse Jože Žohar seems almost erotically attracted to Slovenia, his native land:

> I shall be in you for a very long time
> And you shall be in me
> the eternal serpentine. (*Aurora Australis*, 11)

The crucial question for him seems to be how to reconcile in himself the two lands: he has merely become displaced and never really settled. Almost all of his poems are written in Slovenian, although his good command of English would certainly allow him to write poetry in English as well: Slovenian, however, remains the language of his heart.

The displacement and dividedness that characterise Žohar's *Aurora Australis*, shows how he deals with the migrant's sense of estrangement in the new world, his search for a true mother country and, interestingly, a possible acceptance of the new land, Australia. In an earlier poem written and published in English ('Let's Go Home'), after the initial description of the migrant's suffering, the lines towards the end rather unexpectedly suggest an identification of the Sydney suburb of Penrith as a new home. Home is capitalised and accepted by the speaker as a new reality:

In our quiet, great desire,
In hidden suffering we burn.
Maybe after all
Somehow, someday
To the land of our birth
We'll finally return.
But there's the beauty
Of the Blue Mountains that we have
Yet to see, and to discover ...

With new zeal
From the sadness we shall sustain,
And agree: 'Let's return to Penrith.
Let us go Home! (1981)

Žohar's collection of verse *Aurora Australis* features an artistically intriguing poetic cycle entitled 'Apple Poems', written during a sleepless night in a motel in Orange in April of 1987. They transcend the typical migrant nostalgia and again reflect the poet's erotic relationship with his homeland, tinged with thoughts about death. The external flight is replaced, and thus balanced, by the withdrawal into an 'inner exile' that remains laden with existential anguish: 'We are drowning, drowning, oppressed and twisted, deafened by the howl inside ...' (*Aurora Australis*, 25). These poems are characterised by unusual tropes, paradoxical comparisons and very private symbolism. An apple as the symbol of

'Slovenianness' has turned into mere apple peel, Australia having squeezed out all its juices of life. Elsewhere, only sour, sulphured wine remains, as in the poem 'We Are Apple Peel'. Žohar's stream-of-consciousness technique enables him to make ample use of private hermetic symbols which are difficult to decode. 'Apple Poems' also point to the multiple alienation of the speaker of the poems (geographical, personal, social). The 'black sister' which appears in some of the poems metaphorically stands for the night, death or a prostitute, with an Eros-Thanatos relationship firmly in place. The poet contends that there is no easy or relaxed erotic connection between man and woman, but rather a constant mutual self-denial and fear, a search for something else, a fear of spiritual chaos and hallucinations caused by separation. Frequent sound effects and typography, not devoid of semantic significance, show the poet's postmodern *penchant*.

It all betrayed me.
Even the sun and the sky.
Through a blind pane the black sister
Stares black into my Eye

BEFORE DAWN I have to wash my face
With the blood of the sky, bloodless and restless
For apple-trees, for apples …

APPLE-TREES MIGRATE with overripe faces
Into my dreams that are for me by the town of Orange.

THE APPLE WIND from the apple ships
Is breaking through the cracks of the tired windows.
The galleon oars are rowing into darkness.
Oh, Man, why are we so alien to each other,
Why is there no Sybilla, no words among us? …

WE ARE APPLE PEEL and nothing can save us.
The black sister squeezes us black
Among the apples in the green press. (*Aurora Australis,* 26)

183

The Eros-Thanatos relationship is clearly recognisable in the final stanzas of the twelve-poem cycle 'Apple Poems', where night, death, the poet's mistress, and by extension his homeland, all metaphorically merge into one:

SATISFY ME, oh Night! Make me
A statue, a beam, something
That knows no nightmares and peaceful dreams.
But you are growing pale, retreating from the room!
Far behind the mountains you take off your clothes,
The black robe, and you are white. You are hope.
You are faith. (*Aurora Australis*, 27)

The second part of *Aurora Australis* in particular shows the poet's predilection for linguistic experimentation in the fields of Slovenian lexicon and syntax, which is difficult to render in English translation. He is, for example, fond of homonyms, synonyms, phonetic intensifications; he deftly uses onomatopoeia, occasionally adds alliterations, internal rhymes, assonance, interlocking and end-rhymes, and the like. The poetic cycle 'Mourning Poems' is tinged by the hue of sometimes pathetic migrant nostalgia. The speaker of these poems longs for a spiritual and physical *néant* and laments the fact that he shall forever try in vain to return home:

Only you shall never sleep
In these beds between the furrows,
Your own with your people.
You are too far. A disconnected joint.
In vain searching for the way back. (*Aurora Australis*, 66)

As a migrant poet in Australia Jože Žohar finds himself in a double exile; as a migrant from his native country and as an artist, thus by definition an outsider in society at large. His verse has nevertheless managed, metaphorically, to span two continents, Europe and Australia. He has found a striking balance between his memories of the old country, Slovenia, and the experiences in the new country, Australia, with an emphasis on the characteristic Australian landscape, this paramount Australian literary trope. In contrast to many other migrant poets, there is no place for pathetic, maudlin and self-centred melancholy in *Aurora Australis*. The two elements causing schizoid displacement in his verse are geographical distance and the poet's past. Hence his constant departures and returns create an impression of the transitoriness of life:

> Every time I come back, there are fewer warm hands,
> Ready to be shaken.
> And there are more and more of those
> Who cannot recall me.
> At least I know how I fade into nothingness …
> And southerly wind blows
> Over white bones. (*Aurora Australis,* 40)

In summary, in his very first collection of poems, *Aurora Australis*, Jože Žohar states that he does not acknowledge the division between a 'physical' and 'spiritual' migration, since the two appear to him complementary. In his almost erotic link with not only his native Prekmurje, but with all of Slovenia, which is to remain in him as 'the eternal serpentine', he feels that the key question is how to reconcile the two countries within himself. He became 'dis-placed' and never finally 'trans-placed', remaining a cultural hybrid, half Slovenian and half Australian, which in his case represents a sort of homelessness (see Maver 1992; Jurak 1997). It should be stressed that in the different thematic clusters of this first collection he reveals a gift for linguistic experimentation, which suggests an allied formal significance, reflecting his dividedness between the 'old' and the 'new' homeland (Suša 1999). The initial homely sentimentality is replaced by the existential anguish of a migrant and a person *per se.*

Žohar's second collection is called *Veku Bukev* [To the Crying of Beeches] (1995), which can refer to a chronological definition of his youth spent among the beeches but also crying after it; that is, an ode to a Proustian 'time lost', time spent among the reeds, poplars and beeches (See Maver 1995 and 2003). Geographical locale is again of prime importance in the book and it appears in a typical dual relationship: the Prekmurje and the Australian bush country are constantly contrasted and juxtaposed. This second collection of the poet's verse represents his attempt to identify Australia as his new home; yet Žohar remains caught 'in-between' and sings to the Australian 'harem of camels in the desert, tombstones under the eucalypt trees, the waves broken on the shore, kangaroos, run away from bush fires' (*Veku Bukev* 29; my translation). Žohar revives alliterative verse, amply uses paronyms (words that are identical but have a different meaning in a changed context) and palindromes (that can be read forwards and backwards and may have the same or a different meaning), amasses numerous homonyms, synonyms and uses onomatopoeia. However, the question remains: has Žohar really migrated? Certainly physically, but not (completely) spiritually. As in his first collection *Aurora Australis*, Žohar still remains set asunder in the pain between Eros and Thanatos, between the erotic experience of the homeland, Slovenia, and a wish for a physical and spiritual nothingness in the vicinity of death that can only bring 'salvation'. This dichotomy also accounts for the poet's ambivalent attitude towards his homeland, which on the one hand urges him to become erotically involved with it, and on the other, makes him suffer, triggering off a wish for death because of the abandoned homeland. The poet's dilemma is how to 'reconcile' the two homelands, Slovenia and Australia, within himself. Indeed, he remains displaced and has never completely migrated to the newly adopted land.

In Žohar's new collection, a specific geographic environment again appears in a typically dichotomous relationship: on the one hand there is the poet's native Prekmurje and Goričko, the river Mura, and on the other the Australian desert landscape. They are being constantly juxtaposed in his verse. In his melancholy, the poet is constantly returning home and at the same time bidding farewell to it: he wants to be 'one in the two, to be there and to be here', which he finds a special privilege that especially excites him (*Veku Bukev*, 9). However, it is not that he thus finds himself in a sort of homelessness and a divided position, he who describes himself as 'an excited galley-slave between Scylla and Charybdis'? (*Veku Bukev*, 29). Žohar's displacement and geographic schizophrenia never become a self-centred, pathetic lamentation or weeping. The poetic account of Žohar's migrant experience is clearly set into the Slovenian-Australian context, although it could represent any migrant or exilic experience. A certain thematic development in the collection is represented by the poet's Heraclitean preoccupation with the transience of everything, with the flow of time which, in his view, runs in a circle, with the approach of old age and, with the poet's shame from his running away from himself, 'into a non-day, non-being' (*Veku Bukev*, 21).

The collection structurally consists of four cycles, each of which comprises several sections or units, which could only conditionally be called stanzas, for the poems are written in free verse, with occasional embracing and internal rhymes. Žohar's linguistic experimental vein is also strongly present in *Veku Bukev*. Not only does he experiment with typography (for example, in the verse sections 'a mar rama' and 'mure erum'), sound colouring and ballad characteristics, but he tries to revive the old Germanic alliterative verse, which is an important novelty in contemporary Slovenian poetry.

Žohar uses rather sophisticated paronyms and palindromes. His experimentation with words, the changing of individual letters in them which completely changes the meaning and the poetic description of his stream of consciousness represent a significant development in contemporary Slovenian poetic expression. The surprising introduction of alliteration into contemporary Slovenian poetry is perhaps the result of Žohar's knowledge and attachment to the Anglo-Saxon, Germanic

187

accentual-syllabic metrical system, while the palindromic arrangement of letters and the search for new or similar meanings, lexical and syntactical experimentation, the accumulation of homonyms, synonyms and onomatopoeic sound colouring, places the poet among successful Slovenian (postmodern) verse experimenters. It should be pointed out however that his puns and word games are practically impossible to translate into English.

In the first poetic cycle of the collection *Veku Bukev* titled 'Emigrants' Žohar asks himself about the motives of Slovenian migrants to go and live in Australia 'by the muddy rivers', 'in the Snowy Mountains' or on the sugar cane plantations of northern Queensland (*Veku Bukev*, 6). He mentions the attraction of displacement, of leaving one's homeland for an exotic land. In Žohar's descriptions nature is completely indifferent to the fate and life of an individual, a migrant – 'the beeches in the Panonian marshes do not care' (*Veku Bukev*, 6). The poet is 'an erring figure', the prodigal son who has to write his poems, odes to 'the time of beeches that is no more', which turn out to be elegies (*Veku Bukev*, 6). The last part of this artistically effective cycle is partly surrealistic and full of painful awareness of approaching old age and passing away.

The second cycle of the collection, 'To the Time of Beeches', establishes Žohar's life paradox: 'To grow there. To grow up here.' The poet tries to identify himself with the beech and to define himself by a series of original metaphors. He suffers because of the separation from home, which is, however, not characterised only by nostalgia for time lost, but also by the wish to actively participate in the growth and development of the now independent homeland, Slovenia, 'to witness the burgeoning of the land'. Žohar's verse at times becomes painfully trapped in merciless nihilism: he merely sees living corpses around himself that travel through the day into a 'non-day' (*Veku Bukev*, 21). The poem becomes an invisible apron string which ties the poet to this 'eternally young woman', the homeland (*Veku Bukev*, 23). The cycle ends with two short typographic stanzas, which clearly express the poet's allegiance and feelings: instead of 'hare krishna', Žohar cries out 'mura mura' (*Veku Bukev*, 25).

'I Am In-between, I Am In-between', the third cycle of the collection, is the longest one. The speaker suffers because he is split between the two countries, Slovenia and Australia, he is 'in-between', 'a mixture, a conglomerate of both, the blood of the blood of generations, departed beyond their boundaries' (*Veku Bukev*, 35). He is aware of his flight that has found expression in 'crying' from 'the time of beeches', which opens itself as a spiral and at the same time closes and collapses within. The attitude of the poet towards his homeland is very telling: in his first collection the erotic relationship between a man and a woman comes to the fore, while in *Veku Bukev* it is complemented by the relationship ('old') baby-('ancient') mother. Biblical allusions represent another thematic novelty in Žohar's collection – 'I lay myself down on beech-nut, crucified I lay down on it' (*Veku Bukev*, 39), and assume apocalyptic significance – 'until the return of the Shaman who will be a snake' (*Veku Bukev*, 39). Painful departures and returns characterise this third verse cycle.

The collection is thematically and structurally concluded by the fourth cycle, 'The Dry Shadow-Time', which is not set in the Australian setting by coincidence. The cycle is dedicated to Australia, which in his eyes is a dry, deserted and empty 'stolen continent' (*Veku Bukev*, 45), this is the environment where the poet now lives, 'the kind second home, surrounded by the power of oceans' (*Veku Bukev*, 44). There is a biblical allusion to the saviour – 'him who shuns the grave' (*Veku Bukev*, 45), who is to return 'from the sky'. But according to the poet, the saviour is not going to arrive there, 'there will be no sky with clouds above the poor consumed by fire'. Žohar's allegorical journey across the Australian desert countryside is described in a masterly manner. The ironic label 'Lucky country' refers to the description of a kind of hell, where the Australian Aborigines live. They are identified with the land, which represents for them 'a bowl of memory' and is no hell to them (*Veku Bukev*, 47). Žohar envies them, for in contrast to him, the migrant, they are on their own piece of land and they feel at one with it, with 'the land into which they are cursed' (*Veku Bukev*, 47). How to win over time and transience in the dead, dried-out country? The poet answers it by describing a metaphysical search in a love act between two people, who 'pant into the sky and the earth, who hold back, prolong the moment' (*Veku Bukev*, 48), with which they would at least for a moment experience this illusion. Just as the black Aborigine blows the memory of ancient times into his *didgeridoo*, the poet at the end of the poetic cycle cries out for darkness and water for the dried-out land. It should drink till it is drunk, which he himself also desires: to forget.

In Žohar's most recent verse collection *Obiranje Limon* [Lemon-picking] (2004) he has remained true to his bold linguistic experimentation. As a migrant he constantly tests the borders of Slovenian poetic expression, and in this book for the first time he uses rhythmical prose, representing the dark inventory of the poet's life via the metaphor of lemon-picking in Australia. This rhythmical prose or poems in prose also represent a sort of reconciliation with the anguish of a migrant abroad and the significance of 'homeland', reflected in 'Wanderings' for an emigrant as 'one of us, displaced, with home away from home. Jernej. Domen. The tenth child. And much more' (*Obiranje Limon*, 49; my translation). Žohar intimately yet only partly accepts Australia as his new homeland, because as a migrant he remains constantly displaced and not fully transplaced (Maver 2004). He sees his life as an endless process of saying goodbye and claims there is each time less of himself, whether departing from Slovenia or Australia, where, as the prodigal son, he tries to find his peace but also poetic inspiration. In 'Complaints, Conciliations' he writes:

> Where you are now, there is June, when lemons and oranges become ripe, time when you leave all behind and everybody leaves you behind, because you want it like this for a change. For you know full

well that among lemon trees sensually rich poems happen too. Find
yourself shelter among them. (*Obiranje Limon*, 29; my translation)

The poet's new collection of poems *Obiranje Limon* contains seven
cycles or thematic clusters: 'At Home! At Home! At Home! (The Two of
Us)', 'Symposion', 'From Apple-tree Orchards', 'Indian Fragments',
'Lemon-picking', 'Nameless', and 'Word Anguishes'. The first cycle
represents the poet's most explicit wording of his migrant experience and
the overpowering sense of homelessness. 'Lemon-picking' consists of
lengthy poems in prose, and the cycle 'Nameless' features puns and
linguistic experimentation. Žohar's poems in rhythmical prose are a new
form for him, and he shows his essential dividedness between the two
'homes' in 'Lemon-picking':

> You feel: there is less of you with each new coming back. Anywhere
> you go, you are merely saying good-bye. From everything and
> everybody. From bays and beaches.
> From the Blue Mountains, when they dwell cold in silence or
> when they speak out in fire.
> From the house which is the home of Home. From eucalypts,
> magnolia. From fences and walls between wordless neighbours.
> From new roots. Yes: from new roots. You feel: there is no more of
> you with each new coming back. You bite into a ripe lemon,
> Suck out its juice. The tongue pricks you. The tongue that is
> called …
> You feel like crying. (Obiranje *Limon* 35; my translation)

The poem in 'Word Anguishes' cycle are consistently written in rhymed
stanzas, and here as in his earlier work, he establishes an erotic
relationship with his homeland personified as a woman:

> Who is this coming back
> down the muddy road? An old man
> to see his bride. (*Obiranje Limon*, 65; my translation)

The cycle 'Symposion' re-establishes the image of a dark 'aurora australis' (Australian dawn), the themes and the allusions and elements taken from Greek mythology are, however, quite new for Žohar. In the third cycle 'From Apple-Tree Orchards' expresses the poets melancholic nostalgia, not only for a home left behind (characterised by apple trees) but also for one's own lost youth at the realisation of man's fragility and transience, which drives him to an Australian pub where he does not find solace nor does he feel at home.

The cycle titled 'Indian Fragments' represents an important novelty in Žohar's poetic opus, although certain references to Buddhism (or Hinduism in his most recent collection) can already be found in the collection *Veku Bukev*. In 'Pilgrimages', Man's anguish at the realisation of his own transience suddenly strikes the poet – a Man, a migrant, as Everyman and as a pilgrim through life – as less dense and pressing during his visits to India, for he seems to be able to find a way out of it in an afterlife voyage and search for a new life after death:

> Scented flames, –
> O, bright flames of cremation,
> Anoint the body that through you
> Offers itself to the gods.
> There is the time of search and migration.
> All the destinations and terminals are also the returns. (*Obiranje Limon*, 18; my translation)

It is interesting that the speaker's experience and thinking about life (abroad) ends with a projection into the future, into what is for him a more 'neutral' locale and culture, India – not Slovenia and not Australia. India represents for him, physically and symbolically, 'something in-between', the phrase he uses to describe himself in a previous collection, a Slovenian migrant to Australia ('Pilgrimages', 'For Indira', and 'Vishnu'). Jože Žohar's *Obiranje Limon* connects descriptions of man's existential anguish with questions of migration.

Conclusion: The Future Culture/Literature

Does the future culture/literature of the newly settled migrant countries such as the United States of America, Canada, and Australia belong to the ethnic mosaic, a transnational hybrid or a new fusion of various ethnic identities? Polyvocality and hybridity are recently introduced concepts, in addition to the already well-established multiculturalism. Homi Bhabha (1994) argues that the concept of hybridity as a form of cultural difference, while sometimes regarded as manipulative, allows the voices of the Other/migrant, the marginalised and the dominated to exist within the language of the dominant group whose voice is never fully in control. In recent theoretical debates, diaspora and diasporic writing have been connected to the constructed and transnational nature of identity formation, since the concept refers to both voluntary and involuntary migrations and movements. In the future, migrant/diasporic writing should be examined for how it represents 'otherness' in a text and how it brings this otherness to bear on the actual experience of reading. Contemporary theory of diasporic literature perceives Home as several locales, liberated from the spatial concept of location, which is at the same time deeply embedded in the cultural memory of a migrant and her/his own personal biography. In Jože Žohar's poetry dis-placement and trans-placement and the fluid diasporic identity, as well as the changing position of the subject in the globalised world, show his contemporary, dynamic global view. The sense of movement in his verse underscores his themes. The two remain the source of an original and assured artistic inspiration in his poetic opus.

Considering the numerous – over a hundred published books (Milena Brgoč, 1996) – and increasingly noteworthy literary works by Slovenian migrants in Australia, at least two ideas for the future suggest themselves. Artistically, important works ought to be more adequately represented in the anthologies of the unified Slovenian literature within the so-called common Slovenian cultural space, a syntagm very rarely heard during the past years; and secondly, literary critics and editors should try to publish and republish individual literary works, especially if they were previously published in Australia with success. With the increasing number of verse collections and books of prose published during the last years, the situation is improving, yet the status is far from satisfactory.

Among the literary genres in Slovenian migrant writing, (confessional) poetry is by far predominant, followed by short fiction, biographical and documentary fiction and, more recently, novels. Within the Slovenian migrant community there emerges the problem of the literary language, English, which is mastered fully by the second generation of authors – Michelle Leber and Irena Birsa – and by some representatives of the first-generation of migrants to Australia – Bert Pribac, Pavla Gruden, Danijela Hliš, and several others. The most important body of migrant writing is, of course, still published in Slovenian, although works by Slovenian migrants written in English (or bilingually), one may claim, also belong within the framework of Slovenian literary sensibility and creativity, a phenomenon that can be found also with other migrant-emitive European nations. Bilingual collections of poems result from a longstanding physical and spiritual displacement, whereby many migrants artistically and intimately increasingly experience Australia as their new or 'second homeland'. Slovenian migrant experience has recently seen its first major literary expression (and film version) outside the Slovenian diaspora, in the novel by the Tasmanian writer Richard Flanagan, *The Sound of One Hand Clapping* (1997). Flanagan based his book on the tragic life story of his wife Sonja, a Slovenian migrant who had arrived in Australia at an early age with her parents after the Second World War (see Jurak 2000).

Slovenian migrant literature in Australia, despite its relatively short history in comparison with that in the USA deserves special mention and research due to its swift growth and artistic quality. By the beginning of the new millennium quite a few of its *literati* have independently published their collections of poems or prose works in Australia and in

Slovenia, and they have seen a warm reception. The most productive and successful among them justifiably ask themselves why they have not been included in the most significant Slovenian literary anthologies and histories (and thus become 'canonised'), in light of the publicly proclaimed artistic merit of their literary work. They do not wish to be pushed, in Slovenia too, into a kind of ghetto, in which some migrant writers still at times find themselves despite the Australian 'multicultural' environment. Many factors, among which artistic merit is of prime importance, speak in favour of including individual migrant works in the Slovenian literary canon. They frequently transcend the thematisation of the Slovenian migrant experience in Australia and adopt a cosmopolitan existential stance which addresses readers internationally, in Slovenia and abroad.

In the present processes of globalisation, all migrant literature is valuable and should not be treated separately or ghettoised, certainly not for the geographical 'tyranny of distance' and even less so for its artistic merit, which in some instances is high indeed. This has been acknowledged also by 'emitive' nations much larger than Slovenia, with a considerable migrant body living abroad. Spiritual and physical dividedness in which many migrant authors have found themselves may even represent an advantage for artists as, less burdened and with a greater critical (di)stance, they can reflect the world around them, the new migrant environment, and also the world they left behind 'at home' in Slovenia. It is true, however, that their country of origin is also changing quickly and is no longer as it was when they left it. Slovenian migrant writers in Australia translate reality in two different systems, which is why their work can be enriching to both cultures, the source and the target one: thus they emerge as 'transcultural' writers in the best sense of the word, figuring both in the unified Slovenian cross-border cultural space worldwide and the Australian multicultural society. Their empowered literary voice and vision have pluralised and globalised Australian as well as Slovenian literary production *per se* and the spaces they have created in their diasporic writings are fully open enabling a constant construction, deconstruction and reconstruction.

Works Cited

Bhabha, Homi. *The Location of Culture*. London: Routledge, 1994.

Birsa-Škofic, Irena. *Slovenians in Australia*. Ed. Keith Simkin. Bundoora: Birsa and La Trobe University, 1994.

Brgoč, Milena. *Opisna bibliografija slovenskega tiska v Avstraliji* [An Annotated Bibliography of Slovenian Books and Periodicals Published in Australia]. Melbourne: Brgoč, 1996.

Burnik-Legiša, Ivan. *Klic k Bogu: pesmi* [The Call of God: Poems]. Adelaide: The Author, 2008.

——. *Hrepenenje in Sanje* [Yearning and Dreams]. Adelaide: The Author, 1995.

——. *Za Pest Drobiža* [For a Handful of Coins]. Adelaide: Slovenci južne Avstralije [The Slovenes of South Australia], 1993.

——. *Jesensko Listje* [Autumn Leaves]. Adelaide: The Author, 1991.

Cimerman, Ivan (ed.). *Lipa šumi Med Evkalipti* [A Lime-Tree Rustles among the Eucalypts]. Ljubljana: SIM and SALUK, 1990.

Flanagan, Richard. *The Sound of One Hand Clapping*. Sydney: Pan Macmillan, 1997.

Gregorič, Stanka. 'Pesniška zbirka Petra Košaka' [A Verse Collection by Peter Košak]. *Misli* 55.5 (2006): 9.

Gruden, Pavla. *Ljubezen pod džakarando* [Love under the Jacaranda Tree]. Ljubljana. Prešernova Družba, 2002.

——. *Snubljenje Duha* [Courting the Mind]. Ljubljana: SIM, 1994.

Hliš, Danijela. *Hideaway Serenade*. Kings Meadows, Tasmania: Silvereve, 1996.

——. *Whisper/Šepetanje*. Wollongong, NSW: Five Islands Press, 1991.

Jurak, Mirko. 'Slovene Migrants in Richard Flanagan's Novel *The Sound of One Hand Clapping*.' In *Essays in Australia and Canadian*

Literature. Eds. Mirko Jurak and Igor Maver. Ljubljana: ZIFF, 2000, 107–18.

——. 'Slovene Poetry in Australia: From Terra Incognita to Terra Felix.' *Acta Neophilologica* 19.1–2 (1997): 59–67.

——. 'Poetry Written by the Slovene Immigrants in Australia: Types of Imagery from the Old and the New Country.' *Australian Papers*. Ed. Mirko Jurak. Ljubljana: Filozofska Fakulteta, 1983, 55–61.

Kobal, Ivan. *Možje s Snowyja* [Men Who Built the Snowy]. Gorica: Goriška Mohorjeva Družba, 1993.

——. *Men Who Built the Snowy: Men without Women*. Newtown, NSW: The Saturday Centre, 1982.

Košak, Peter. *Ko Misel Sreča Misel* [When a Thought Meets another Thought]. Maribor: Samozaložba Stanka Gregorič, 2006.

——. *Iskanje* [The Search]. Melbourne: The Author, 1982.

Lapuh, Ivan. *Potok Treh Izvirov* [The Brook of Three Sources]. Melbourne: The Author, 2000.

Majnik, Janko. *Diary of a Submariner*. Inglewood: Asgard, 1996.

Maver, Igor. 'Slovene Immigrant Literature in Australia: Jože Žohar's Aurora Australis.' In *The Making of a Pluralist Australia 1950–1990*. Eds. Werner Senn and Giovanna Capone. Bern: Lang, 1992, 161–68.

——. 'The Mediterranean in Mind: Bert Pribac, a Slovene Poet in Australia.' *Westerly* 39.4 (1994): 123–29.

——. 'Zbirka *Veku Bukev* ali oda Izgubljenemu času, času med Bukvami, Topoli in Obmurskim Trstičjem.' In *Veku Bukev* [The Crying of Beeches]. Jože Žohar. Murska Sobota: Pomurska Založba, 1995, 52–57.

——. *Literarno ustvarjanje avstralskih Slovencev v angleškem jeziku* [Literary Creativity of Australian Slovenes in English]. In *Slovenska Izseljenska Književnost, Evropa, Avstralija, Azija*. Eds. Janja Žitnik and Helga Glušič. Ljubljana: ZRC SAZU, 1999, 305–17.

——. 'Four Recent Slovene Migrant Novels in English.' *Contemporary Australian Literature between Europe and Australia*. Sydney:

University of Sydney, Sydney Studies in Society and Culture No 18. Nottingham: Shoestring Press, 1999, 75–84.

——. 'Jože Žohar, Izseljenski Pesnik med Prekmurjem in Avstralijo' [Jože Žohar, a Migrant Poet between the Prekmurje and Australia]. *Sezonstvo in Izseljenstvo v Panonskem Prostoru/Seasonal Work and Emigration in the Panonian Space*. Ed. Marina Lukšič-Hacin. Migracije 4. Ljubljana: ZRC SAZU, 2003, 423–28.

——. 'Jože Žohar, Slovenski Izseljenski Pesnik med Prekmurjem in Avstralijo' [Jože Žohar, a Slovenian Migrant Poet between the Prekmurje and Australia]. *Obiranje Limon*. Jože Žohar. Ljubljana: Cankarjeva Založba, 2004, 71–75.

Peršič, Marijan. *Na Usodnem Razpotju: Per Aspera ad A(u)stra)(lia)*, [At the Fatal Crossroads: Per Aspera ad A(u)stra(lia)]. Ljubljana: SIM, 2001.

Prešeren, Jože et al., eds. *Zbornik Avstralskih Slovencev* [Anthology of Australian Slovenes]. Ljubljana: SIM; Sydney: Slovenian-Australian Literary & Art Circle, 1988.

Pribac, Bert. *Tam daleč pod Južnim križem* [Far Away under the Southern Cross]. Ljubljana: Združenje SIM, 2010

——. Kiss Me, Koštabona = Poljubi me, Koštabona: Ljubezenske Pesmi in Baladice. Koper: Capris, 2003.

——. 'Književnost Avstralskih Slovencev' [The Literature of Australian Slovenians]. *Glasnik Slovenske Matice* 27–28.1–2 (2003–04): 68–75.

——. *Bronasti Tolkač* [The Bronze Knocker]. 1962. 2nd rev. ed. Koper: Capris, 2000.

——. *Prozorni Ljudje* [Transparent People]. Ljubljana: MK, 1991.

——. *V kljunu Golobice* [In the Beak of a Dove]. Canberra: The Lapwing Press, 1973.

Rudolf, Neva. *Južni Križ* [The Southern Cross]. Trieste: The Author, 1958.

——. *Avstralske Črtice* [Australian Sketches]. Trieste: The Author, 1958.

Slovenian-Australian Literary and Art Circle. *Zbornik Avstralskih Slovencev*. Ljubljana: SIM; Sydney: SALUK, 1985.

Sluga-Škof, Ivanka. *Skozi Ogenj in Pepel* [Through Fire and Ashes]. Ljubljana: SIM, 1999.

Štravs, Marjan. *Pesmi iz Pradavnine* [Poems from Ancient Times]. Sydney: The Author, 1993.

Suša, Barbara. 'Literarno ustvarjanje Slovencev v Avstraliji v slovenskem jeziku: Jože Žohar' [Literary Creativity of Slovenians in Australia in the Slovenian Language: Jože Žohar]. In *Slovenska Izseljenska Književnost, Evropa, Avstralija, Azija*. Eds. J. Žitnik and Helga Glušič. Ljubljana: ZRC SAZU, 1999, 267–303.

——. 'The Slovenian Language among the Slovenians in Australia.' *Ethnic Literature and Culture in the U.S.A., Canada and Australia*. Ed. Igor Maver. Frankfurt: Press. Lang Verlag, 1996, 295–98.

Zabukovec, Victoria. *The Second Landing*. Adelaide: Anchorage, 1993.

Žagar, Cilka. *Goodbye Riverbank: The Barwon-Namoi People Tell Their Story*. Broome, WA: Magabala, 2000.

——. *Magdalena med Črnimi Opali* [Magdalene among Black Opals]. Ljubljana, MK, 2000.

——. *Barbara*. Celje: Mohorjeva Družba, 1995.

——. *Growing Up Walgett*. Canberra: Aboriginal Studies Press, 1990.

Žohar, Jože. *Obiranje Limon* [Lemon-Picking]. Ljubljana: Cankarjeva Založba, 2004.

——. *Veku Bukev* [To the Crying of Beeches]. Murska Sobota: Pomurska Založba, 1995.

——. *Aurora Australis*. Ljubljana: Mladinska Knjiga, 1990a.

——. 'Emotions Exposed to Draught are Just Fine, They Will Not Catch Cold.' Interviewed by Milan Vincetič. Trans. Igor Maver. *Delo*. Ljubljana: Književni Listi: 1990b, 7.

11

A MODEL OF MULTICULTURAL LITERARY PRODUCTION: THE UKRAINIAN-AUSTRALIAN LITERARY FIELD

SONIA MYCAK

More than two hundred languages are spoken in Australia today, across at least as many ethno-cultural communities. What kind of literary activity is enacted within these culturally and linguistically diverse communities? To answer this question at least in part, I refer to a project I undertook[1] to study the literary culture(s) of a selected group of Australians: writers who came to Australia as refugees (so-called displaced persons) immediately after the Second World War.

Arriving from war-torn Europe during the years 1947 to 1954, some 170,700 refugees came to Australia under the auspices of United Nations International Refugee Organization resettlement and the Australian government's Displaced Persons Scheme. Department of Immigration statistics at the time revealed that most of the refugees were from Poland, the former Yugoslavia, Latvia, Ukraine, Hungary, Lithuania, the former Czechoslovakia, Estonia, Russia, Germany and Romania. Although the immigrants were penniless on arrival, they quickly formed communities and organised a social and cultural infrastructure by establishing cultural and artistic organisations, dance troupes, choirs, theatrical societies,

---

[1] For details of the scope of the project and the empirical methodology see Mycak 2003.

orchestras, women's groups, youth and scouting associations, sporting clubs, co-operatives, learned societies, newspapers, presses, meeting halls, churches and schools. Within each of the ethno-cultural communities a lively literary life also flourished, and a distinct literary culture emerged which included writers' associations and readers' clubs, recitals and festivals, competitions, and the production of periodicals and books.

According to official statistics, of the 170,700 refugees who arrived through the Displaced Persons Mass Resettlement Scheme, 14,500 were Ukrainians, who arrived in the years from 1948 to 1951 (qtd. in Kunz 43). Eugene Seneta (1989) has calculated a higher figure of 21,000, because ethnic Ukrainians could have given their country of birth as Poland, Russia, Austria, Romania, Czechoslovakia, Hungary or Germany, due to the changing borders of Ukraine and volatile wartime experiences (88). A significant number were also classified as 'stateless' and thus would not have figured within the official number of Ukrainians (Seneta 1986). In 1989 the number of persons of Ukrainian ancestry in Australia was estimated at some 32,000 (Seneta 1989); and it was further estimated that the number of Australian-born Ukrainians was approaching half of this total. Recent figures from the 2006 Census of Population and Housing indicate 13,666 persons were born in Ukraine, although it should be noted that this figure is not derived solely from the postwar wave of immigration but includes more recent arrivals subsequent to the dissolution of the USSR. In the 2006 Census figures, the number of persons of Ukrainian ancestry is given as 37,584.[2]

Ukrainian-Australian publishing began in July 1949 with the appearance of the first newspaper *Vil'na Dumka* [Free Thought].[3] Distributed as a weekly, by August the newspaper was publishing literary

---

[2] Census data taken from the Australian Bureau of Statistics and circulated by the Australian Federation of Ukrainian Organisations.

[3] Transliteration of Ukrainian titles and names of authors in this paper follows that used by the Library of Congress.

works by immigrant writers (Nytczenko 1998, 656). With the production of Ukrainian-Australian books (the first appeared in 1951), the newspaper became an important forum for the review of new material. Both publishing and reviewing literature is a practice which continues in *Vil'na Dumka* to this day. Other periodicals were also established – *Iednist'* [Unity], *Nashe Slovo* [Our Word], *Tserkva i Zhyttia* [Church and Life], *Ukraïnets' v Avstraïi* [The Ukrainian in Australia], to name a few – also acting as valuable publishing and reviewing outlets.

It was not long before literary associations (for both readers and writers) were founded as part of the cultural network within each city. The most active writers' association was the Vasyl' Symonenko Literary-Artistic Club, established in Melbourne in 1954. Membership was open only to active and reputable authors and artists. Literary recitals and 'authors evenings' were held (Nytczenko 1998, 656). This association also paid particular attention to younger writers, organising recitals for them and holding 'Young Writers' creative writing competitions, for which it awarded monetary prizes and organised the publication of winning entries.

The initiator and driving force behind the Vasyl' Symonenko Literary-Artistic Club was the late Dmytro Nytczenko, a consistent and key networker who encouraged potential writers and created opportunities for recital and publication. Nytczenko himself wrote under the pen name of Dmytro Chub, but he was also conscious of maintaining a tradition of Ukrainian-Australian literature and a community of writers. The community of writers functioned within the larger Ukrainian cultural community, and Nytczenko understood and to a large extent created the necessary relationships between the two.

One of Nytczenko's most important activities was the editing and production of *Novyi Obrii* [The New Horizon], a literary 'almanac' published every five years, beginning in 1954. Subtitled *Literatura, Mystetstvo, Kul'turne Zhyttia* [Literature, Art, Cultural Life], it remains the most significant journal and record of Ukrainian-Australian literary culture, and is still published to this day. Nytczenko also compiled two anthologies: a collection of poetry entitled *Z-pid Evkaliptiv: Poezïi* [From under the Gumtrees: Poetry] published in 1976; and *On the Fence: An Anthology of Ukrainian Prose in Australia*, translated into English by Yuri Tkach (1985). In 1980 an anthology of poetry was published in Adelaide by the local association, the Language and Literature Group of Adelaide, entitled *Pivdennyi Khrest* [Southern Cross].

My research led me to some eighty Ukrainian-Australian writers of fiction[4] (including those born in Australia of Ukrainian parentage). These are authors who self-identified as ethno-culturally Ukrainian through community involvement or participation in community-driven publishing. Some feature in R.H. Morrison's *Australia's Ukrainian Poets* (1973), the only other collection of translated works. But most of the work is circulated solely within the Ukrainian community. Written in Ukrainian for this specific audience, prose and poems are recited, and plays performed, at concerts and festivals. Many of these writers have published books. However, community newspapers and other periodicals have also provided a major avenue of publication for their work. Some have been regular contributors for decades. Others send work occasionally. And others write occasional literature. The international Ukrainian diaspora is also an audience, and similar communities in North and South America and Europe have provided significant publishing opportunities for these Australian writers. Many authors have

---

[4] I refer here to writers of prose, poetry, novels and plays. This includes the type of writing now commonly referred to as life writing (memoirs, autobiography and biography or works which combine elements of these with fictional devices). A significant number of authors also write essays. These feature in a wide range of subject and style including prose compositions about literature and the arts, issues of social and cultural significance, historical and political topics, and didactic or polemical pieces. Versatility in literary output is also reflected in other types of literary activity such as editing, translation, and bibliography. Those who wrote only non-fiction or journalism were not included in this study.

contributed to newspapers, cultural magazines and literary anthologies published overseas. Many have also now had work featured in Ukraine. This has been a relatively recent development, since the collapse of the former Soviet Union and Ukraine's independence in 1991 has resulted in a new intellectual freedom and the possibility of links with the original homeland. Writers have work published in literary journals such as *Literaturna Ukraïna* [Literary Ukraine] or have their own books published. Some submit their writing. Some works are solicited. Some of the authors belong to the Spilka Pys'mennykiv Ukrainy [Association of Ukrainian Writers]. In 1993 an anthology of Ukrainian-Australian literature was published in Kyiv – *Ridni Holosy z Dalekoho Kontynentu: Tvory Suchasnykh Ukraïns'kykh pys'mennykiv Australii* [Voices of the Homeland from a Far Away Continent: Works of Contemporary Ukrainian Writers of Australia]. Many of the books published in Australia now circulate in Ukraine.

How is such a literary culture best accounted for? In my view neither a critical interpretation nor a bibliographical description would fully account for the way in which this culturally and linguistically diverse literary culture functions. In my case study, community cultural infrastructure is responsible for the creation and circulation of a body of literature. Within each ethno-cultural community there are networks – there is a structure – by which literary texts are produced, distributed and consumed. For the individual writer, the network supplies an audience/market-place, infrastructural and moral support, and the means of publication. For the community, the network provides a viable and dynamic literary culture that answers the psychological needs of members to maintain their original language and cultural formations.

What then is the best way to theorise how a multicultural writing community such as this functions in Australia? To understand the complex interactions that secure the very existence of the writing, one needs to examine both the socio-historical context and the institutional or material base. Community cultural networks are vital for the texts created and read by these postwar immigrants, and the writing of postwar displaced persons cannot be fairly assessed without understanding the literary cultures of these communities. Since these writing communities function as identifiable and self-contained literary systems within Australia, what is needed is an institutional approach based on field theory, as exemplified by the work of Dutch scholar Kees van Rees and his colleagues, many of whom publish their findings in the scholarly journal *Poetics: Journal of Empirical Research on Culture, Media and the Arts*. Van Rees is one of an interdisciplinary group of researchers based at Erasmus University Rotterdam in the Netherlands.[5] He has formulated a model which schematises the contemporary literary field in Western European countries and has conducted extensive empirical research investigating certain dynamics and structures through which literary fields operate.[6]

Van Rees drew inspiration from Pierre Bourdieu's sociological account of the cultural field, and in particular his article 'The Field of Cultural Production, or the Economic World Reversed' which was published in *Poetics* in 1983 and positioned as the 'institutional approach to the literary field' (1983a, 2001). Van Rees' own conception of the literary field as outlined in 1996 (with Jeroen Vermunt) and 2001 (with Gillis J. Dorleijn) is particularly useful. Here the literary field is defined as 'the set of literary institutions, organizations and agents involved in the material and symbolic production and in the distribution of reading materials' (van Rees and Dorleijn, 333). This conception of the literary field

> is a model of a particular historical situation: Western Europe during the late twentieth century ... However, it may illustrate the different parties that are at stake and their interactions, and may incite students

---

[5] His colleagues include Susanne Janssen, Nel van Dijk, Marc Verbood, and Wouter de Nooy.

[6] A recent project compared the Dutch and US trade book field.

of other cultural and historical settings to specify the agents relevant to their domain. (van Rees and Dorleijn, 333)

This is my aim: to specify the agents and institutions relevant to my particular case-study and adapt the existing scheme of the literary field in contemporary Western societies to create a model which illustrates the structure by which literature is produced, circulated and consumed within the Ukrainian community in Australia. This model of Ukrainian-Australian literary production will exemplify the literary culture(s) of communities and writers who immigrated to Australia as displaced persons immediately after the Second World War.

Van Rees' Scheme of the Literary Field

Van Rees (1983a) defines the literary field as a network comprising of literary institutions. ' "Literary institution" must be taken to mean any formation or collection of agents performing specific tasks in the production, distribution or promotion of fiction' (292). This includes the organisations involved in the material production and distribution of books (publishing houses, public libraries, booksellers and book clubs), literary agents (who function as brokers of new manuscripts), trade organisations (such as writers' unions or associations), and arts councils which advise national and local authorities on public subsidies for the arts. Equally as important are the groups of people, loosely organised, who are most directly involved in the process of symbolic production (literary critics and teachers of literature). 'The whole body of interrelated institutions constitutes the literary field' (1983a, 292).

Looking at van Rees' scheme of the contemporary literary field (cf. Figure 1) we see 'The literary field is the set of literary institutions' (van Rees and Vermunt, 319). Clear also is the fact that the literary field is a dynamic and relational entity. Van Rees explains:

The literary field embodies a varied network of relations. Members of different institutions engage in specific professional activities with respect to literary texts. These activities are shaped by the institutional framework. Therefore, to gain insight into an agent's functioning and its effects one must take into account the rules and conventions governing both the institution to which s/he belongs and its relations with the other institutions in the field. (van Rees and Vermunt, 320)

The relational nature of the literary field can further be understood in two important ways. First, the position of any one specific institution is always relative to other institutions in the field. Van Rees states clearly: 'The position of any of these institutions at a given moment cannot be determined independently of the other institutions' (1983a, 295). This functional interrelatedness is partly what defines each institution: 'The literary field is made up of the institutions functioning within it ... each institution in the field partly owes its specificity to the network of relations it maintains with the other organisations active in the field' (1983b, 402). Second, the relational nature of the literary field is evident in 'the interdependency of material and symbolic production and consumption' (van Rees and Dorleijn, 331); the fact that material production and symbolic production are interconnected processes, which in turn affect the consumption of literary texts.

'A book's material production must have a positive sequel in the process of symbolic production' (van Rees and Vermunt, 318). Symbolic production can be seen as the attribution of (aesthetic or literary) quality or value to the text, the process through which a text is recognised as a legitimate form of art. Assigning value to literature is a process which is 'regulated and controlled' (1983a, 288) by specialised institutions, the most important of which is the institution of literary criticism.

Critics are persons who are authorised to make judgements about the artistic/literary qualities of texts, and make pronouncements which award a certain degree of artistic/literary merit to a text. Three types of critics make up the institution of literary criticism: journalistic, essayistic,

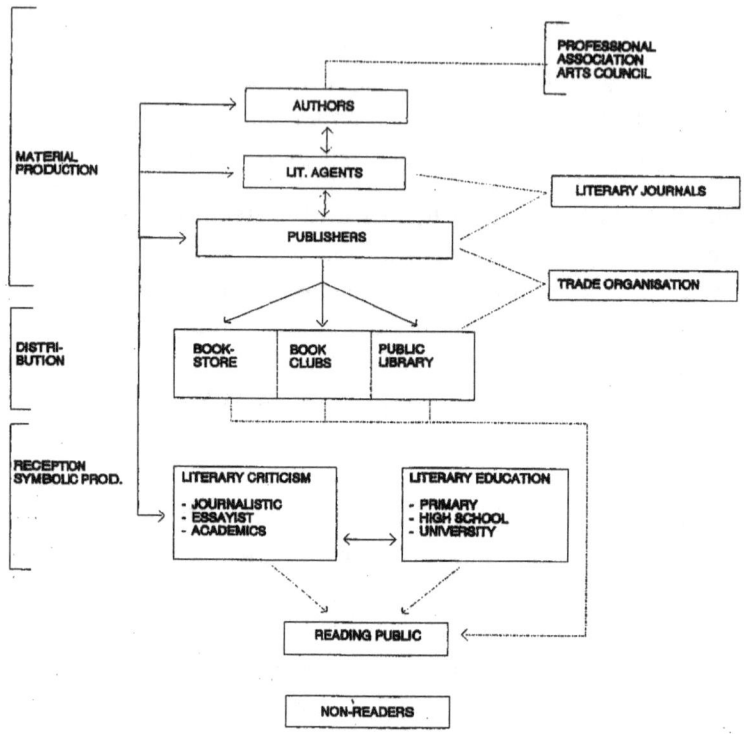

Figure 1: Diagram of the Twentieth-Century Literary Field

and academic. Each type of critic has a certain level of 'legitimizing competence' which can be defined as 'his socially accepted qualification to force, by means of his discourse, public recognition of a text as a literary text which has a certain degree of quality, compared with other literary texts' (1983b, 403). Despite functioning with different levels of 'legitimizing competence', the three types of critics co-exist within the one literary institution because they are engaged in a similar project – have a 'common aim and way of achieving this end' (1983b, 402). First, each type of critic strives to make descriptive, interpretative and evaluative statements on literary texts. Second, the activities of all three types of critics lead to a hierarchical classification of these texts according to their supposed (literary) quality (1983b, 400). As van Rees further explains, each segment of criticism decides (with respect to the repertory coming within its scope):

    i.   which texts are held to be legitimate forms of literary fiction

    ii.   to which rank a particular text is entitled in the hierarchy of literary works

    iii.   which statements on these texts represent proper ways of dealing with literature, viz. which 'do justice' to the text under discussion. (1983b, 402)

Literary critics assign specific qualities to literary works. They award value to literary works, based on the qualities. Thus literary criticism assigns both qualities (properties) and quality (value) to literature. Literary critics rank literary works relative to other texts, thus they decide the degree of legitimacy to which a particular literary work is entitled. They also decide on the legitimate ways of discussing texts. As van Rees clarifies: 'reviewers and critics, as professional judges of literature, possess the socially accepted authority to ascribe specific properties to a work, to suggest in what literary tradition it might be set and how it is to be ranked' (1987, 280).

Despite these common goals, there are differences between the three types of critics. First, with regard to a newly published literary work, they occupy different positions in time. At the point of its publication, a text is not simultaneously discussed by a reviewer, an essayist and an academic critic. A newly published text is first assessed by a journalistic review. Subsequently, the text may (or may not) go on to be assessed in essays or academic criticism. This sequence is designated by van Rees thus: 'In a purely temporal sense, the work of the journalist, the essayist and the academic critic can be designated as "primary", "secondary" and "tertiary" criticism' (1983b, 403).

Temporal distinction is significant; however, other important factors distinguish these three types of literary criticism. Notable differences are to do with the scope of the repertory from which each type of critic selects texts to discuss. The role of primary criticism is to report on the contemporary output of literary publishing houses. The number of books available for review is huge, and journalistic critics select texts through certain indicators: the reputation of the author, or the good name of the publishing company. A primary critic is further constrained. As van Rees points out, 'the journalistic critic has to show great restraint in his references to non-contemporary authors' (1983b, 403). Non-contemporary authors are only relevant insofar as they provide a general background and can be used to make comparisons with the contemporary author under scrutiny.

The first task a reviewer must undertake is to select a work for discussion, or, if invited by a publisher or review editor, to decide whether or not to pay attention to the work. In selecting a particular book for review, a primary critic implies it is of potential importance, either because of the standing of the author, or (in the case of a debutant writer) the status of the publisher. Therefore, being selected for review is in itself confirmation of a certain literary status. By writing a positive review, the primary critic positions the text as indeed important; conversely, a negative review will reject the importance of the work. Reviewers have the power to withhold their attention and give no consideration to a new work. A newly published work that fails to attract the attention of reviewers risks falling into oblivion. Negative reviews of works by lesser-known authors are also institutionally significant because they fulfill the function of setting a 'global average standard' by means of which the 'rarity value' (the high quality) of renowned authors and texts can be gauged.

The repertory of primary criticism is comprehensive. From this body of texts, only a small number will be selected by essayists and academic critics for attention, and thus reach the repertory of secondary and tertiary criticism. Compared with primary criticism, van Rees defines secondary criticism this way: a critical essay comprises a far greater number of words; it often devotes attention to highly esteemed literary works; but most importantly, it is published in a medium other than a daily or weekly newspaper. In other words, essayists publish their 'discourses on literature' in literary reviews/periodicals. Academic criticism, by comparison, is 'the concern of people with a university education' (1983b, 407), publishing their findings in scholarly journals and publications.

As a general rule, academic criticism does not concern itself with recent authors whose work has not received undivided attention of journalistic critics. Similarly, 'in dealing with contemporary authors, an essay will nearly always cover work which primary critics have by common consent spoken of positively' (1983b, 407). Therefore 'the selection made by secondary and tertiary criticism amounts to a narrowing down of the space allotted to contemporary authors in the repertory of highly esteemed literary texts' (1983b, 406). While the journalistic reviewer is institutionally limited to the supply of contemporary literature, the number of non-contemporary authors belonging to the repertories of essayists and academic critics is substantial. There is, in fact, a 'demarcation of domains' whereby the literature of previous periods is almost exclusively the province of academic criticism.

The vastness of the domain from which texts are selected leads to a difference in the cultural prestige attached to each distinct form of criticism. The enormity and the 'unexplored nature' of the terrain from which primary criticism selects texts to be discussed have a negative effect on the prestige of journalistic criticism.[7] On the other hand, the relatively limited number of authors and texts that become the subject of secondary and tertiary criticism bespeak a greater level of prestige. Essayists and academic critics base their own selection upon selections

---

[7] No doubt the discursive form of the journalistic review – short pieces published in daily and weekly newspapers – is also partly why such criticism 'is sometimes reproached with being superficial' (van Rees 1983b, 406).

made by former generations of critics, and are thus seen to pay attention only to important authors and texts.

If secondary and tertiary critics enjoy higher levels of social prestige, so too do their judgements and pronouncements about literary works. The process by which a text is assessed first by reviewers and then by essayists and academic critics is a 'grading process' (1983b, 408) by which a text is awarded a certain degree of quality relative to other texts:

> The respective types of criticism form the complementary parts of a selection process which is, at the same time, a ranking process by means of which a text, when compared with other texts, grows in importance and eventually may obtain the status of masterpiece. (1983b, 403)

The higher prestige associated with tertiary criticism means it has the greatest impact:

> attention being given to a text by academic critics is a necessary prerequisite if it is to be assigned the status of 'timeless masterpiece.' Thus, works consecrated by academic criticism do hold the highest rank in the canon of literary texts. (1983b, 404)

The grading process by which critics rank literary works is 'socially recognised', meaning that critical discourse has an impact upon other institutions in the literary field. As van Rees explains: 'members of the institution of criticism succeed in getting members of other literary institutions as well as non-professional readers to believe that the properties they attribute to a work inhere in it' (1987, 281). Indeed, literary criticism affects the production, distribution and consumption of literature, which is why it is the most important agent of symbolic production.

First, a critic's discourse is itself a form of reception that can in turn affect consumption by influencing the reading public and the institution of literary education. Individual readers may be more likely to obtain a text that is favourably reviewed, and critical reaction is decisive in whether or not a text appears on primary, high school or university curricula. Second, a critic's discourse can affect the distribution of texts, especially via bookshops and libraries. Booksellers may estimate the saleability of a text, and librarian book selectors may assess the lendability of a title, by taking into account the reaction of critics, either to the newly published work itself, or to earlier works by the same author. Third, a critic's discourse can affect the further production of literary texts. Favourable critical attention may influence a publisher's decision to keep a title in print. A publisher may also be more inclined to publish a new manuscript by an author if previous work was critically acclaimed. Positive critical attention may help the author to obtain financial support to produce new material by way of grants or prizes. Work may be anthologised if critics award it a high degree of quality. In summary, then,

> Not only the decisions of the publishing, the book selling and the library fraternities, but also the preferences of individual book buyers and borrowers are to an important degree affected by the opinions set forth by members of the reviewing community. (van Rees 1987, 282)

It is not difficult to understand why in van Rees' model 'Criticism is presented as one of the institutions in the cultural field that play a major role in the assignment of quality to both cultural products and their material producers' (van Rees and Vermunt 318). It is also not difficult to understand 'criticism's dominant position with respect to the other institutions in the field' (1983b, 409). Nonetheless van Rees makes the point that all institutions in the literary field participate in some way in the decision process in which a text is awarded a certain degree of quality (1983a, 295).[8] Further to this, 'The specific ways in which literary

---

[8] This is connected to Bourdieu's concept of 'belief' which functions at all levels of production, distribution and consumption: 'Institutional analysis makes it plain that the activities of all literary institutions jointly contribute – albeit to a varying

institutions analyse the problem of quality largely accounts for their ways of operating within the literary field' (van Rees 1983a, 293). It seems, then, that in understanding processes of symbolic production we come to understand the very ways in which the literary field itself works: 'the study of the way in which literary institutions attribute quality to literary works constitutes a good starting-point for gaining insight into the nature and functioning of these institutions and, consequently, into the dynamics of the literary field' (van Rees 1983a, 297).

The Ukrainian-Australian Literary Field

The Ukrainian-Australian literary field bespeaks a minority literature, taken here to mean a body of writing produced by members of a community which is culturally and linguistically diverse and expresses a specific ethno-cultural identity. Statistical evidence of readership is not known. Nonetheless there are specific institutions of material production, distribution, and reception/symbolic production and these constitute a dynamic and viable literary field. The following model of the Ukrainian-Australian literary field is derived from van Rees' scheme of the twentieth-century literary field (Figure 2).

---

degree and in very different ways – to the kind of (surplus) value an artwork is thought to possess. From this viewpoint, inquiry into the production and consumption of art objects is inevitably involved with inquiry into the production of belief, as Bourdieu's title ['La production de la croyance,' 1977 and 'The Production of Belief: Contribution to an Economy of Symbolic Goods,' 1980] suggests: belief in the symbolic surplus value of art; belief in the consecrating and legitimising activities of critics and connoisseurs; belief in the art producing talent of this or that artist; belief in the edifying and distinctive function of art consumption' (van Rees 1983a, 296).

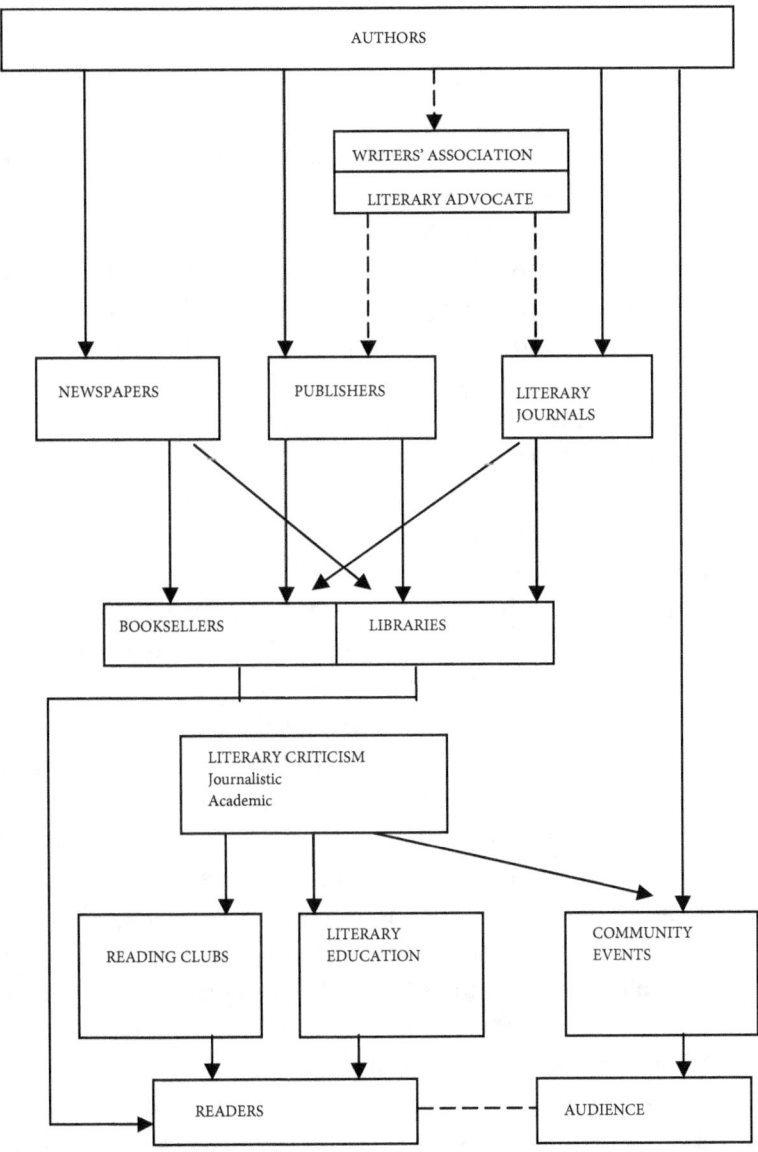

Figure 2: The Ukrainian-Australian Literary Field.

I. Material production

Authors are not professional, in that they receive no remuneration for producing literature. While it could be argued that even in a mainstream literary field often writers do not earn an adequate income from writing, they do attempt to make writing (or related literary activities) a paid occupation and consider themselves to be writing professionally. By contrast Ukrainian-Australian writers do not intend to earn any income from writing. Writing is not regarded by them as a form of employment. It is not an occupation undertaken as a means of livelihood.

Authors write literary fiction (poetry, prose, novels and drama) and have three avenues of publication. First, they can approach community *newspapers*, and send work directly to the editor (the category of 'newspaper' also includes community newsletters and bulletins). Second, authors can negotiate directly with *publishers* to have a book published. In this category publishers can also work as printers, in the sense that they can produce a book in exchange for payment from the author, without necessarily taking on an editing role. Before the advent of computer desktop publishing, publishers who acted as printers provided an important service given that most of the material was written in Ukrainian and relied on a limited number of presses that would print in the Cyrillic script. Third, authors can submit work directly to *literary journals* (the most substantial being *Novyj Obriy* [The New Horizon]).

Authors may join a *writers' association*. These exist in most capital cities and provide valuable moral support for those engaged in writing, an opportunity for feedback on work in progress. In the Ukrainian-Australian literary field, there is no role for a literary agent. Authors do not engage a representative who acts on their behalf to promote their work, negotiate book contracts, organise readings and the like. Instead authors manage their own literary affairs, and liaise directly with publishing and other outlets. However, there is the need to configure a different kind of agency – *the literary advocate* – a networker or facilitator who acts on behalf of the community of writers. In the Ukrainian-Australian case, this role was fulfilled by the late Dmytro Nytczenko. He was the convenor of the most active writers' association, which is why the institutions of writers' association and literary advocate are connected in this scheme. Authors have a choice of whether to work with the writers' association and the literary advocate (the dotted line signifies that they may or may not be connected). Authors may also reach publishers and literary journals through the writers' association and/or literary advocate (for example, the South Australian writers' association produced an anthology; Nytczenko was able to negotiate the publication of books and anthologies with publishers, and he himself was editor of the most substantial literary journal). The words of one author explain the significant role the advocate and writers' association played in motivating her to write:

> I like poetry very much and I started writing from very early age but it was all left at home in Ukraine. But I showed a few things to Mr Nytczenko and he encouraged me. He was always at me, why don't I write, so I joined the [Vasyl' Symonenko Literary-Artistic] club and started writing.

II. Distribution

There are two institutions available for distribution, and both directly reach a readership. *Booksellers* are not bookstores as such. The Ukrainian-Australian community is not large enough to support shops that sell only printed material. Instead, outlets that sell an array of cultural material (music, clothes, artifacts, educational goods, etc.) will also sell newspapers, material provided by publishers, and literary journals. Booksellers will also distribute books provided by the authors themselves. Authors often function as booksellers, in that they will sell their books directly to the public. Books are often sold at cost.

Libraries are not independent institutions as such but are maintained by cultural organisations within the wider Ukrainian-Australian community (churches, schools and local community organisations established and maintained small but significant lending libraries).

The Ukrainian-Australian literary field is non-professional, and literary activities undertaken by the institutions in the field are in a sense non-commercial. It is true that some of the institutions are engaged in commerce or trading, and that products which may be traded are produced. However, the material production and distribution of literary texts in the Ukrainian-Australian literary field cannot be seen to be 'commercial' if we take into consideration the other OED definitions of that word as meaning 'viewed as a mere matter of business' and 'looking toward financial profit'. The field may be regarded even less as commercial if we look to the Macquarie Dictionary's definitions of the word: 'capable of being sold in great numbers', 'setting possible commercial return above artistic considerations' and 'preoccupied with profits or immediate gains'. While authors may hope that their book will sell in order to recoup the cost of publishing it, they are not motivated by the intention of making any profit from their work. While institutions of material production and distribution need to make enough money to cover their costs, they largely function as not-for-profit organisations, hoping only to be able to continue their work.

III. Reception/Symbolic Production

Literary criticism is an important avenue for the promotion of literary work. The 'tripartition of criticism' (van Rees 1983b, 401) evident in van Rees' model is here collapsed into two types of critics: 'journalistic' and 'academic'. In keeping with the non-professional nature of the field, journalistic reviewers are not paid for their work. Nevertheless they write reviews of new material, which are published in the community newspapers. There are no literary reviews in that there are no periodicals devoted solely to publishing critical essays on literature, and so the category of secondary/essayist criticism does not exist in the Ukrainian-

Australian literary field. There are, however, academic critics whose critical work values and ranks literary texts.

The work of academic critics is particularly influential upon another institution of symbolic production, that of *literary education*. There are three ways in which potential readers can be introduced to Ukrainian-Australian literature through literary education. First, community ('Saturday') schools, which aim to teach Ukrainian language and culture may include Ukrainian-Australian literary material within their syllabus. Second, students in mainstream secondary schools have the option of taking a course in Ukrainian language that can count towards their final year leaving certificate (in New South Wales this is called the Higher School Certificate [HSC]). Ukrainian-Australian literary material may be included in this program of study. Third, tertiary courses in Ukrainian language and literature have been available through two universities in Australia (Monash University in Melbourne and Macquarie University in Sydney). Ukrainian-Australian literature may be included in the reading lists of such courses.

Literary critics may also influence the agenda of *reading clubs*, another institution of literary reception. These are quite formal organisations that meet regularly to read and discuss literature. At times a reading club can also function as a writers' association. The Knyholiuby (Booklovers) club in Sydney, for example, provides an opportunity for people to recite and discuss their own writing as well as read material previously published by others.

Community events also provide a form of literary reception. On occasion authors are invited to recite their work at concerts, festivals and commemorations within the Ukrainian-Australian community. Their literary reputation and the quality of their work as valued by academic critics no doubt influence the decision as to who is invited to take part. Authors participate directly in this form of literary reception. Recitals at community events provide an immediate audience, who may or may not be a part of the author's usual readership.

The 'interdependency of material and symbolic production and consumption' within the literary field (van Rees and Dorleijn, 331) is evident in the ways in which reading clubs, literary education and community events can be causal factors in both the creation and consumption of texts. Authors will write occasional texts for national days of commemoration in order to perform at concerts and festivals. Some write new material specifically to be read at meetings of reading clubs. For at least two authors, literary education proved an instance of both production and reception as they created literary material for community Saturday schools. Indeed one author began her writing career in this way. Finding a lack of suitable material for children to recite at school and community concerts, she began to write her own poems, short plays and vignettes. Another told of how she produced teaching material for a Ukrainian Saturday school in Melbourne.

> First of all, I *like* writing, that's the main thing, I think. And later when we came here to Australia there was very little literature in Ukrainian language, and I started working in Ukrainian school, and we didn't have any teaching materials, so it started from there. I started to write about our classics, about our people who were fighting for our freedom and so on, so that our young teachers could [have materials to teach with]. That's how I started first.

Such literary education can function as an effective agency of literary reception. One second-generation author felt exposure to Ukrainian culture during her childhood had been responsible for her developing a love of poetry 'through having to learn poems in Ukrainian [Saturday] school'. She also appreciated the poetry recitals at Ukrainian community concerts for giving a sense of 'legitimacy' to literature. These influences proved instrumental in her decision to write her own poetry.

IV. General Characteristics

A Non-Commercial Field

The Ukrainian-Australian literary field is non-professional, and literary activities undertaken by the institutions are not driven by profit. This minimises two forces that underpin a mainstream literary field: relationships of commercial competition and relationships of commercial support. Van Rees' homology thesis (2004) charts relationships of competition by which individual authors compete with other authors; material producers (such as publishers) compete with one another; and symbolic producers (such as critics) also compete with each other. At the same time, there are relationships of support between authors and their material producers (publishers); there are relationships of reinforcement between material producers (publishers) and symbolic producers (critics); and ultimately this results in confirmation or reinforcement on the part of a consumer group (who will show support by buying/borrowing/reading). While it would be naïve to think that there are no relationships of competition in a non-professional literary field, it would be accurate to say these relationships are quantifiably different and different in kind. Similarly, relationships of support must be different (for example, while a publisher may provide moral support for an author, the publishing company would not be able to pay an advance for the author to write a book, or fund a promotional tour once a book is published).

The non-commercial nature of the literary activity has had an important effect on the structure of the field. A number of agencies which function within the conventional twentieth century literary field are here absent. The realm of material production sees no role for a literary agent as the writing is without commercial gain. As there are no professional writers, there is no 'trade organisation' to represent their interests or 'arts council' from which they can draw financial subsidy or occupational support. The 'literary advocate' and 'writers' association' which do feature in the Ukrainian-Australian field are qualitatively different agencies; both depend on voluntary labour and so the scope of activity is determined according to the amount and type of expertise available at any one time.

Perhaps the most marked difference about the Ukrainian-Australian field is the way in which the authors have unmediated access to publishing outlets and readers. Material production of texts is reliant upon authors liaising directly with newspapers, publishers and literary journals, either with or without the assistance of the literary advocate and writers' association. Authors also self-publish, thus a certain level of personal initiative and financial commitment further drives publication in this field. Individual resourcefulness is paramount, as the experience of one author showed. When asked how his books were published, he explained: 'Some subsidised by Ukrainian community, and mostly on my own expenses.' The community support upon which he drew involved sponsorship from large organisations (such as the Ukrainian Studies Foundation in Australia) together with what he called 'collection from people'. This was in effect a type of literary subscription whereby groups and individuals donated small amounts of money, which accumulated to cover the cost of publishing a book. For each book published this way, the author had kept a detailed list of sponsors and their donations. For those he had paid for, he had largely managed to recoup his money: 'Mostly what I published, I got my money back for selling it.'

The chain of distribution in the Ukrainian-Australian field mirrors the non-commercial nature of the material production. Libraries are much less substantial an institution, given they are not funded and are maintained solely through voluntary labour and donated material. With no commercial outlets, the 'bookseller' is a more diverse institution than the 'book store' which functions in a conventional literary field. The Ukrainian-Australian bookseller comprises an array of agencies which on-sell literary texts, often without any financial reward. This may involve a business with a shop-front but also includes annual bazaars, occasional markets set up at concerts and community events, distribution through community organisations, and the authors themselves.

Non-commercial literary production also means that the relationship between material and symbolic production is somewhat loosened. Whereas in a conventional literary field underpinned by professional and commercial needs, the judgements cast by the critical establishment are crucial in determining the success of a text and career of an author, in the Ukrainian-Australian case the attribution of quality does not play as dominant a role.

Authors often pay for their work to be published. With the publisher not carrying a financial risk, saleability is not a deciding factor in whether to produce a book. Book production is therefore not so dependent upon an author's reputation or the opinion of reviewers (both of which would normally be used to assess the commercial viability of a text). Self-publishing does not necessarily carry a loss in prestige, rather it is seen as a reality and practicality given the small size of the Ukrainian-Australian community. Authors may act as booksellers and directly reach their readers while bypassing the institutions of symbolic production. Such dynamics are near impossible in a conventional commercial field which depends upon a sizeable market-place, sophisticated systems of distribution, and a high turnover of products.

While the structure of the field reflects the fact that the literary activity is driven by a not-for-profit motive, that which is produced similarly reflects a non-commercial orientation. Since there is not as much emphasis on creating a commodity that can be bought and sold, there is a high proportion of transitory literary products, texts written for recital at reading clubs or a concert or commemoration, not intended for publication. Literary ephemera written for a particular occasion effects a particularly close and immediate relationship between author and audience – another striking feature of the Ukrainian-Australian literary field.

International Linkages

The Ukrainian-Australian literary field is embedded within the wider Ukrainian-Australian community. This literary field firmly relates to the wider socio-cultural structure by which those who identify as ethno-culturally Ukrainian can relate to one another and engage in cultural practices. The authors here referred to are members of the Ukrainian-Australian community, which provides a readership/audience and functional agencies such as newspapers and libraries. As one author stated, 'I began writing for myself and then later on I wrote for [the] community.' Organisations within the community may provide (minimal and sporadic) funding for the publication of texts. The Ukrainian Studies Foundation in Australia, for example, has on occasion provided authors, writers' associations and publishers with a financial subsidy towards the cost of publication. Community organisations are responsible for staging community events at which authors can recite their work. Hence institutions within all three realms (material production, distribution and reception) are functional entities of a wider Ukrainian-Australian community at the same time as relating to each other in the form of a literary field.

There are processes of international cultural transfer which are supportive of the Ukrainian-Australian literary field, mainly through providing additional opportunities for publication and distribution. In the past connections were with the international Ukrainian diaspora (largely in North America); more recently authors have established links with (post-Soviet) Ukraine. One author explained succinctly where his work had appeared, saying 'in Ukrainian publications in Australia, Canada, USA, in Ukraine'. Another spoke of his short stories in this way:

> I think that it's the Ukrainian community who reads them. Of course, I have a larger reader[ship], a wider public when I send stories to 'Novi Dni' because 'Novi Dni' [is] published in Canada ... they have more readers than Australia has. Also, you have American readers and

all over the world, they sell that magazine everywhere. Today, [the Australian-Ukrainian newspaper] 'Vil'na Dumka' also goes [all over the world], many copies go to Ukraine. So they also read my stories there in Ukraine.

Authors such as these have achieved a measure of success within Ukraine, while working consistently and productively within the field in Australia. A question arises as to how such international connections should be positioned. I would argue that at the point of engaging with overseas literary institutions – publishers, journals and associations in Ukraine – authors step into another literary field, that is, they enter the contemporary Ukrainian literary field. There are several interesting ways in which this passage from one field to another has been accomplished. One author who wrote short stories, at his own initiative and expense, produced a series of illustrated books about Australia (about the Great Barrier Reef, Australian flora and fauna, and aspects of Australian history). These books were written in Ukrainian and aimed specifically at an audience in Ukraine. 'I decided that Ukraine would need knowledge of Australia. I wanted people in Ukraine to know about Australians.' These publications were distributed in Ukraine and intended to serve as constructive tools of cultural exchange.

Two years after Ukraine achieved independence, an anthology of Ukrainian-Australian literature was published in Kyiv (Mykhailenko). This was the product of a relationship between a Ukrainian journalist, literary advocate Dmytro Nytczenko, and a number of Australian benefactors (including Ukrainian-Australian associations, and the authors themselves). This was arguably the first publication to have been produced collaboratively at an institutional level and hence the first transnational venture between the Australian-Ukrainian and Ukrainian fields. It took some fifty years after Ukrainians first migrated to Australia – and the collapse of the Soviet Union – before such a venture could succeed.

Post-Soviet Ukraine would go on to offer intellectual opportunities for those in the diaspora through what might best be described as an opening of the Ukrainian literary field. One writer's short story 'based on truth about the hunger in 1933' was solicited and published in 1996 by a newspaper produced in the region in Ukraine in which the author had been born.[9] This author had written on only one point of history he himself had lived through – "just about that horrible 1933 year … the Ukrainian famine' – when millions of people starved to death at the hands of Soviet collectivisation of farms. It was not possible to produce or distribute this kind of material in Ukraine during earlier decades of Communist censorship, but now it could serve as valuable historical source material. Australian-Ukrainian literary activity and expertise was beginning to aid in the cultural and educational reconstruction of the newly autonomous nation.

This bespeaks an important point about the literary activity enacted within the Ukrainian-Australian field: like the community within which it is embedded, it is inherently connected to a Ukrainian ethno-cultural identity and the maintenance of Ukrainian language and culture. As one author explained, in writing she was 'spreading the knowledge about my country, my culture … trying to spread the knowledge about Ukrainian culture among the general population'. Indeed, within the Ukrainian-Australian community, all forms of cultural production have promoted the Ukrainian language and culture, which for the most part remained suppressed under Soviet dictatorship. The very existence of the community and its cultural products lent symbolic support to the struggle for self-determination in Soviet-occupied Ukraine.

The writing of Ukrainian history from a counter-hegemonic (that is, counter-Soviet) perspective is a particular aim, as authors have been motivated by a need to record their experiences. Historical fiction was

---

[9] The story, written by Tykhin Korinec, was titled 'Halia Radianska' and published in a newspaper called *Ridnij Kraj*.

produced early in Ukrainian-Australian literary life. *Potolocheni Khliba* [Trampled Harvest] by Ivan Stockyj was published in 1954. It told of the arrests, interrogations, and incarcerations that were part of Soviet rule in Ukraine. Yevhen Zoze's personal account of Soviet occupation of Ukraine entitled *Likvidatsia* [Liquidation] is a relatively recent work (1997), as is Olexander Lysenko's autobiographical novel about the genocide of Ukrainians through the artificially created Stalinist famine of the 1930s, *Prokliati Roky: Spohady Svidka* [Cursed Years: Memoirs of a Witness], published in Ukraine in 1993. Lysenko spoke poignantly of repression and dissidence in his early life in Ukraine and the effect it had of silencing him.

> When I went to university ... I tried to write some lyrics and some poetry. But it was very dangerous in those days to write anything because at that time I was in Kharkiv just when they started this what you can say [call] pogrom [of] Ukrainian intellectuals, like Khvylovyj and other writers. Yes, so it was very dangerous to write anything because if they find something in your possession, something that they don't like, well, that's it! And this one fellow student ... was arrested just because on his bedside cupboard in the dormitory they found, or somebody reported him of course, they had reporters everywhere, and they found one of those books ... of those writer's organisations and he was arrested and it was nine months [in prison] ... And so I didn't write.

Notwithstanding difficult conditions during the early years of settlement in Australia, Lysenko, like others, eventually found the motivation to write.

> Mainly I wanted to leave something for the younger generations to read, to read about what was going on because during that Soviet regime, you couldn't print anything, you couldn't even talk about those things, so those people grown up, they don't know what was going on. So I try to leave something to read, for them to read and understand what really was going on.

It would not be accurate to imply that all authors working within the Ukrainian-Australian literary field write so that (as another author explained it) 'readers can ... learn about ... aspects of life past and present ... under oppressive regime of the USSR'. Nonetheless, sentiments such as this do reflect the common psychology of a people who immigrated in a single wave as persons displaced by the Second World War and made political refugees of the Soviet Union. The literary products which are the direct result of this specific socio-historical situation now intervene into the contemporary Ukrainian literary field. As another author explained:

> When I went [in] 1992 to Ukraine, many people did not know what happened in their own country. Those people in Ukraine they did not know until I told them that what happened to me and to my family ... and I said ... I [will] publish in Ukraine ... And I did.

Relations with the Australian Literary Field

This model sees no links between the Ukrainian-Australian literary field and the Australian mainstream cultural establishment. This is because such connections do not exist in any systematic way.[10] The Ukrainian-Australian literary field is a self-contained system which, for the sixty-odd years of its existence, has functioned independently of the Australian

---

[10] Possible exceptions may be found within the institutions of academic literary criticism and literary education, in the form of academic (Ukrainian studies) positions within Monash and Macquarie universities. It is from these positions that a professor can engage in academic literary criticism of Ukrainian-Australian literature or include Ukrainian-Australian material while involved in the literary education of secondary or tertiary students. These institutional positions, however, cannot be fully regarded as interventions by the Australian literary field since these academic positions have always been maintained (funded and supported) by Ukrainian-Australian community organisations. These institutional positions have never operated solely as an initiative or function of the mainstream Australian educational or cultural establishment.

literary field and mainstream recognition or support. There is effectively no audience, no opportunities for publishing, and no institutional support that comes from conventional literary circles or wider Australian society. Only one author interviewed had drawn upon any cultural infrastructure outside of the Ukrainian community in that she had participated in workshops and writers' groups organised by the Fellowship of Australian Writers or government agencies such as her local Migrant Resource Centre. Aside from the writers who were of the second generation,[11] she was the only writer who had had work published outside of the Ukrainian community. While she had successfully published in small-scale non-commercial outlets, she nonetheless spoke of the difficulty and disadvantage multicultural writers face when confronting the prospect of publication in Australia:

> For non-English speaking background people is *very* very difficult; they have language problem, sometimes they have a lot to say but they need a lot of advice and help and encouragement ... I think it's *very* very difficult for non-English speaking background to get accepted, for instance, by mainstream magazines. I think it's extremely difficult.

Her sentiments were echoed by the few Ukrainian-Australian authors who had hoped, and tried, to have their work published within wider Australian society. As one author said despondently, 'I was trying. With no hope.' Australian publishers, he had found, were simply 'Not interested.'

Why is there such a dislocation of the Ukrainian-Australian literary field from a mainstream readership and publishing world? Why have the literary networks established within the Ukrainian-Australian field not extended into any systematic connection with the Australian literary field? One reason concerns the use of language. Authors working within

---

[11] Second generation refers to those born in Australia or who immigrated at a very young age and thus received their primary socialisation in Australia.

the Ukrainian-Australian literary field write largely in Ukrainian.[12] This is mainly to do with perceived levels of proficiency. While these authors had acquired a good working knowledge of English, they felt limited in their capacity to use the language for literary purposes. As one author explained, 'I have enough knowledge [of English] to talk, but not to write.' By contrast they felt themselves to be fully fluent, articulate and expressive in their native Ukrainian tongue. The few who felt able to write in English most often chose not to. As one said, 'I wrote some of my stories into English but I must say that I write much better in Ukrainian because my weapon is much sharper.'

The blockage between literary fields due to the use of a language other than English may have been overcome had there been consistent efforts at translation. There appear not to have been any arrangements made at an institutional level to engage translators, obtain funding or liaise with publishers. With the responsibility resting with the authors themselves, translation did not feature as a realistic possibility. As one author explained:

> When my book was finished I went to that community service [Ethnic Affairs Commission] and ask if they would like to translate to English. You see, translation it costs me a lot of money and I can't afford.

Occasionally an author would undertake to translate a text, although not necessarily his or her own work. Helen Boris was committed to translating texts from Ukrainian to English. Her motivation, however, was not to circulate her own writing but 'to get Ukraine, Ukrainian culture, on the world scene'. She translated a number of texts by famous Ukrainian writers. 'In this way I think I put a drop into spreading the knowledge about Ukraine', she said. Another author was interested in the reverse flow of cultural transfer: introducing Ukrainian-Australian

---

[12] Exception lies only with the writers of the second generation, who write in English, their native tongue.

readers to iconic Australian literary works. Stepan Radion translated a series of Australian short stories (mostly those of Henry Lawson) into Ukrainian and published them in journals intended to be circulated within the Ukrainian-Australian community.

A collection of translated poetry appeared in 1973; one of prose in 1985. Taken together with the very few instances of author-initiated translation, it appears there were only sporadic possibilities for translation within the Ukrainian-Australian literary field. Whether it was due to a lack of resources or a lack of expertise, there has been no ongoing systematic or strategic activity aimed at getting Ukrainian-language material translated into English and into print. As Helen Boris noted, translation did not seem to be a high priority: 'to spread the word to show that Ukraine has culture, has literature and so on, there is no support for that idea among the community'.

Use of a language other than English is certainly one reason why there has existed a disconnection between the Ukrainian-Australian and Australian literary fields. However, I contend there is another, more obtuse, dynamic at play. The words of one author give us a clue:

> I tried to publish one short story in English, but, I send it to few publishers, every publisher just knock it back. They haven't got any interest because it wasn't written in [the] way English people think, and something different for English-thinking publisher, they just can't take it, that's it.

Although written in English, the author felt his text did not appeal to the aesthetic norms or literary conventions that mark Australian literature. In fact, he sensed that he was confronting an altogether different mindset. If, as the work of Bourdieu and literary sociologists suggest, judgements about literature are not objective or absolute but are socially and culturally determined, what this author confronted was a specific set of beliefs about literature as an art form, a set of beliefs which contain certain attitudes about and expectations of a literary text. Such a set of beliefs is what van Rees has called a 'conception of literature': 'a system of explicit or implicit essential definitions or norms, pertaining to the nature and function of literature' (1981, 52).

A 'conception of literature' is a kind of 'literary ideology.' It may be defined as a set of premises and normative ideas which are believed to specify the nature and function of literature, together with the literary techniques used and their alleged effects on readers (van Rees 2001, 340). The mainstream Australian literary field functions according to a particular conception of literature. The Ukrainian-Australian literary field, however, employs another set of aesthetic norms, is informed by other literary traditions, and draws upon historical, political, social and cultural antecedents that constitute a very different conception of literature. Put simply, Ukrainian-Australian writers are writing and Ukrainian-Australian readers are reading according to their own conception of literature. This conception of literature – this set of beliefs about literature – is similar to those found within the other literary cultures studied in my research project. In other words, there is a shared conception of literature across the literary cultures of writers and communities who immigrated to Australia as so-called displaced persons immediately after the Second World War. But their common conception of literature is very different from the one which functions in wider Australian society.

In approaching Australia's mainstream cultural establishment, the authors working within the Ukrainian-Australian literary field confront a conception of literature with which their work does not comply. This makes it improbable – perhaps even impossible – for the work produced within the Ukrainian-Australian literary field to be accorded value or status in mainstream terms. This does not mean that the work is intentionally negated or deliberately marginalised by agents and institutions within the Australian literary field. It does however mean that those agents and institutions, charged with the authority to make judgements as to the qualities (properties) and quality (value) of literary texts, assess the multicultural texts against a set of standards to which they do not conform. Van Rees' notion of the conception of literature is a useful way of understanding why products of the Ukrainian-Australian literary field have not entered the mainstream literary and publishing world. Indeed the dislocation between the Australian literary field and these writers and their texts may be seen to be largely a consequence of clashing conceptions of literature.

Australian Multiculturalism: A National Context

The dislocation between the Ukrainian-Australian and Australian literary fields is troubling, given the multiculturalism for which Australia is renowned. Australia now has a population approaching 22 million people. About twenty-five per cent of the people were born overseas. A further twenty per cent have at least one parent who was born overseas. Australians identify with more than 200 ethnic ancestries and speak well over that number of languages. While English is the national language, more than fifteen per cent of Australians speak a language other than English at home.

Australia, then, is one of the most multicultural countries in the world. The cultural and linguistic diversity within Australian society is the consequence of a sustained immigration policy which is 'global and does not discriminate on racial, cultural or religious grounds.'[13] There is an official commitment to multiculturalism, a term which is used in two senses in Australia. Firstly, the word 'multiculturalism' is used to describe the social reality and lived experience of diversity given that contemporary Australia is a place in which people from different countries and of different cultures live. Secondly, 'Australian Multiculturalism' refers to the public policies and legislation designed to manage this ethnic diversity. The impact of immigration and multiculturalism is officially sanctioned, as this statement by the

---

[13] Australian Government, DFAT. *Australia in Brief: A Diverse People.*

Australian Government shows: 'Australia has a tolerant and inclusive society made up of people from many different backgrounds. Cultural diversity is a central feature of our national identity'.[14]

The Australian Government's approach to multiculturalism is reflected in a range of programs designed to assist non-English speaking settlers and foster harmony within Australian society. The *Diverse Australia Program,* for example, is 'a community-based educational initiative for all Australians and aims to address issues of cultural, racial and religious intolerance by promoting respect, fairness, inclusion and a sense of belonging for everyone'. This program 'provides funding, education and information to help organisations create a spirit of inclusiveness and helps ensure all Australians are treated fairly regardless of their cultural background or circumstance'.[15] Specific multicultural initiatives also exist within the arts and culture sector. The Australia Council for the Arts is the Australian Government's arts funding and advisory body. It provides grants to artists and arts organisations involved in community cultural development, dance, literature, music, new media arts, theatre, visual arts/crafts and Aboriginal and Torres Strait Islander arts.[16] The Australia Council administers a *Languages Other than English (LOTE) Publishing Initiative* which supports the translation and publication of works. Australian publishers who wish to translate into English and publish the work of living Australian authors may apply for assistance for a writer's and translator's fees and some production costs. 'The *LOTE Publishing Initiative* is intended to encourage partnerships

---

[14] Australian Government, DFAT. *About Australia: Australia: A Culturally Diverse Society.*

[15] Australian Government, DIAC. *Diverse Australia Program – About Us.*

[16] Australian Government, DFAT. *Australia in Brief: Culture and the Arts.*

between writers, translators and publishers and to introduce the work of LOTE writers to a wider Australian readership.[17]

While the intention is to facilitate mainstream recognition of non-English language writing, restrictions associated with this program would render many prospective applicants within a minority literary field ineligible. Only professional publishers are permitted to apply for funding under this program, which would effectively disallow those working within the Ukrainian-Australian literary field.

> This initiative is open to Australian publishers who are registered with the literature board. To register, publishers must be legally constituted as an organisation, have previously published at least five titles (not necessarily literary), at least two of which must have been published in the two years prior to application. Publishers must also have works commercially available for sale with effective national promotion and distribution systems. Publishers who receive payment from writers to publish their works are not eligible for registration.[18]

That the government of Australia considers multicultural policy and practice a success is evident in government discourse such as that produced by the Department of Foreign Affairs and Trade:

> Australia recognises, accepts and respects cultural diversity. There are few countries in the world where migrants have achieved the level of economic, political, social and cultural participation that they have in Australia.[19]

Yet despite multicultural policies and initiatives across all levels of government, there remains a severe disjunction between mainstream

---

[17] Australian Government, Australia Council, *Grants: Languages other than English Publishing – Literature*.

[18] Australian Government, Australia Council, *Grants: Languages other than English Publishing – Literature*.

[19] Australian Government, DFAT. *Australia in Brief: A Diverse People*.

cultural fields and forms of cultural production within ethno-cultural communities.

The Ukrainian-Australian literary field has functioned in a kind of solitude, separated from Australian literary networks and wider Australian society. Has this solitude been a welcome freedom from interference or an imposed loneliness? Until connections are made between such multicultural solitudes and the Australian literary field, Australia's national literature will not truly reflect the multifaceted reality of Australian society. How such connections should be made poses a difficult question, as it involves overcoming the barriers associated with non-English language use and clashing conceptions of literature. Resources and expertise are needed to overcome the former; pathways of cultural exchange and communication are needed to combat the latter.

Conclusion

Australia has arguably always been culturally diverse given the differences between settlers from England, Ireland, Scotland and Wales, and an intake (albeit a small one) of immigrants from around the world. However, it was after the Second World War that Australia embarked upon a long and sustained period of immigration, destined to change the ethno-cultural makeup of Australian society. The literary history of multicultural publishing largely coincides with the massive post-war immigration program, which has brought settlers from all over the world to Australia over the last sixty years.

Given the Second World War is a pivotal point in the history of immigration and migrant settlement patterns, a focus upon writers who immigrated to Australia as displaced persons directly after the war and their communities which were formed in the immediate postwar period is fitting. Since this was the first government policy designed to bring significant numbers of non-British immigrants into Australia, the Displaced Persons Scheme was a milestone in Australia's history. The intake of refugees under the Displaced Persons Scheme was the precursor of the entire postwar immigration program[20] and a forerunner to the cultural diversity which marks Australian society today.

Whilst I have outlined the methodology of my project and presented empirical data elsewhere, my aim in this paper has been to theorise a model which illustrates the structure by which literature is produced, circulated and consumed within the Ukrainian community in Australia, as a prototype of the literary culture of writers who immigrated to Australia as displaced persons after the Second World War. It is hoped that this will have wider applicability as a study of immigrant community writing in Australia and can serve as a model for other community-based culturally and linguistically diverse literary fields.

My project addresses an important research question: exactly how is culturally and linguistically diverse literature produced and circulated in Australia? The model I propose accounts for literature produced outside of the mainstream cultural establishment and within ethno-cultural communities. It accounts for work that circulates outside the conventional realms of the Australian publishing industry because it is linguistically and culturally diverse. It goes towards explaining how it is that small literary cultures which are not commercially viable can exist and continue to function. Like all the literary cultures encompassed within my case-study, the Ukrainian-Australian literary field may be small in terms of conventional publishing industry markers but it is dynamic – and its dynamics are a significant part of Australia's cultural and book history.

---

[20] Due largely to the success of the Scheme, by the time Australia's intake of European refugees had ceased, the principle of accepting large numbers of non-British immigrants had been established (see Murphy, 150; Collins, 55; Borrie, 251; Kunz, 247).

Works Cited

Australian Government. Australia Council for the Arts. *Grants: Languages other than English Publishing – Literature.* [Accessed 2 June 2010]. www.australiacouncil.gov.au/grants/grants/languages_other_than_english_publishing_-_literature.

Australian Government. Department of Foreign Affairs and Trade. *About Australia: Australia: A Culturally Diverse Society.* [Accessed 2 June 2010]. www.dfat.gov.au/facts/culturally_diverse.html.

Australian Government. Department of Foreign Affairs and Trade. *Australia in Brief: A Diverse People.* [Accessed 2 June 2010]. www.dfat.gov.au/aib/society.html.

Australian Government. Department of Foreign Affairs and Trade. *Australia in Brief: Culture and the Arts.* [Accessed 2 June 2010]. www.dfat.gov.au/aib/arts_culture.html.

Australian Government. Department of Immigration and Citizenship. *Diverse Australia Program – About Us.* [Accessed 2 June 2010]. www.harmony.gov.au/aboutus.htm.

Australian Bureau of Statistics. *Census Data 2006.* [Accessed 27 June 2007] www.abs.gov.au/websitedbs/d3310114.nsf/home/Census+data.

Kunz, Egon. *Displaced Persons: Calwell's New Australians.* Canberra: Australian National University Press, 1988.

Language and Literature Group of Adelaide. *Pivdennyi khrest.* Adelaide: Language and Literature Group of Adelaide, 1980.

Lysenko, Oleksander. *Prokliati Roky: Spohady Svidka.* Poltava, Ukraine: Krynytsia, 1993.

Morrison, R.H., ed. and trans. *Australia's Ukrainian Poets.* Melbourne: Hawthorn, 1973.

Murphy, Brian. *The Other Australia: Experiences of Migration.* Cambridge: Cambridge University Press, 1993.

Mycak, S. 'The Role of Networks in Australian Multicultural Literature: Post-war "New Australians" as an Empirical Case Study.' *Empirical*

Study of Literature. Ed. Steven Totosy de Zepetnek. Spec. issue of *Sun Yat-sen Journal of Humanities* 17 (Winter 2003): 19–30.

Mykhailenko, Anatolii, ed. *Ridni Holosy z Dalekoho Kontynentu: Tvory Suchasnykh Ukraïns'kykh pys'mennykiv Avstralii*. Kyiv: Veselka, 1993.

Nytczenko, Dmytro. 'Z Literaturno-vydavnychoho Zhyttia v Avstraliï: Bibliohrafichna Rozvidka.' *Ukraïntsi u Avstraliï: Tom II*. Melbourne: Australian Federation of Ukrainian Organizations, 1998, 656–86.

—— [Dmytro Chub], comp. *On the Fence: An Anthology of Ukrainian Prose in Australia*. Trans. Yuri Tkach. Melbourne: Lastivka, 1985.

——. *Z-pid Evkaliptiv: Poeziï*. Melbourne: Prosvita, 1976.

Seneta, Eugene. 'Ukrainians in the 1986 Census.' In *Ukrainian Settlement in Australia: Fourth Conference, Sydney, 22–24 April 1988*. Eds. Ihor Gordijew and Halyna Koscharsky. Sydney: School of Modern Languages, Macquarie University, 1989, 88–93.

——. 'Ukrainians in Australia's Censuses.' *Ukrainian Settlement in Australia: Second Conference, Melbourne, 5–7 April, 1985*. Ed. Marko Pavlyshyn. Melbourne: Department of Slavic Studies, Monash University, 1986, 1–27.

Stockyj, Ivan. *Potolocheni Khliba*. Sydney: Free Thought, 1954.

van Rees, Kees, and Gillis J. Dorleijn. 'The Eighteenth-century Literary Field in Western Europe: The Interdependence of Material and Symbolic Production and Consumption.' *Poetics* 28 (2001): 331–48.

van Rees, Kees, and Jeroen Vermunt. 'Event History Analysis of Authors' Reputation: Effects of Critics' Attention on Debutants' Careers.' *Poetics* 23 (1996): 317–33.

van Rees, Kees. 'Indicators of Institutional Performance in the Literary Field: How to Measure Interactions between Literary Institutions that Yield Classifications?' Paper presentation. 'Literary Communities' workshop. 'The Social Context and Literary Production and Consumption.' SOAS, University of London. May 2004.

239

——. 'How Reviewers Reach Consensus on the Value of Literary Works.'
Poetics 16 (1987): 275–94.

——. 'Advances in the Empirical Sociology of Literature and the Arts:
The Institutional Approach.' *Poetics* 12 (1983a): 285–310.

——. 'How a Literary Work becomes a Masterpiece: On the Threefold
Selection Practised by Literary Criticism' *Poetics* 12 (1983b): 397–
417.

——. 'Some issues in the study of conceptions of literature: A critique of
the instrumentalist view of literature theories' *Poetics* 10 (1981): 49–
89.

Zoze, Yevhen. *Likvidatsia*. Adelaide: self-published, 1997.

12

GENERATION V: THE SEARCH FOR VIETNAMESE AUSTRALIA[1]

HOA PHAM AND SCOTT BROOK

The Vietnamese community has now been in Australia for over thirty years but are still, in spite of producing a large number of *tho* (poems) and *van* (stories), 'invisible' in mainstream Australian literary culture (see Appendix 1 for a selective bibliography of Vietnamese-Australian writers and texts).

Vietnamese migration to Australia has come in three waves: post-1975 after the fall of Saigon; during the 1980s with the so-called economic refugees; and the ethnic Chinese fleeing persecution in the 1990s. The Vietnamese community in Australia is seen as a fluid one and not homogenous, with the notion of the Vietnamese as a diasporic community coming under question (Thomas 1999; Dorais 2002). It has been suggested that the overseas Vietnamese community is better described as transnational – since overseas Vietnamese maintain their strong links to homeland and often return home, with their links being from kinship rather than a collective political force (Dorais 2002). One description of the Vietnamese-Australian community is that there 'are networks and a notion of connectedness, as there is also some degree of spatial concentration in certain geographical locations' (Thomas 1999,

---

[1]This chapter was first published in *Reading Down Under: Australian Literary Studies Reader* edited by Amit Sarwal and Reema Sarwal (New Delhi: SSS Publications, 2009, 311–20).

14). This notion of connectedness includes an attachment to the land of Vietnam, with life in Australia being described as having 'two faces, one looking forward and one looking back' (Thomas 1999, 186). Another description of the Vietnamese transnational is that of the 'mobile exile' (Carruthers 2007) since there is still a strong feeling of anti-communist sentiment and nostalgia for Vietnam pre-1975, along with the ability of the Vietnamese to go home.

Vietnamese-Australian literature to-date has taken a wide range of forms. Autobiographical novels such as *A Child of Vietnam* (1987) by Uyen Loewald, *Red on Gold* (1991) by Nam Phuong and *The Dragon's Journey* (2004) by Duy Long Nguyen detail the authors' war and refugee experiences. Such experiences are depicted in *Only the Heart* (1997) by David Chiem; as well as books which detail the present day Vietnamese-Australian experience, like David Chiem's *The Full Story* (2002) and my own work – *Quicksilver* (1999), *No One like Me* (1998) and *49 Ghosts* (1998). There has been one anthology todate of Vietnamese-Australian short stories and poems titled *Cau Noi: The Bridge* (2004), and numerous short stories published in anthologies such as *Dark Dreams: Refugee Stories* (2004) and Nam Le's *The Boat* (2008). Vietnamese-Australians seem to be most prolific in play form, covering a wide range of subjects including survivors of the Vietnam/American War in *Market of Lives* (2002), *Meat Party* (2002) and *A Graveyard for the Living* (2002) by Duong Le Quy, Binh Duy Ta's work on Vietnamese-Australian experiences, and Dominic Golding's search for identity in *Shrimp* (2007).

This article will discuss a number of Vietnamese-Australian artists and their search for Vietnamese-Australian identity. I set out to profile the different variations of Generation V, that is, generation 1.5 of the Vietnamese community by talking to a number of Vietnamese-Australian artists. I interviewed five Vietnamese-Australian artists, four of whom are of the 1.5 generation – Dominic Golding, David Nguyen, Chi Vu, and Tony Le Nguyen – born in Vietnam and raised in Australia, and Binh Duy Ta who was born and educated in Vietnam where he trained in acting and mime but defected to (or 'settled' in) Australia as an adult in 1988 after attending the 1988 Interplay Festival in Sydney.

1.5 Generation Vietnamese-Australians as Cultural Mediators

Although the phrase '1.5 generation' is a term used by academics to refer to migrants who were born overseas and whose education took place both in their home and adopted countries, it is also used more widely to describe the experience of being 'between' cultures in generational terms. Typically, it is represented as the awkward experience of being between the 'parent culture' of first-generation migrants, and the 'host culture' of the adopted country. For popular media and government agencies, as well as for many first-generation Vietnamese-Australians, the 1.5 generation Vietnamese-Australian subject condenses hopes and anxieties about the migration of pre-adult bodies from one societal context to another: the hope such subjects will form a bridge between the 'parent' and the 'host' culture; and the concern they might fall between. To fall between cultures is to be 'without roots' or *mac goc*, having a foundation in neither culture. While many representations of migrant families in Australian literature focus on the relation between first and second generation as a site for debates between parents and their children over cultural maintenance and cultural adaptation, representations of the 1.5 generation subject often stage this conflict as a much more existential and internal kind of struggle. The idea of an experience that is specific to a 1.5 generation has been a powerful metaphor for catalysing the arts of young Vietnamese, resulting in the literary anthology *Cau Noi: The Bridge* as well as the visual arts exhibition *Mac Goc* or 'lost roots'.

At the same time, it is often the 1.5 generation of Vietnamese-Australians who are looked to by the Australian media for evidence of improvement in the situation of the Vietnamese community overall, and are often represented in terms of a 'rags to riches' narrative of social mobility. For instance, a *Sydney Morning Herald* review article published on the occasion of the thirtieth anniversary of the Fall of Saigon begins by focusing on the high profile 'Do brothers'. Khoa and Anh Do came to Australia as refugees in the early 1980s and have together built successful careers in the film and television industry; Khoa Do is a well known film director and recipient of Young Australian of the Year, while Anh Do has been a comedian for many years and appeared in numerous television series and advertisements. After contrasting their current success with the horrors of their escape from Vietnam by boat, the article writes 'as a new generation emerge from the torment of a long lost war, it is stories like theirs that guide the diaspora towards the fabled shores of freedom, prosperity and acceptance' (Kremmer, 27).

Diasporic Vietnamese 'Return Narratives'

If 1.5 generation artists are looked towards to mediate public perceptions of the Vietnamese-Australian community generally, then they have also acted as cultural intermediaries in producing representations of contemporary Vietnam for Western, non-Vietnamese audiences. At a global level, many diasporic Vietnamese authors and directors have been able to act as 'brokers' between the new, post-*doi moi* (economic reform) Vietnam and Western audiences who are curious about the country as it forges links with the West in the post-Cold War era. Since the mid-1980s when the government of Vietnam proposed to embrace a less economically isolationist policy under the renovation policy of *doi moi* (1986), and especially since (under mounting international pressure) Vietnam relinquished its occupation of Cambodia (1989), Vietnam has opened up to substantial foreign investment capital, development aid and tourism. Australia had a significant role to play in Vietnam's opening-up to the West, having had a closer relationship with North Vietnam before the end of the war, as well as a closer relationship with Vietnam since the war's end. In June 1990 Australia signed a bilateral trade agreement and with almost no investment capital in Vietnam prior to 1991, by September 1993 Australia was ranked third with total projects worth US$ 727 million. By 1994 bilateral trade had grown to US$ 898 million. In

1991 Australia was the first country to send development aid to Vietnam (US$200 million in 1992) (Logan, 192).

The process of relaxing relations between Vietnam and the West has been ambivalent for the predominantly refugee diaspora, as this has resulted in the withdrawal of automatic refugee status for Vietnamese who flee Vietnam (since 1989), with many refugees being either forcefully repatriated or stranded for significant periods of time. This period has also seen attempts by the government in Vietnam to reach out to the diaspora and encourage return visits through bilingual publications with titles such as *Vietnam My Homeland* (1989). Although 'returning' to Vietnam was a politically contested act within the diaspora for a period in the 1990s, with many older Vietnamese embracing an 'exile' narrative, many Vietnamese-Australians return to Vietnam to visit family, pursue business interests and for holidays.

It is in this broad context that we can usefully describe many of the films and novels produced in the Vietnamese diaspora as 'return narratives'. However, there can be many different kinds of 'returns' taking place in these stories. Well-known American examples would include the film *Three Seasons* (1999) in which an American Vietnam veteran (played by Harvey Keitel) returns to Saigon to find the child he had had with a Vietnamese women but never met. Similarly, Andrew Pham's *Catfish and Mandala: A Vietnamese Odyssey*, an autobiographical novel published in 1999, follows the author as he returns as a bicycle tourist to the country his parents fled. In this novel the presence of the narrator's bicycle is a paradoxical motif in that it lets him 'blend in' with the local Vietnamese – at one point he locks his bike up, then takes a cyclo into town but lets the driver sit in the back while he does the pedalling – and simultaneously marks its rider as a foreign tourist, an eccentric *Viet Kieu* ('overseas Vietnamese') who wastes all his energy by riding everywhere.

In the Australian context, we might note Pauline Chan's feature film *Traps* (1993) – filmed in Vietnam, a radical adaptation of the novel *The Dreamhouse* (1986) which re-sets Kate Grenville's social drama in French

Indochina in 1954; Hoa Pham's novel *Vixen* (2000), a magical realist allegory of the postcolonial period in Vietnam narrated by a spirit-being who migrates to Australia, and returns as a tourist; Chi Vu's bilingual theatre production *Vietnam: A Psychic Guide* (2003), a surrealist, bilingual play and short-story that stages the psychical breakdown of a Vietnamese tourist on a visit to Hanoi; Dai Le's *Operation Babylift* (2004), a documentary in which the film-maker accompanies a Vietnamese adoptee to Vietnam to locate her biological mother; and Dominic Golding's play *Shrimp*, an autobiographical play about the author's return to Saigon to find his birth parents. For many of these authors and their narrators the physical journey to Vietnam is an occasion for asking questions about history and social memory, as well as raising more personal questions about culture and identity. As Chi Vu puts it in *Vietnam: A Psychic Guide*: 'I could not take photos because I didn't know who the person pressing the button was.' As this well demonstrates, the figure of the tourist-narrator provides an effective medium with which to explore these questions in a form that can relate to the interests of a broader, non-Vietnamese audience, even as it dramatises the very *different* relations to culture and history experienced by returning diasporic Vietnamese compared to Western tourists. Although most return narratives are addressed to an English-speaking audience, Chi Vu's play is unique in that it was performed as a bilingual production, and thus attracted a large number of older Vietnamese-Australians, while the short story it was based on was also disseminated in a bilingual edition by the author as a chapbook (developed by Quynh Du, the translator) and the online Vietnamese journal *Tien Ve*. *Vietnam: A Psychic Guide* was therefore able to reach audiences of established literary journals such as *Meanjin*, as well as audiences for Vietnamese literary work within the diaspora.

Return narratives often balance the interests of a broader audience with community-orientated forms of address. It is at this level that return narratives set the scene for powerfully intimate forms of collective identity formation within the diaspora. Consider the opening section from *Vietnam: A Psychic Guide*:

> Airport
> The City is located within a large airport. Metal and leather armchairs occupy the kilometers long lobby. Waiting, always waiting, people will pass the time by asking where you had arrived from and which ticket you had purchased to get there.
>
> A small friendship is struck, cheering up both parties momentarily. The complete strangers will ask to see each other's tickets. With the little glossy paper in our hands we build centuries of history from each other's seat number.

Calling Australia Home?

For the Vietnamese diaspora in Australia 'home' can be a fraught term. For Binh Duy Ta, playwright, and Tony Le Nguyen, founder of Australian Vietnamese Youth Media, Australia is emphatically home. This is shown dramatically in Binh Duy Ta's play 'Conversations with Charlie' (2000) where the young Vietnamese artist is introduced to Australia by a woman representing the 'Spirit of the Old Land' (Ta, 96) and they sing and dance together. They were the oldest of the Vietnamese artists I spoke to, the others are in their early to mid thirties.

However for war orphans such as Dominic Golding whose play *Shrimp* was on tour around Victoria in May and June of 2008, 'home' is a more problematic construct:

> I think of Footscray as my home and I don't call Mt Gambier my home or Adelaide because it's too white for me to feel comfortable … but I wouldn't 'call' Australia my home as such and that Australia is John Howard's Australia … so-called great Australia. I would call Footscray [home] which is basically where I live but I like Bankstown and I like Cabramatta in Sydney. (Golding, personal communication 2006)

Similiarly David Nguyen from SCRAYP theatre company based at the Footscray Community Arts Centre clarifies home is where he feels most accepted and that isn't necessarily Australia:

> it's where I feel most accepted. And that's not necessarily my family for that matter although I'm not fully accepted by the Australian community. I'm sort of out of place there. I think it boils down to places and individuals that make me feel comfortable, quite often it's an art setting and amongst artists I feel more at home because I can use both identities and receive validation, and in my writing and how it's received and in short stories and poetry. I feel pretty much at home where I can express myself, that's not always a tangible place. (Nguyen, personal communication 2006)

This theme is carried on by Chi Vu, writer and artist at Western Edge who indicates that home is where they feel most accepted and it may be the artists of the community:

> I just came back from France and in France I was hanging out with my uncle who lives in Germany and has lots of French-Vietnamese artist friends. I felt really at home in that environment, as well obviously whenever I speak to Asian-Australian artists I feel at home. I feel very at home bushwalking, there are all these facets to one's identity and personality. I felt at home in Berlin, it had the same sort of vibe like you might find in Fitzroy. I think in terms of getting the Vietnamese cultural fix, I can get it anywhere, it has a different flavour in Paris, it has a slightly different flavour in Los Angeles, Orange County and in Vietnam and I can go to Vietnam to feel at home but I don't have to. (Vu, personal communication 2006)

This confirms that 'home' in the sense of the diasporic 'homeland' is a place that cannot be returned to, even if one can visit the geographical space of 'home' (Brah 1996).

These younger artists are transnational in the sense that they can feel at home in at least two countries. This finding differs from previous work done on the Vietnamese-Australian diaspora, such as that by Mandy Thomas and Ashley Carruthers. This may have to do with the age of the interviewees in this study, both Mandy and Ashley dealt with older populations. It emphasises that home is 'intrinsically linked with … processes of inclusion or exclusion … and are subjectively experienced under given circumstances' (Brah, 192). These artists are accepted as artists in the world.

Having been personally accepted as an author in Australia, I will automatically say Australia is home, not Vietnam. But at large I do not feel at home in Australia because Howard's policies[2] have alienated me, and I too feel like an outsider at times.

Race Politics

Exclusionary processes are something that these artists have in common. As David Nguyen points out:

> I had to reject it [Vietnamese identity] to fully understand it and I learnt it through not liking it and putting out at the start what I disagreed with, like having rigid boundaries around expression of self and I wasn't able to do that very well, also the framework around family and how you express yourself and it was very difficult for me to understand and I rejected that early because I could not express myself and so I rejected it and if anything took on an Australian identity stronger and more free than I was, for example over-emphasising the Australian accent so people would think that I was Australian despite the fact I had black hair and round eyes, as well as getting into yobbo culture, growing up in West Heidelberg you get a lot of racism, easier to be Australian than it was to be Vietnamese. (personal communication 2006)

I can relate to David's experience, I remember drawing pictures of myself with blonde hair when I was six because I thought that was what was

---

[2] John Howard was Prime Minister at the time of writing.

desirable. With the proliferation of skin-whitening products and eye augmentation operations particularly in Asia, this beauty myth continues to proliferate into the twenty-first century regardless of the integration of Asian communities in white societies.

> kids and teachers would say that I'm outside of Australia ... in high school it was all about social isolation and having to come to terms with that group, racial slurs and asking how do they relate to me and finally working out that the racial slurs linked up with war. (Golding, personal communication 2006)

The war continues to be a marker for Vietnamese-Australians and Australians who can only relate to Vietnamese people as war refugees. Being asked whether your parents came from the north or the south is a common question whilst the reality is more complicated – many families fled from north to south after 1954.

Yet these artists identify with being Vietnamese-Australian. So what is being Vietnamese-Australian?

Being Double Agents

> Obviously I'm obviously Vietnamese and then I came over to the country of Australia and become an Australian citizen in that way ... just automatically I became Australian ... and at the same time I cannot avoid my Vietnamese identity naturally it became the two parts of my life, the Vietnamese, and in some ways of course it keeps changing but still I can find that my Vietnamese part is quite strong, I don't know why, it may be because I was born there and I have a lot of Viet training and education that's why but it seems slowly slowly it ... the Australian part is getting stronger the more time I spend in this country the more time I work and live in this country it seems that the Australian part is getting stronger. (Ta, personal communication 2006)

> I'm lucky I'm the 1.5 generation. I'm privileged to go in and out of both cultures but no one totally accepts you. You always live on the

margins and I've accepted that. When you're younger it can be a killer, the older you get you become a double agent except you can die easily – you can mediate but also be seen as the enemy. (Tony Le Nguyen, personal communication 2006)

When I was very young it was a Vietnamese living in Australia … and then as an adolescent I was neither Vietnamese or Australian however feeling like you existed in both cultures … and then at some point, I think actually after I returned to Vietnam for the first time, I think we left that, I felt that I was very privileged to have both cultures so from neither to both and … I'm in a position to pick and choose rather than having to be a slave to both cultures … (Vu, personal communication 2006)

These three different stories of straddling both cultures illustrate how diverse responses can be. I used to emphatically say I was Australian and it took me a long time to connect to my Vietnamese origin, especially since in the 1970s and 1980s it was preferable to assimilate and fit in.

Dominic Golding as a Vietnamese war baby adoptee has yet another view:

I myself and a lot of younger Vietnamese Australians … we embody the dual but that comes in many different shapes and sizes in society …

But for me it is actually quite distinctive in that I'm an adoptee as opposed to a strictly 1.5 generation … as an adoptee most of us, a lot of us don't speak the language and at the same time being an adoptee allows you to connect with being Vietnamese in a very distinctive way, we don't try to reject being Vietnamese, like some Vietnamese would say 'you are not Vietnamese' or 'you're not Vietnamese because you don't speak the language' … we accept the fact that we are from Vietnam but we also accept the fact that we are of our adopted country. (Golding, personal communication 2006)

For Dominic Golding, his play *Shrimp* (2007) is essentially about his search for his identity, returning to Vietnam in search of his parents. For

251

him the search did not come to a ready resolution as can be seen from this extract:

> I knew the orphanage held no truths about me, now I know that it wasn't to be.
> Am I happy?
> Yes … and no.
> I'm not alone in this world.
> I know that I'm Vietnamese-Chinese-Australian.
>
> --
>
> There I realised something, the question is not what others see of me but who I want to be. I'll never find my real parents, like a UFO, Unidentified Family Origins.
> In Saigon I found only ghosts of the past. (39)

In Chi Vu's work, she describes how her exploration of identity in her writing has changed over time:

> In my earlier work I might have explored Vietnamese-Australian identity through the plot or the characters in the work, but my more recent explorations have tended to do this through the theme or form of the work. In my current work I am looking at genre.
> For example, 'A Story of Soil' is made up of three parts. The first is that of the protagonist trying to run away from her Vietnamese family. The second part is her trying to run away from her Anglo-Australian boyfriend, and in the third part (The Third Space), she is alone with the new soil that she must live on.
> In comparison, 'Vietnam: A Psychic Guide', is composed of postcards from the protagonist's trip to Vietnam alternating with the pages of a forbidden book written by a local dissident writer. The postcards explore the theme of travel and biculturalism, while the form of the whole work suggests the reasons why many people have escaped Vietnam in the first place. The form suggests the political and artistic repression beneath the tourist images. (personal communication 2006)

The 'Story of Soil' (2002) is explicitly a work about a young Vietnamese-Australian woman trying to find her identity with her Anglo-Australian boyfriend.

Binh Duy Ta describes his work as such:

> I think it comes out in nearly every work and every play and every creative work I am doing because I think it is the way to do art, my way as an artist is as a Vietnamese-Australian so what I write comes out as half Vietnamese part and some from the Australian part, the same as my life, all my work it comes out in a different way, some work is stronger in the Vietnamese part some stronger in the Australian part and it keeps changing, in all my work it comes out, that is the mix between the Vietnamese part and the Australian part without trying. (Ta, personal communication 2006)

His plays 'Conversations with Charlie' and *Monkey Mother* (2000) explore Vietnamese identity in Australia. In *Monkey Mother* the tension between a Vietnamese mother and her son who has an Anglo-Australian girlfriend is the dramatic focus of the play.

Identity issues are not the prime focus in my own work but the tension between Vietnamese and Australian cultures does feature in my fiction and playwriting.

Like most migrant communities, individuals are exposed to at least two cultures and can carve out a 'third space' (Bhahba 1994) in which to operate. It seems like the ongoing search for Vietnamese-Australian identity and the return home is a pressing tension for Vietnamese-Australian artists of the 1.5 generation and features strongly in Vietnamese-Australian works. This is an ongoing journey in the Vietnamese community and for most Australians at large.

Works Cited

Bhabha, Homi K. *The Location of Culture*. New York: Routledge, 1994.

Brah, Avtar. *Cartographies of Diaspora: Contesting Identities*. New York: Routledge, 1996.

Carruthers, A. Paper presentation. 'Asian-Australian Identities 2' conference. Melbourne, June 2007.

Chiem, David. 'The Full Story – The Next Step on the Journey.' *Viewpoint: On Books for Young Adults* 11.2 (Winter 2003): 6–7.

——. *Only the Heart*. St Lucia: University of Queensland Press, 1997.

Chiem, David, and Brian Caswell. *The Full Story*. St Lucia: University of Queensland Press, 2002.

Dechian, Sonja, Millar, Heather and Eva Sallis, eds. *Dark Dreams: Australian Refugee Stories*. Kent Town, SA: Wakefield Press, 2004.

Dorais, Louis-Jacques. 'Defining the Overseas Vietnamese.' *Diaspora* 10.1 (2002): 3–28.

Golding, Dominic. In *Shrimp*. Brisbane: Currency, 2007.

Grenville, Kate. *The Dreamhouse*. St. Lucia: University of Queensland Press, 1986.

Huang, Ngoc-Tuan, ed. *Cau Noi: The Bridge – Anthology of Vietnamese Australian Writing*. Liverpool Area, NSW: Casula Powerhouse Research Centre, 2004.

Kremmer, Christopher. 'Generation V.' *Sydney Morning Herald* 30 April 2005: (News Review), 27.

Le, Nam. *The Boat*. Ringwood, Victoria: Penguin, 2008.

Loewald, Uyen. *A Child of Vietnam*. Melbourne: Hyland House 1987.

Logan, William S. 'The Angel of Dien Bien Phu: Making the Australia-Vietnam Relationship.' In *Australia and Asia*. Eds. Mark McGillvary and Gary Smith. Melbourne: Oxford University Press, 1997, 178–202.

Nguyen, Duy Long, and James Knight. *The Dragon's Journey*. Pymble, NSW: HarperCollins, 2004.

Operation Babylift. Dir. Dai Le. Prod. Anna Grieve and SBS Independent. Film Australia, 2005.

Pham, Hoa. *Vixen*. Sydney: Hodder Headline 2000.

——. *Quicksilver*. Sydney: Addison Wesley Longman, 1999.

——. *49 Ghosts.* Sydney: Addison Wesley Longman, 1998.

——. *No One like Me.* Sydney: Addison Wesley Longman, 1998.

Pham, Andrew X. *Catfish and Mandala: A Vietnamese Odyssey.* London: HarperCollins, 1999.

Phuong, Nam. *Red on Gold.* Sutherland, NSW: Albatross, 1991.

Quy, Duong Le. *Market of Lives.* Sydney: Currency, 2002.

——. *Meat Party.* Sydney: Currency, 2002.

——. *A Graveyard for the Living.* Sydney: Currency, 2002.

Ta, Binh Duy. 'Conversations with Charlie.' *Diaspora – Negotiating Asian-Australia.* Spec. issue of *Journal of Australian Studies* 65 (2000): 88–105.

——. *Monkey Mother. 3 Plays by Asian-Australians.* Donald Batchelor, Ta Binh Duy, Anna Yen, and Indija N. Mahjoeddin. Brisbane: Playlab, 2000, 8–31.

Tai, Le Van. *Waiting the Waterfall Falls: Concrete Poems.* Melbourne: Dept. of Asian Studies and Languages, Victoria University of Technology, 1997.

——. Empty Arms – Surrounded by Warm Breath. Melbourne: The Author, 1987.

——. *Ocean, Salt's Handkerchief: Poems.* Ferntree Gully, Victoria: Aztec Studios, 1985.

Three Seasons. Dir. Tony Bui. Prod. Tony Bui, Jason Kliot, and Joana Vicente. Script. Tony Bui. Perf. Harvey Keitel, Duong Don, and Diep Bui. Giai Phong Film Studios and October Films, 1999.

Thomas, Mandy. *Dreams in the Shadows.* Sydney: Allen & Unwin, 1999.

——. 'Electra and the Fire Eaters.' *The Australian Literary Magazine* 6–7 July 1985: 6.

Tien Ve (webzine). 2002–07. 14 June 2007 www.tienve.org/home/activities/viewActivities.do

Traps. Dir. Pauline Chan. Prod. Jim McElroy. Script. Pauline Chan and Robert Carter. Perf. Saskia Reeves, Robert Reynolds, and Jacqueline McKenzie. Australian Film Finance Corp., 1993.

Viet Nam Que Huong Toi/Vietnam My Homeland. Hanoi: Su That and
Vietnam Tourism, 1989.

Vu, Chi. 'Vietnam: A Psychic Guide.' *Fine Writing and Provocative Ideas*.
Spec. issue of *Meanjin* 60.1 (2001): 34–47.

——. 'Vietnam: A Psychic Guide.' Basement Theatre, Footscray
Community Arts Centre, Melbourne. 2001.

——. 'Vietnam: Sach Huong dan tam Linh.' *TienVe* (webzine). 2002–07.
14 June 2007 www.tienve.org

——. 'Story of Soil.' Basement Theatre, Footscray Community Arts
Centre, Melbourne. 2000.

Appendix 1

Selective bibliography of Vietnamese-Australian writers.

Chiem, David. 'The Full Story – The Next Step on the Journey.'
Viewpoint: On Books for Young Adults 11.2 (Winter 2003): 6–7.

——. *Only the Heart*. St Lucia: University of Queensland Press, 1997.

Chiem, David, and Brian Caswell. *The Full Story*. St Lucia: University of
Queensland Press, 2002.

Dac, Hop. 'The Mud-Walkers.' In *Scrapbook to Somewhere*. Eds. Lou
Smith and Eve Vincent. Fitzroy, Victoria: Breakdown, 2004, 20–24.

Do, Khoa. 'Cabramatta Story.' Cabramatta, NSW. 2003.

Duong, Xuan. *War and Pieces*. Bankstown, NSW: Integration, 2005.

——. 'Smiles on Your River.' *Newswrite: The NSW Writers' Centre
Magazine* 131 (October 2003): 33.

——. 'Your Freedom.' *Overland* 168 (Spring 2002): 12.

——. 'The July Rain.' *Overland* 168 (Spring 2002): 20.

——. 'Mateship of Wartime.' *Overland* 168 (Spring 2002): 20.

——. *Refugee Kosovo*. Bankstown, NSW: Integration, 1999.

Golding, Dominic. In *Shrimp*. Brisbane: Currency, 2007.

Huang, Ngoc-Tuan, ed. *Cau Noi: The Bridge – Anthology of Vietnamese Australian Writing*. Liverpool Area, NSW: Casula Powerhouse Research Centre, 2004.

Huong, Ho Xuan. 'Weaving a Double Cloth.' In *Weaving a Double Cloth: Stories of Asia-Pacific Women in Australia*. Eds. Myra Jean Bourke, Susanne Holzknecht, and Annie Bartlett. Canberra: Pandanus, 2002, 5–23.

Huynh, Helen. 'Kim's Story.' *Dark Dreams: Australian Refugee Stories*. Ed. Eva Sallis. Kent Town, SA: Wakefield Press, 2004, 111–17.

Huynh, Kim. 'Fathers, Flags, and Modern-Day Fanaticism: A Short Story About Cold War Grand Theories and Ordinary Vietnamese Australian People.' In *Alternatives: Global, Local, Political* 28.5 (November-December 2003): 517–28.

Kiep Nguoi van Nuoc. Melbourne: Vietnamese Language and Culture Publications for Committee for the Preparation of Vietnamese Reading Materials, 1990.

Le, Hung. *Barry Noodles and DaKillerBs*. Milsons Point, NSW: Random House, 2005.

——. *The Yellow Peril From Sin City*. Ringwood, Victoria: Penguin, 1997.

Le, Nam. *The Boat*. Ringwood, Victoria: Penguin, 2008.

Loewald, Uyen. 'Austlalian' are Stupid.' *Neighbours: Multicultural Writing of the 1980s*. Ed. Ronald Frederick Holt. St Lucia: University of Queensland Press, 1991, 114–22.

——. *A Child of Vietnam*. Melbourne: Hyland House 1987.

Nguyen, David. 'Monsoon Dome.' Arts Centre, Melbourne. 2 November 2003.

Nguyen, Duy Long, and James Knight. *The Dragon's Journey*. Pymble, NSW: HarperCollins, 2004.

Nguyen, Hai-Van. 'Journey to Freedom.' *Dark Dreams: Australian Refugee Stories*. Ed. Eva Sallis. Kent Town, SA: Wakefield, 2004, 198–204.

——. 'Journey to Freedom.' In *AIR!, Australia is Refugees: Winning Essays and Stories, 2002*. Eds. Eva Katerina Sallis and Heather Millar. Fitzroy North, Victoria: Australians Against Racism, 2002, 5–7.

Nguyen, Tranh Hoang. *Tho*. Cabramatta, NSW: Tien Ve, 2003.

Nguyen, Tu. *Niem Yeu Dau Con Hoai*. Liverpool, NSW: The Author, 2000.

——. *Doi La Kho: Tap Truyen Ngan*. Toronto: Lang Van, 1993.

——. *Cat Lo*. Petersham, NSW: Tram Lang, 1990.

——. *Hoa Nang Tren Cao: Truyen*. Petersham, NSW: Tram Lang, 1988.

——. *Nguoi Tu O Lai*. Petersham, NSW: Tram Lang, 1987.

——. *Dem Lang Quen*. Sydney: The Author, 1986.

——. *Ben Troi Lan-Dan: Tho*. Sydney: The Author, 1986.

——. *Dang XuaDang Xua*. Sydney: The Author, 1985.

——. *Goi Nguoi Ben Ay: Tho & Van*. Sydney: The Author, 1984.

Pham, Hoa. *Vixen*. Sydney: Hodder Headline 2000.

——. *Quicksilver*. Sydney: Addison Wesley Longman, 1999.

——. *49 Ghosts*. Sydney: Addison Wesley Longman, 1998.

——. *No One like Me*. Sydney: Addison Wesley Longman, 1998.

——. 'On the Continent.' *Aurealis: Australian Fantasy & Science Fiction* 20–21 (1998): 73–82.

Pham, Andrew X. *Catfish and Mandala: A Vietnamese Odyssey*. London: HarperCollins, 1999.

Phan, Viet Thuy. *Dung Nhan: Tho*. Ho Chi Minh City, Vietnam: Kim Viet, 1970.

Phuong, Nam. *Red on Gold*. Sutherland, NSW: Albatross, 1991.

Quy, Duong Le. *Market of Lives*. Sydney: Currency, 2002.

——. *Meat Party*. Sydney: Currency, 2002.

——. *A Graveyard for the Living*. Sydney: Currency, 2002.

Quynh, Da. *Hai Muoi Nam*. Melbourne: The Author, 1999.

——. *Ngay Xua Hoc Tro*. Melbourne: The Author, 1994.

Ta, Binh Duy. 'Conversations with Charlie.' *Diaspora – Negotiating Asian-Australia*. Spec. issue of *Journal of Australian Studies* 65 (2000): 88–105.

——. *Monkey Mother. 3 Plays by Asian-Australians.* Donald Batchelor, Ta Binh Duy, Anna Yen, and Indija N. Mahjoeddin. Brisbane: Playlab, 2000, 8–31.

Tai, Le Van. *Waiting the Waterfall Falls: Concrete Poems.* Melbourne: Dept. of Asian Studies and Languages, Victoria University of Technology, 1997.

——. *Empty Arms – Surrounded by Warm Breath.* Melbourne: The Author, 1987.

——. *Ocean, Salt's Handkerchief: Poems.* Ferntree Gully, Victoria: Aztec Studios, 1985.

Tam va Nam. Pascoe Vale South, Victoria: Vietnamese Language and Culture Publications for Committee for the Preparation of Vietnamese Reading Materials, 1984.

The Last Train Journey, Or, Chuyen Xe Lua Cuoi Cung. Pascoe Vale South, Victoria: Vietnamese Language and Culture Publications for Committee for the Preparation of Vietnamese Reading Materials, 1984.

Thomas, Mandy. *Dreams in the Shadows.* Sydney: Allen & Unwin, 1999.

——. 'Electra and the Fire Eaters.' *The Australian Literary Magazine* 6–7 July 1985: 6.

——. 'Landlocked.' *Overland* 98 (April 1985): 50.

Tuyen Tap Nhung Cay But Uc Chau. 1. Bankstown, NSW: NSW Chapter of the Vietnamese Community, 1997.

Vinh, Le Quang. *Defy the Death Spirit: An Autobiographical Novel.* Bassendean, WA: The Avery Publ. Co., 1995.

——. *Moon Festival.* Bassendean, WA: The Avery Publ. Co., 1990.

Viet Nam Que Huong Toi/Vietnam My Homeland. Hanoi: Su That and Vietnam Tourism, 1989.

Vu, Chi. 'Vietnam: A Psychic Guide.' *Fine Writing and Provocative Ideas.* Spec. issue of *Meanjin* 60.1 (2001): 34–47.

——. 'Vietnam: A Psychic Guide.' Basement Theatre, Footscray Community Arts Centre, Melbourne. 2001.

——. 'Vietnam: Sach Huong dan tam Linh.' *Tien Ve* (webzine). 2002–07. 14 June 2007 www.tienve.org

——. 'Story of Soil.' Basement Theatre, Footscray Community Arts Centre, Melbourne. 2000.

13

'LONGING FOR SYDNEY': DIDIER COSTE'S *DAYS IN SYDNEY*

ROBERT PICKERING

A grand metropolis sprawling out to suburbia, the whole intimately known, recreated and possessed; echoes of other places (Paris, Barcelona, London, New York), but present only to highlight the central reference; lives in 'disarray',[1] haunted by the past yet pictured in their becoming; a consuming abandoned love, to which, as the writing puts it, testifies an array of 'witnesses', themselves portrayed in the ups and downs of a hurried existence; interpersonal relationships of considerable psychological and emotional density: all the ingredients are present to constitute some kind of higher-class 'soap' – all the more since the pseudonym of Jacques Voisin, one of the two central characters and who has recently published in *Poetry Australia*, is 'James *Neighbour*'[2] – or a remake of David Lodge's sceptical and disillusioned intellectuals embroiled in the trivia of academe (Voisin is Reader in French at the University of Sydney).

From this backdrop grounded in the banality of 'real life' Didier Coste has fashioned a work, *Days in Sydney* (2005), of remarkable

---

[1] *Le désarroi de son récit de vie* (*Days in Sydney* 93) which, by almost homonymic equivalence, typically discreet, becomes the powerful image of 'dry rot' (*Days in Sydney*, 83).

[2] My italics. The proximity to the television series *Neighbours* (1985–present) is certainly coincidental, but none the less intriguing.

resonance and depth, which adds a distinctly new dimension to Australian creative writing. The blurb to the book gives a necessarily succinct overview of some of the aspects underscoring this achievement, but falls well short of doing full justice to the latter's extraordinary complexity. In taking Sydney as a focus the writing adheres to a well-established strain in Franco-American literature (Dos Passos in particular, but also several French writers of the nineteenth and twentieth centuries, Verhaeren, Jules Romains and the 'Unanimist' school, the Sartre of the trilogy). Influence of the French analytical novel could also perhaps be traced. The novel is also of obviously experimental nature, in tune with the kind of ambition which characterises a truly exploratory vision of things. The blurb accentuates these aspects (a contemporary Odyssey traced by 'absurd separation and unfailing memory', yet the uniqueness also embracing the 'Australianness' of Sydney), particularly the 'contrapuntal' strain which inhabits the book, and points to the narrative technique adopted, French and English weaving together the 'strands' of a 'unique story'.

In an obvious way, this book is experimental, if only by the demands made on comprehension by the two alternating languages. Coste passes effortlessly from one to the other, yet remains critically aware of the expressive potential and limits of both – an aspect to which I will return later. Alternating sequences are complemented by the interpolation, in French or in English, of the other language, signified by two typefaces (bold for French, lighter for English). There is nothing particularly novel in such use, which can be dated back at least to Mallarmé's *Un Coup de dés jamais n'abolira le hasard* (1898), but it is helpful when, as often occurs, snatches of conversation or inner monologue in one or the other language are interpolated in a segment otherwise dominated by one language alone. Despite certain precedents – Milan Kundera's *La Valse aux adieux* (1976) springs to mind – it is experimental also in its structure and narrative technique: seven 'days' (and nights – the French chapter title *journées*, implying both, includes some fine passages devoted to nocturnal description) provide an overall structural hub, the first six concluding with an 'interlude' (*intermède*) whose function is to widen the scope of events and commentary and to relate them to the present of awareness or composition. On the surface the time span is therefore circumscribed and kept in check; in addition, remembrance of the past and its relation to the present can be situated across the seven 'journées' between the beginning of the 1970s and 1992. But this fundamental temporal architecture is only the starting point for both frequent flashbacks and anticipation, which interact with an elaborate web of interpersonal connections. In addition, the blurb speaks of the 'narrative fresco' thereby put in place: experimental in this regard as well, it would be wrong, despite the traditional 'end', to expect a clearly linear treatment along well-trodden lines. The events characterising the two principal lives and loves of Jacques Voisin and Matilda Jones are progressively unravelled, but there the comparison with tradition stops. Segments and 'glimpses' (*Days in Sydney*, 138) are here the stuff of creativity, implying constantly oscillating viewpoints and 'voices' (*Days in Sydney*, 173). Point of view is therefore plural, perfectly suited to the 'special geometry'[3] whose contours the writing enacts in the constellation of characters surrounding the central Voisin-Jones axis, running parallel yet also intersecting at times with the latter. Characterisation adheres to these changing planes of vision, since none of the characters are given to the reader as all-of-a-piece: in a real way we watch them make their way and participate with them as they construct their paths in life.

In this sense, that of a work which takes up the very difficult challenge of depicting lives in their becoming, this novel is not just experimental but above all situated at the sharp edge, for the reader, of a real *experience*. The French word *expérience* (*Days in Sydney*, 193;

---

[3] 'The science of geometry says that parallels never intersect. But it seems that witnesses have their own special geometry which does not obey Euclidian laws' (*Days in Sydney*, 30)

l'expérience actuelle) has the virtue of encompassing both these meanings. At the beginning Coste hints at the profound nature of his enterprise: language is to be used in order to liberate us from a 'minimal threshold of meaning', and to situate us beyond the 'baseline of information, in the hidden strata of speech',[4] homing in on that past 'sole happiness', mercurial and aphasic, which constantly haunts the writing and takes the form of the oft mentioned 'unforgivable' (*Days in Sydney*, 16; more frequently referred to as *l'impardonnable*). Beyond a linear, teleologically loaded quest for this past happiness, now glimpsed now lost, the novel charts an onward moving thrust towards its *possible* apprehension, with all that such a movement implies of the restive, the variable, the paradoxical and the indeterminate. Language is used here as a living instrument for plumbing the ambiguous nature of what seems to be an ever receding (self-)identity: the vision proposed is, in part, founded in one direction of Coste's literary criticism, where the concept of 'language as communication' occupies a central place. I would here like to accentuate the fact that Didier Coste has always, admirably, considered literature not as just a scholarly pursuit or worse still a pedagogical chore, but as a living experience in 'getting through' to the listener (see Coste 1989).

Hence a view of language and of its use which is embedded in a sense of both its living presence, capable of searching for the inner recesses of the mind and the emotions, and its opacity, its elusiveness. Jill, one of Jacque's former loves, sums it up, 'knowing all too well that the thick curtain which had fallen between them was largely a web of words that she had woven herself' (*Days in Sydney*, 138). Other references to the negative or elusive resonance of this type of lapse in communication occur, throwing a shadow over immediacy of exchange (Jill and Jacques, shying away from 'naming' the event which henceforth deprives them of

---

[4] 'Ces paroles au-dessous du seuil minimum du sens … sous le plancher de l'information, dans les souterrains de la parole' (*Days in Sydney*, 11).

intimacy[5]). Jacques, attempting to conflate inner and outer perception, realises that *cet espace n'avait pas de nom* (*Days in Sydney*, 194). The ramifications of this view of the disconcerting plurality language can accommodate are to be seen on various other levels as well – on that of names, for example (various instances of alias or abbreviation: Matilda Jones, frequently becoming 'Mattie' or just 'M'/Carol Matthews; Robert/Youssef Abdallah; Ella/La), that of 'voices' and identity (*Days in Sydney*, 99; 'Who is speaking? … Who's who?'), and particularly on that of the insufficiency of expression which, in an interesting commentary, encapsulates both 'fiction' and 'reality'.[6] Such an approach to literary creativity serves powerfully to place this writing in a special conceptual and stylistic field of its own, which can only be described as original: the problematic of identity which can be taken as a fundamental dynamic of the vision proposed is articulated through a questioning of the very adequacy of language, style and form to give it presence and meaning.

For all these reasons Coste places the stakes of readability and reception very high. This all the more since, working out via rich cross-cultural references – French, Australian and Aboriginal primarily, but not exclusively – towards the apprehension of what it means to live in contemporary Australia, his objective according to the blurb is to enact through language the cultural diversity of 'that oldest and ever new world', alone capable of rendering the 'voices' which are the stuff of his creativity. The novelist makes the incompatible 'old-new' terms used here, encapsulating a well-known dictum attempting to define Australian identity, reach well beyond the banality of their normal contextualisation.

---

[5] *comme si l'événement auquel ils ne savaient encore donner un nom devait désormais les priver d'intimité* (*Days in Sydney* 21).

[6] 'Fiction doesn't know a thing about feeling, it doesn't understand a thing about knowing, it's completely obsessed with believing. And reality can't feel, can't understand, can't even believe, which is all that's left to dumbos' (*Days in Sydney*, 99).

The writing is frequently pitched at the level of the apparently contradictory, particularly as regards Jacques' view of the world (16; *cette monotonie de la diversité*) or even at the very heart of intimacy – Jacques and Kathy Powell, *séparément ensemble* (196). Kathy, musing on her relationship with Jacques, perceives their situation as 'being in the world and out of it' (202). On the level of landscape and of objects, the text can become inextricably enmeshed in their 'entire visibility' (the blurb speaks, rightly, of the 'hyper-realism' which invests the text), yet also their refusal to be apprehended and rendered, a refusal verging on the invisible.[7] The 'too precise' (22), assuming a false necessity, signals passages where the paradoxical apprehension of the presence–absence of things becomes, for Jacques, a landmark in his own mental landscape. In such circumstances a more tangible 'necessity' of the self, 'naturalised' into its Australian context, can be glimpsed:

> *Que toute chose fût si proche, mais intégrale, d'une irréductible, envahissante immédiateté, c'était cependant cela la plus pure absence, la nôtre peut-être, peut-être imminente, car tout nous atteignait, nous pénétrait de son affirmation, nous évidait de notre manque … La lumière était telle que voir devenait un acte de reconnaissance … On n'avait plus rien à faire … rien à oublier ni à démentir pour être accepté, réconcilié, naturalisé, nécessaire et donné sans hésitation à la générosité du paysage.* (*Days in Sydney*, 59)

The difficulties of self-possession and self-identification are thus translated in the texture and style of the writing itself. The interpolated hypotheses (emphasis placed on *perhaps* here, reinforced by the oft-

---

[7] *ce visage et cette voix [Matilda], agrandis jusqu'à la dissolution (comme dans Blow Up) jusqu'à la dissolution, jusqu'à la réfraction et à la division continues, étaient si généralement confondus avec le paysage qu'ils auraient seuls pu expliquer comment sa totale visibilité se rendait elle-même invisible, insaisissable … par son seul être visible, ni nouveau ni ancien, non daté, non précédé et non suivi'* (*Days in Sydney*, 15).

repeated 'it seems/seemed',[8] points to a central dynamic and to a wider understanding of the work), and the sequence of past participles in the final sentence place the writing in a perspective of continuing self-analysis and self-appreciation. Through style, and not only content, the reader is invited to embrace the fullness of experience. This, despite the plenitude born of adhering to *'what is'*,[9] to the strangely blinding immediacy of light and the giddying perspectives which the latter can open up. On the one hand, luminous clarification; on the other, indeterminacy. It is this difficult path that *Days in Sydney* has chosen to tread.

The resonance of such a complex 'mental landscape' (*Days in Sydney*, 81), with its deeply affective and sensual ramifications – dismissed by Voisin as yet another abstract 'academic exercise' yet experienced with total fidelity to its real presence – is such that a brief appraisal cannot but fall short of complete appreciation. Certain axes of approach can nevertheless be identified, each requiring far fuller analysis than can here be given.

The Characters and Their Making

The inchoative nature of Coste's book, and the way in which it grows upon the reader as unfolding experience, can largely be traced to particularities in characterisation. The segmentation of moments of thought and perception, oscillating freely from one character to another yet retaining discreet coherence with events, is entirely consonant with a view of characterisation placing the latter in a context of progressive

---

[8] Examples abound of this dubitative, questioning or hypothetical mode of writing. In one of many instances, an entire paragraph is given over to 'seeming' in the *Cinquième intermède* (*Days in Sydney*, 160).

[9] My italics. '*il [Jacques] recevait de plein fouet le choc de la plénitude et de l'adhésion à ce qui est comme une chute vertigineuse dans le puits sans fond s'ouvrant parfois sous les pas du rêveur* (*Days in Sydney*, 188).

becoming, not of that ponderous 'realistic' portrayal denounced by Nathalie Sarraute (1956). A becoming which is not set, moreover, on the level of certainty: style is often placed in an interrogative mode, in keeping with that meteorological indeterminacy to which Coste frequently has recourse at the beginning of the seven major *journées* (*Days in Sydney,* 9; *Il voulait pleuvoir*).

We learn of course a lot in terms of objective information regarding the two principal characters especially, whether in their own terms or through others' eyes. Jacques in particular: 'forty-six years old' (80), 'a scholar who lectured all over the world' (71), blending 'incoherence and systematicity' and wishing to 'abolish discrepancies between imagination and reality' (79), incapable of grasping felicity in terms other than 'too much or too little' (112), ambiguous in his relationship to Australia and difficult to pin down (119; 'evanescent'), as Rita, the novelist in the book, discovers when attempting to place him in her writing (119; 'invented' by Matilda, but left 'unfinished'). In less complimentary wording, the text homes in on a 'depressive, decadent intellectual' (95) and on his 'egocentricity' (194).

Matilda too is delicately etched, particularly in her loneliness and her search for a stable core to self-identity. Much could be written concerning male attempts to circumscribe female consciousness, feeling and view of the world – yet another of the challenges which Coste sets himself in this book. There are numerous precedents, from Flaubert's *Madame. Bovary* (1857) to Mauriac's *Thérèse Desqueyroux* (1927) and beyond. If the vision proposed cannot by definition purport to encompass complete feminine awareness, Matilda and Kathy Powell are nevertheless portrayed with very considerable sensitivity. Formerly a painter, subsequently a teacher of geography 'in a private High School' (156), Matilda is not just statically depicted but assumes an ongoing substance before our eyes: her regrets, her aspirations become a springboard to understanding a temperament remarkable in its otherness and in its distinctive peculiarity.

In particular the characters, faced with their past, must 'reinvent themselves'. Jill, another of Jacques' lost loves, speaks of him as always being 'a settler' (*Days in Sydney*, 114), with all this implies in 'counterpoint' of the unsettled. But Coste makes of this outlook far less an indication of instability than a drive towards constant becoming and regenesis. In typically questioning mode Matilda wonders whether she can 'reinvent' (124) the self she had abandoned on leaving Jacques. Despite its 'end', the novel cannot leave the reader with certainty in this regard, its 'open' structure precluding such definitiveness.

In order to reach out to his characters, Coste uses the fullest range of stylistic nuance. There is a distinct narrative line, but not in its usual teleological acceptance: a story is unravelled, from Jacques' initial musing to the 'end' of the book. Be they segmented, the levels of discourse and changing points of view re-appropriate preceding incidents or states of feeling and of mind, conferring on the whole a perfectly coherent narrative texture. Careful reading also identifies possible premonitory allusions which allow us to link up with preceding events or perception: the writing passes over an unexplained lapse in Jacques' conversation (164; *je ne suis pas malade*), only to return to the hypothesis, following his fatal accident, of 'stress, a heart attack' (215). Problems of the heart intersect with banal, but also necessary in narrative terms, heart problems. But these strictly narrative devices are not allowed to gain the upper hand. Criss-crossing direct conversation, the interweaving of dream sequences (see 33, 91, 151, 179), and above all the interpolation of inner monologue confer on the writing its peculiar density, requiring very attentive reading.

L'impardonnable

If there is an existential and experiential core in the remarkable density of such writing, it is certainly to be found in what Jacques repeatedly terms the 'unforgivable'. Recurring in numerous contexts, the latter acquires something of the status of an experiential nexus. Its definition is not easy.

It is associated with the 'dry rot' (93; *désarroi*) and the 'dereliction' (23) of the story of his life; it links up with wider thoughts on 'desertification', yet remains constantly attuned to that inner world of experience[10] which Coste succeeds admirably in conflating with the conditions, expectations and limits of contemporary Australian living. Seeking 'deliverance' (110) which obstinately refuses to come, Jacques situates what he perceives to be the 'unforgivable' of the past against the 'absurd', the 'ineffable' and sheer 'boredom' (121) of his being in life. Many other references associate this thematic element with his 'vain amour' (122; see also 133, 169, 171, 178, 182, 187–88, 195), or the constant striving for a lost centre of living. The constantly changing viewpoint allows Kathy to reflect at the end on having to bear the weight of the compounded 'oblivion and self-neglect' (210) which is that of both Matilda and Jacques.

Weather, which conspires until the end not to be apprehended (193), or in existential terms, 'being in the world and out of it' (202), shroud vision in their indeterminacy. To the end the text emphasises that the 'unforgivable', never far from the surface of Jacques' perception of existence, does not admit of easy description. The weight of the past, on which the 'unforgivable' turns, and continuing self-appraisal, place the writing in the context of an 'open-ended' work in which the conclusion has a somewhat artificial place.

Sydney Long(-ing)

Counterbalancing this backdrop of the indeterminate, *Days in Sydney* is obviously rooted in a sense of place. Starting from the first 'interlude', place – houses – loom large in the text. The state capital Sydney, however subjectively posited as being of 'universal' significance (59; *un univers*

---

[10] Intertextuality here gives an indication of the author's discreet erudition in situating the 'margins' of an inner 'desert' (*Days in Sydney*, 182) – both Rimbaud's 'Les Déserts de l'amour' (1872) and Mauriac's *Le Désert de l'amour* (1925) having given due place to the 'desertification' of emotion and the aridity of feeling.

d'univers), is much more than just a décor: it interacts with another essential hub of the evolving points of reference in the writing, that of Sydney Long's painting 'The Music Lesson' (1904). In other contexts one might allude here to *ekphrasis* (description of a work of art); but the properly experiential dynamic of Coste's narrative technique makes of this fundamental reference a central point in exploring self-identity, or its eclipse. By virtue of name, and far more significantly as a result of its totally organic pertinence to the thematic of the 'unforgivable', Long's painting is an essential pointer to deciphering the mysterious overtones of the latter.

In addition to regularly recurring allusions, an entire 'segment' whose density would require specific analysis is devoted to Long's painting 'The Music Lesson' (76–79) which, with the 'unforgivable', is manifestly situated at the heart of the novelist's creative vision. The Aboriginal girl foregrounded in the painting, remaining 'nameless' since she is 'eternal',[11] becomes progressively enmeshed in the quest for that 'territory of the imagination, a symbolic estate, that clearing in the wilderness of reality' (76) which could pertinently define an essential aspect of Jacques' longing. Exemplified in a painting in the Art Gallery of New South Wales, a very significant dynamic of the novel revolves around this reference, and seems to be posited in powerful 'counterpoint' to the 'unforgivable'. The attentiveness to painting is echoed in the characters' consciousness of colour, which can on occasion assume symbolic resonance.

The Bilingual Challenge

Over and above such literary and pictorial concerns, the question remains: why write a novel in two languages? For Didier Coste, having native fluency in both, the answer can partially be located in that imperative of 'communication' in which he sees an important function of

---

[11] *Elle n'a pas de nom, parce qu'elle est de tout temps* (*Days in Sydney*, 72).

narrative. Herein lies of course a real difficulty, that of readership and reception. In historical and cultural terms the impact of France and the French on an emerging Australian national consciousness cannot be qualified as essential. True, pre-1770 charting by a handful of intrepid French explorers has left a legacy still traceable to certain place names; but the same is true of the Dutch. The twentieth century alone (after the Chinese of the nineteenth century) brought incalculable enrichment from several European countries; India, the Middle and Far East, to name only a few sources, have added to this fertilisation of an emerging national identity. But in the multi-ethnic and multi-cultural texture which is now one of the nation's assets, French outlook and the French language are not clearly discernable. The demands made on the reader by Coste's creative ambitions are thereby compounded. Without possessing at least a reading competence in French, who will be able to bring to this book the kind of understanding which its acute and complex 'presence', as well as its 'vanishing points', unquestionably solicit?

Another possible answer to the question reaches out more deeply than this. In circumscribing identity – not only that of his characters but also that of the landscape and the places to which Coste is so close – all possible means must be brought to bear. In the attempt to seize the contemporary contours of a society characterised from the outset by the vast cultural divide between British mentalities and Aboriginal views of existence, now incomparably enriched by many other languages and social codes, bilingualism would seem to be a fundamental prerequisite. In this sense, the experimental nature of the book cannot be seen in the abstract, as some kind of rather eccentric and shaky motivation for seeing things afresh. On the contrary, it is entirely consubstantial with the portrayal of those mental and emotional landscapes which provide the basic material of the text. To this extent it would be appropriate to speak of the properly organic nature of the relationship in these pages between English and French: to the criss-crossing viewpoints are added the varying subtleties of two languages, each possessed in their finest nuance.

Without purporting to do so, the linguistic fabric of the novel thus projects something of a mirror image of its own content and aspirations. Literally a 'beginning', it is rooted in the humus of a native grounding which has still to be nurtured: a character providing an important counterpoint to the mainstream of unfolding events, Fred Devlin, is not perhaps by chance a nurseryman. Attuned to the complexity of emotions and feeling, inviting us to follow the channels of thought itself in the frequent use of inner monologue, the vision proposed remains in contact with the network of responses and attitudes underscoring an intricate social fabric, of which plurality is one of the keywords.

There is moreover, perhaps another justification for placing standard Australian English, requiring its own level of understanding,[12] in constant juxtaposition with French. Generalisations are at best questionable, at worst perilous; one could nevertheless advance that French serves on several occasions as a vehicle for the rich poetic texture towards which the writing can sometimes turn, as also for the haunting introspection of Jacques Voisin. After all, the latter is French: despite his 'unacknowledged passion for this silent, secretive land' (134), on several occasions characterisation turns on the ambiguity of his responses to Australia – a sense of feeling 'alone and uprooted' (71), and *ce pays vis-à-vis duquel ses sentiments étaient demeurés ambigus* (149). Moments when the all-invasive sense of self is lost in passages of pure perceiving, very close to poetic prose, seem to have a special priority in French – as in the final segment of the *Troisième journée*, writing which is very close to a prose poem and moreover closing in poetry:

> *La flûte et le violon reprenaient en duo les rythmes de la mer enregistrés par la torsion des branches flottées dans le ciel intense. Il était toujours temps de recommencer, les jours et les nuits se prenaient par les sentiments round the clock, les coques des graines éclateraient dans le*

---

[12] The non-Australian Anglophone reader will need to be able to place 'Woolies' (*Days in Sydney*, 63), 'David Jones' (64), 'bull' (106) and 'ockerism' (179).

feu naturel que les yeux des adolescents reflètent pour imager le désir.
Puis nous marchions sur les bords de l'île qui se gondolait comme un
continent de plus en plus éloigné des glaces:
> *Sur un quai de gare en forme de plage,*
> *j'attends le premier train*
> *comme une vague,*
> *j'attends la vague d'amour qui m'emportera au loin.*

(*Days in Sydney*, 97)

This poetic substratum which can sometimes surface in the writing is enhanced by allusions to the fine poetry which Australians have written. The journal *Poetry Australia*, in which some of James Neighbour's 'fluid, subtly allusive' (138) poems are published, is a frequent reference; excerpts from Kenneth Slessor (126), and particularly Alec Hope, figure in the text as obviously admired models. In constant touch with 'reality', Coste seems also to place his special kind of writing in relation to Symbolism,[13] whose influence on French and Australian writing is patent (Brennan via Mallarmé).

If only in terms of the wider reception which this novel certainly demands, a monolingual temptation must certainly be in Coste's mind – not towards French, where national consciousness of Australia, let alone actually living there, is largely limited to exotic and tourist fantasia. Should ever an English-only version be envisaged, it will require an excellent translator – someone not just versed in English and in French, but in close personal contact with the homeland.

'Longing for ...': Vanishing Points

Longing for what? On the surface, the retrieval of a long-lost original love, which others can subsequently replace in part, but never entirely. If

---

[13] Reference is made to Georges Rodenbach (1855–1898), a leading figure in Belgian/French symbolism, and to his influential novel *Bruges la morte* (1892–1894) (see *Days in Sydney*, 194).

one searches for a certain narrative consistency, it is here to be found. This is the stuff of novelistic tradition. What else has Didier Coste to offer?

Days in Sydney acquires sufficient density in its imaginative repercussions for such an appraisal to be totally inadequate. The remembrance of times past, and particularly of a sense of place, imbues the writing with constantly enriched overtones. *Sydney n'avait cessé de donner une leçon de musique au visible* (207): over and above his literary objective, Coste turns here to both music and painting in order to render the fullness of experience. A longing for the 'Matilda Jones' of the novel's narrative ambit cannot but place us in contact with a certain Matilda 'waltzing' across generations of Australian consciousness. Whether coincidentally or deliberately, a central focus of the narrative urges us to situate this very personal account of life and love in Sydney against a much wider background.

It is on a dubitative note – the present approach to the novel makes absolutely no claim to apprehend the full complexity of the writing – that *perhaps*, just to quote the frequently repeated adverb in the text itself, appreciation must conclude.

Rita, a novelist in the text, envisages writing a work entitled *Lignes de fuite*. In pictorial terms, 'vanishing points' imply absence – a foreground receding and disappearing into the distance. A superficial reading of Coste's novel might place the characters, and their relationship to place and events, in a framework of dispersion. The fragmented frames of reference do not provide us with total clarity. Jacque's own awareness of fringing on an *aventure inénarrable* (213) does not help us to place the work in a comfortably circumscribed ambit, be the latter construed in terms of *genre* or of perception and experience.

The novel nevertheless gives a very full account of the 'defeated adventurers' (186) portrayed in the two central characters. This description is entirely pertinent, since it invites us to explore the 'underside' of those 'regions situated beyond standard understanding'

(217; *compréhension normale*). Living and loving in Australia, with both European and Australian roots, are inscribed here as 'adventure'. Defeat? The concluding sequences of the novel seem to abut on this. Towards the end perception homes in on an apparent sufficiency, *Tout était à sa place* (188), but remains subject to the constantly interrogative mode which is a hallmark of Coste's creativity (189; *Pourquoi la plénitude, si on pouvait l'appeler ainsi, lui devenait-elle suspecte?*). Doubt seems to undermine all, and the concluding *Journée*, with its references to death, shrouds the whole in pessimistic overtones. Despite a rather artificial ending, albeit carefully prepared, there remains in this account of life in contemporary Sydney and its surrounds something of the tragic, of anguish and pain. Kathy, bearing Jacques' unborn baby, wishes abortion 'in the tone of a final decision' (215).

There remains, in this darkening prescience of mortality, a glimpse of what must nevertheless constantly *become*. Joël, Jacques Voisin's son, situates the end of his father's life and its compulsive, varied loves against the dawn of awareness which Sydney Long's painting awakens (218). Similarly, Matilda finds a degree of assuagement in her description as seen by others, 'her new selfless self' (202). Pictured against Jacques' 'egocentricity' (194; *égocentrisme*), such contrasting details situate us at the novel's heart, which is born of tension and productive conflict.

Coste's novel *Days in Sydney* is a work demanding certain critical acclaim. Bilingual, with all this implies of very rich intercultural and international understanding, in direct touch with Australian creative writing, it brings to the latter a contribution of the highest distinction. One can only hope for the next.

Works Cited

Coste, Didier. *Days in Sydney: Roman.* Clamecy: Noesis, 2005.

——. *Language as Communication.* Minneapolis: Minnesota University Press, 1989.

Flaubert, Gustave. *Mme Bovary.* 1857. 20 August 2007 www.bibliomania.com/0/0/136/1955/frameset.html

Kundera, Milan. *La Valse aux adieux* [*Valčík na rozloučenou*]. Paris, Gallimard, 1976.

Mallarmé, Stéphane. *Un Coup de dés jamais n'abolira le hazard.* 1897. *Oeuvres completes.* Ed. Bertrand Marchal. Vol. 1. Paris: Gallimard, Bibliotheque de la Pleiade, 1998.

Mauriac, François. *Thérèse Desqueyroux.* 1927. Paris: Le Livre De Poche, 1965.

——. *Le Désert de l'amour.* Paris, Bernard Grasset, 1925.

Neighbours. Creator. Reg Watson. Prod. John Holmes, Tony MacDonald, Dave Worthington, Sally Anne Kerr, and Peter Dodds. Seven Network. 1985–present.

Rimbaud. 'Les Déserts de l'amour.' 1871. *Oeuvres.* Ed. Suzanne Bernard. Paris: Editions Garnier Frères, 1960.

Rodenbach, Georges. *Bruges la morte.* 1892–94. London: Atlas, 1993.

Sarraute, Nathalie. *L'Ere du soupcon.* Paris: Gallimard, 1956.

14

CULTURAL EQUILIBRIUMS AND LINGUISTIC DISLOCATIONS: THE POETRY OF PAOLO TOTARO

GAETANO RANDO

The writing of poetry is an activity carried out by a very small number of the 350,000 Italians who migrated to Australia in the period following the Second World War. From 1947 to the present some thirty-eight first-generation migrants have published eighty-seven volumes of poetry – mostly in Italian with a few bilingual volumes and some exclusively in English – while a few hundred writers have had their work published in edited anthologies such as Abiuso et al. (1979), Rando (1983 and 1986), Cincotta (1989), Genovesi (1991), Polizzi (1994 and 1995), ALIAS (1997), as well as in the Sydney Italian language newspaper *La Fiamma*.[1] Frequently expressed themes include the subjective expression of a personal, emotive response to life and its meaning, to love, to nature, to interpersonal relationships, etc. Nonetheless by far the most distinctively characteristic recurring theme is that of Australia and its interrelationship with and effect on the migrant, the newcomer who has to make sense of a new world and the cultural and linguistic dislocations of this experience.

---

[1] For a detailed survey of Italian-Australian poetry by first-generation writers see Rando 2006. Other studies on Italian-Australian poetry are Savoca 1983; Niscioli 1996; and for oral dialect poetry of migrants from Isole Eolie, see Rando La Cava 1983.

The Australian landscape and its natural beauty are also an integral component of this thematic area. The most representative first-generation Italian-Australian poets are Luigi Strano, Enoe Di Stefano, Lino Concas and Mariano Coreno. However they, as well as other first-generation poets, are little known outside the Italian-Australian community notwithstanding their contacts with Anglo-Australian writers and intellectuals. This situation can be considered one of the many tensions inherent in Australian multiculturalism which has not led to an integral socio-political and cultural inclusion of the CALD (Culturally and Linguistically Diverse) migrant who, as a tolerated object, is never simply present but is 'positioned' in specifically perceived roles (See Hage, 89–90, 136).

Paolo Totaro[2] constitutes an exception for his many years of engagement in 'mainstream' political, cultural and intellectual endeavours. Born in Naples in 1933, Totaro has been living in Australia since 1963 as a result of the diaspora of corporate executives who promoted Italian industry abroad in the wake of Italy's economic miracle. A temporary transfer to Sydney as CEO for Italian car maker FIAT operations in Oceania eventually led to a decision to remain permanently and to acquire Australian citizenship. His considerable managerial skills and his wide cultural interests – he has university degrees in law and music – led him to accept an offer to create the innovative Community Arts Board of the Australia Council in 1975. In 1977 he received a commission from the New South Wales government to research and write a report on the ethnic minorities present in the state. This report, *Participation* (1978), whose introduction is based largely on a not antithetic synthesis of the ideas of the Jesuits of the Istituto Pontano (Totaro's school) and of Antonio Gramsci (see Totaro 2004), was a 600-page book instrumental in determining for the first time multicultural

---

[2] Heartfelt thanks to Paolo Totaro for his constant and generous support and the interesting discussions and exchange of ideas.

policy in New South Wales and proved a blueprint for similar initiatives in other Australian states. It marked the beginning of Totaro's appointment as Foundation Chair of the Ethnic Affairs Commission of NSW, a post that he held from 1977 to 1989. In this role he pioneered many important and fundamental multicultural initiatives. He subsequently held other appointments in positions involving constitutional and legal reform, was for a time visiting professor at the University of Western Sydney and pro-vice chancellor and member of Council at the University of Technology Sydney. He is currently engaged with government institutions and movements working for educational and social reform.[3]

A busy schedule that also includes journalism and television appearances and an interest in science has not prevented him from the practice of chamber music and writing. His short story 'Storia patria' (1996) won the 1993 edition of the literary prize *Premio Letterario 2 Giugno* promoted by the Consulate General of Italy (Sydney). The main theme of the story, expressed through an interesting fusion of emigration and *Risorgimento* and the resulting existential consequences, focuses on how chance is the main factor in determining human events. The story is told through an exchange of letters over 1859–60 between real characters

---

[3] Castles et al. (1992) conclude that in the context of the cultural and social transformations experienced in Australia during the second half of the twentieth century, Italian-Australians have not only contributed by bringing to Australia a range of European cultural perspectives but have also contributed to prepare the country for newly evolving geopolitical realities (397). Paolo Totaro is an emblematic, indeed a unique, case. In a context exclusively dominated by Anglo-Celtic cultural and intellectual traditions, an Italian intellectual became a pioneer of multiculturalism, promoting in a highly detailed and sensitive manner the cause of CALD migrants at a political level. As well as his literary texts and *Participation* Paolo Totaro has authored *Environment and Earthmoving* (1971) and has also contributed to publications in the field of legal reform, the constitution, culture, education, and others.

living in Naples and Sydney who relate facts based on the realities of the period that illustrate the similarity of the human condition in the two cities: colonialism and exploitation; the vitality and the poverty of the indigenous people of Naples and of Sydney; the provincialism of art and society in the two cities; the moral problems posed by the emerging sciences and the consideration of the oppressed as objects of observation, more than comprehension among equals.

A fine prose writer, Totaro's forte in the field of creative writing is, however, poetry. He writes both in Italian and English and was among the first, and is still one of the very few, writers to depict the sound track of Australia's multicultural work environment rich in linguistic dislocations. His collection of over 100 poems, characterised by the search for a possible equilibrium between cultural traditions, is however largely unpublished although a number of his poems have appeared in the volume *Paolo poesie* (1981) as well as in magazines and anthologies – some of his English poems were published in *Two Centuries of Australian Poetry* (1988), making Totaro one of the very few first-generation Italian-Australian poets to be published in a 'mainstream' anthology. His work is worthy of consideration given the unique perspectives it provides, its bold linguistic experimentalism and its subjective introspection that underscores the existential condition of the late twentieth century.

The themes enunciated in Totaro's poetry range from the unforgettable childhood traumas of war, to the dilemma of whether to follow music or other paths, to the expressive tension and a search for possible equilibriums between Catholic and Marxist, humanistic and scientific, Italian and Australian cultures. His early poetry expresses the rebellion of a young intellectual towards the elitist culture of his place of origin. 'Il Comizio' [The Political Meeting], written in 1959, is a *passeggiata* in the ancient historical centre of the city of Naples and a metaphor of the passage from Benedetto Croce's neo-idealistic philosophy, studied by many students in the Italian south at the time, towards Gramsci and Togliatti's brand of Marxism. The poet, then twenty and a student at the Conservatorium, and his friends talk about the fact that Naples presents very few opportunities and that they would soon have to leave, perhaps for the most distant corner of the world that with prophetic perspicacity is identified as Australia. The old, the new, the exotic, the familiar, the stress of constant travel are the themes of 'Sono passato anche per la Guinea' [I've also been through New Guinea] (unpublished), written in 1960 when Totaro travelled the world on behalf of FIAT. Addressing his far-away parents, he invites them to come to Sydney to see his new life. He recalls with yearning the sound of his mother's footsteps when in the dead of night she would get up to make the coffee that would send her back to sleep; the image of his father, and his abandoned land in Puglia with its wine, olives and wheat, another lifetime ago. The exotic totems brought from New Guinea become 'two obscure Christs' that share space on the walls of his Sydney home with two other familiar totems brought from Naples: the miniature portrait of a baroness aunt and the 'mute' square of a Sacred Heart.

Totaro's later Australian poems express the challenge of the awareness that participation in the culture of his adopted country leads to contributing to its transformation. There are explicit references to the diaspora although they are by and large veiled by the need not to indulge in nostalgia. The migration experience is thus perceived as the courageous translocation from one society to another, representing constant dynamic change, a linguistic melting pot, with its challenge of not overlooking the reciprocal recognition of the continuity and dignity of each individual person. In this context Totaro's plurilinguistic lyric experimentation is particularly interesting and displays a rare sensitivity towards the human condition of the migrant. Many of his poems, written in a mix of languages, relate to salient aspects of the presence of CALD first-generation migrants in Australia who account for about 12.5% of its population. Poems like 'Port Kembla', written in 1974, express the theme of the 'non meaning' of life in the punishing environment of the blast furnaces at the steelworks:

Extremadura
coke havens
altiforni hornos
de fundicion
aqui la vita è breve
meaningless
non ha significado

hermanos o calor
red-hot-white
blanco fierro
c'è ancora l'hope
y l'esperanza

da l'Estremadura
tu veinist you came
frade meu
brothero
español ancora
and yet
el pianto mio
my cry
si confounds se mixa
col tuo (Italo-Australian Poetry in the 80s – II 132)

In '6pm Cleaners' plurilingualism becomes the symbol of the brotherhood between workers from Italy, Spain and Latin America:

cuando quando
when

l'office
is close

e l'executivo
todo all tutto
va home

then
entonces allora
quattro four or five
poveri devils
pobre diablos

umildemente

escoban
vacuumclearanno
l'oficio. (Italo-Australian Poetry in the 80s – II 133)

This brotherhood is extended also to Greeks in 'Homer: Fish Shops' (unpublished) and further references to Australian pluriculturalism are found in 'Lydia Nausicaa: In Memoriam' (unpublished), a moving elegy for a young friend.

Totaro's poems on the condition of the migrant worker present interesting parallels with the work of Pietro Tedeschi (*Le rime e le prose del maligno* and *I CAMMINANTI Quasi poesia di Pietro Tedeschi*), a writer of populist origins whose poems relate to workplace experiences of the 1950s and 1960s when newly arrived Italian migrants found themselves at the bottom of the industrial pecking order. Tedeschi's text, 'Acciaierie' [Steelworks], deals with, among other things, the monotony of work and the infernal atmosphere of the steelworks is compared to Dante's *Inferno* (*I CAMMINANTI*: 36–39) and a life severely limited by the requirements of an exploitative industrial process (See 'Hostel '58', *Italo-Australian Poetry in the 80s*, 127). Whereas Totaro articulates the existential plane of the CALD migrant worker experience with expressive sensitivity, Tedeschi, at a more concrete level, has given voice from the 'inside' to a common aspect of the Italian diaspora and articulates the experience of a class that has, by and large, not been able to express what the transition from a largely rural Italian context to the urban industrial environment of Australia has meant.

Totaro's existential plurilingualism, however, also marks crossings with pre-migratory experiences. 'Conversazioni mute' [Mute Conversations] (unpublished), four poems written in July 1985, are inspired by a sudden return to Naples because of the imminent death of his father and articulate memories of past and present relationships with his parent.

'The Lie'
Halfshadowed hospital room
whitish light: a Neapolitan noon.
But for an occasional moan
as he slumbers to and from,
but for his brow
which is furrowed and drawn,
you wouldn't know his pain
since surgery at dawn.
He was cut and quickly sewn
back: nothing could be done:
'His pain will grow and grow.
There are no guidelines,
it may come or go
it may burn or ice'.
The son was told it all:
'The old man is at the ropes'.

Days before, an intercontinental call,
a frankly sad voice:
'Catch the first plane.
You are needed at once'.
In the faraway place
which the son calls home,
the moment ever since dreaded
had now truly come.

The mother's stunted body
clutches her son. Despair and a trace

of joy: 'Figlio mio, ma che tiene?'
Oh white gentleness of lies:
'*Mamma* he will be well again.
Vedrai. Will see. The purple space
and the birds red blue green
of Pittwater. Paoletta. Riccardo
sailing for him on that strange sea …
Shall book a flight. Back with me.
Back, back with me'.

No moment of truth for the ill man
and his wife. They are so frail
and old. Here, you tell only those
who should be told.

'Primo notturno: *le voci di dentro*'

Night signals:
nightnurses' noises
muffled,
and the inner ear's. Wave
upon wave, other voices,
thinner than air. They belong
to the dying man and his son.

'I had to go. To migrate
was fugue and revolt.
Against you? Maybe so;
we always fought a tug of love.
Remember in jest I once said:
my first resistance
as an oppressed minority
was against father's hegemony!
Pater patria potestas. Oh father
your time has come
and you cannot be told.
Here it is not done

you are so tired and old'.

Slow caresses along greyspent hair
searching, bent, halfclosed eyes
as you do with a baby
if you want his smiles.

'Secondo notturno: Food'

'Don't you eat, *babbino* ?
Just this morsel, will you please?'

'No, non posso.
Il sapore. Mi delude'

He remembers taste, smells
of his once upon a time
in a village.
'Pane, acqua,
un poco d' aglio'.
Any effort
to relive his appetite
dies with him.

'Mi dispiace'.

'Terzo notturno: Shelters'

Unreachably tall
he lifted the child,
his arms and chest
a fort and a cradle.
Hell on earth, airshelters:
they ran most nights
and the sky was alight
with mitraille and groundfire.
'Were you scared, *babbo*?'
'For you only. To die

was matter of fact. Four years.
Hell on earth. Airshelters.
The war was your childhood
companion'.

'I remember: till now,
a siren, or the rumble
of the pistons of a slow aircargo
arouse that scream
you taught me not to voice'.

Now as then he tries to shelter
others. His pain his own
to bear. His care is quiet.
Open, stabs the side;
a blade his back *piagato*,
the mouth a cave of fire,
yet he says subdued:
'Mi dispiace'.

Gli dispiace.
When they clean that waste
which was his body
he just says with his eyes:
'Don't tire'.

And the screams
all the screams of a lifetime
of war, of love, of patient
toil do remain
as unvoiced now as then
when he sheltered his son
from mitraille and groundfire.

Paolo Totaro's themes include his relationship with his environment and the people that are important in his life: his Jesuit teachers, his parents, his wife, his children. Enchanting Pittwater, on the coast north of

Sydney and surrounded by an immense national park, on whose shores Totaro lives, constitutes an idealised oasis of peace:

'*Linee diritte*: Straight Lines'

Scure bande di terra
sottolineate dal brulichio bianco
di barche minutamente ancorate.
In alto, larghe onde di eucalipti
intrecciano dita di rosa in riccioli
di nuvole.

'*O rododactyylos eos*[4]
precede d'estate qui in Australia
il vento di nordovest
che fra un'ora
scompiglierà il mare
e le linee ora dritte
saranno, per il resto del giorno,
incertamente increspate.[5]

---

[4] *Aurora dalle dita di rosa*, rosy-fingered dawn.

[5] Many horizons: long ribbons of bush underscored by a dotted white line of boats closely anchored.

On top, gentler lines,
a wave of eucalyptus
interlocks with wisps of clouds:
'O rododàctylos eòs
the rosyfingered dawn
precedes also in Pittsummer-time
the nor'westerly breeze
which in an hour
will tease out the sea.

And those straight lines

This oasis of peace exists in sharp contrast with the hectic and alienating environment of New South Wales politics. In 'Volontà di sorridere' [Wanting to Smile], Pittwater, where the calm dawn sea is later disturbed by the midday trade winds, represents a serenity that perhaps mirrors a conscience disturbed by the tension between a wistful aspiration to interior peace and the reality of social conflict (*Italo-Australian Poetry in the 80s – II*, 130–31). The difficulty of saying things that really count is perhaps another way of expressing that active participation in the culture of the adopted country is a no less wistful aspiration than past participation in the culture of the country of origin.

'Volontà di parlare'
sinceramente
e di tutto.

Se si crea fra persone
anche amatissime
un vuoto di segni,
se il vuoto significa la perdita
del coraggio di comunicare,
se le non molte parole
sembrano solo proiettili
da rintuzzare
subito
senza perdere un colpo
solo:
non c'è che da cominciare
tutto da capo,
se si ha volontà di sperare.

C'è chi crede nella pace
tra la gente

---

will be for the rest of the day
the lines of a shattered face. ('*Linee diritte*: Straight Lines'; author's translation)

ma io mi sto convincendo
che non c'è altra pace
che quella
con sè:
se io fossi in pace
con me stesso,
io saprei dove andare
saprei anche parlare
a te di te,
e a quei tanti altri
che m'illudo di saper
guidare
e che invece trattengo
lontani impauriti
come da loro intrattengo
lontana
la mia natura
rinchiusa tanti anni fa
nella mia prigione
di bambino
insicuro. ('*Volontà di parlare*', Italo-Australian Poetry in the 80s – II:
129)[6]

---

[6] 'Wanting to speak'
sincerely
and of everything.

If between people
who even love each other very much
an emptiness of signs is created
if this emptiness signifies
the loss of the courage to communicate,
if the not many words
seem only projectiles
to drive back
immediately

The above poems provide salient examples of the broad range of themes interlinking life and migration that are found in Paolo Totaro's poetry. They also serve to illustrate the impressive variety of stylistic expression that marks his writing. Paolo Totaro's poetic 'journey', while not losing touch with his point of departure, presents with rare sensitivity

---

without losing a single
blow:
the only thing left is to begin
all over again,
if we are willing to hope.

There are some who believe in peace
among people
but I'm becoming convinced
that there is no other peace
than that
with oneself:
if I were at peace
with myself,
I would know where to go
I would also know how to talk
to you of you,
and to those many others
that I fool myself I know
how to lead
and who instead I hold back
far away frightened
as from them I hold back
far away
my nature
locked up many years ago
in my prison
of an insecure
child. ('*Volontà di parlare*' [Wanting to Speak], *Italo-Australian Poetry in the 80s
– II*, 129 – my translation)

the many different aspects of the recesses of his soul as well as the collective experience of the migrant diaspora. For a number of Italian-Australian poets the transition to a new world and a new life is not only accepted but seen as a means of personal, cultural and linguistic enrichment. For others, the long crossing has failed to live up to its promise: the dream did not become reality, their allegiance is torn, they fail to reach a personal and cultural equilibrium and nostalgia becomes an overriding though not entirely negative element.[7] For Paolo Totaro, who has actively participated in the social, political and cultural life of his adopted country making significant contributions, emigration is an integral part of a life whose transformations are lived positively and critically, where linguistic and other dislocations can be overcome by the sense of one's origins and the sense of brotherhood with the other human beings that are part of one's world, both equally important in the search for cultural and personal equilibrium.

Works Cited

Abiuso, Giuseppe, Michele Giglio, and Valerio Borghese, eds. *Voci nostre Antologia italo-australiana di novelle, commedie, poesie e ricordi, scritta da emigrati italo-australiani.* Melbourne: Tusculum, 1979.

ALIAS, ed. Antologia A.L.I.A.S. 1996–97: *Antologia del quarto premio letterario internationale: poesia e narrativa.* Avon Heights, Victoria: ALIAS, 1997.

Casella, Antonio. 'Literature of Nostalgia: The Long Voyage.' In *Literary and Social Diasporas: An Italian Australian Perspective.* Eds. Gaetano Rando and Gerry Turcotte. Brussels: Peter Lang, 2008, 43–54.

---

[7] Recent critical work on Italian-Australian literature has argued that nostalgia is in fact a constructive element in coming to terms with the long-term cultural and identity issues posed by the migration experience, see Papalia 2007; Casella 2008.

Castles, Stephen, Caroline Alcorso, Gaetano Rando, and Ellie Vasta, eds. *Italo-australiani. La popolazione di origine italiana in Australia.* Turin: Edizioni della Fondazione Giovanni Agnelli, 1992.

Cincotta, Vincenzo, ed. *Italo-Australian Poetry in the 80s – II.* Wollongong, NSW: Department of Modern Languages, University of Wollongong, 1989.

Ethnic Affairs Commission of New South Wales. *Participation: Report of the Ethnic Affairs Commission of New South Wales on Participation, June 1978.* Sydney: Government Printer, 1978.

Genovesi, Piero, ed. *Compagni di viaggio.* Carlton, Vic: CIS Publishers, 1991.

Hage, Gassan. *White Nation: Fantasies of White Supremacy in a Multicultural Society.* Sydney: Pluto Press, 1998.

Niscioli, Paola. Migrant Writing and Beyond: The Voices of Four Italian-Australian Poets: Lino Concas, Mariano Coreno, Enoe Di Stefano and Luigi Strano. MA Thesis. The Flinders University of South Australia, Adelaide, 1996.

O'Connor, Mark, ed. *Two Centuries of Australian Poetry.* Melbourne: Oxford University Press, 1988.

Papalia, Gerardo. 'Nostalgia: Elaborating New Diasporic Identities.' In *La Diaspora italiana dopo la Seconda Guerra Mondiale. The Italian Diaspora After the Second World War.* Eds. Jim Hagan and Gaetano Rando. Bivongi, RC: International AM Edizioni, 2007, 373–84.

Polizzi, Umberto, ed. *Antologia ALIAS 1995: Poesia, Prosa, Teatro.* Keilor, Victoria: ALIAS, 1995.

——, ed. *'Antologia' ALIAS: Poesia e Prosa.* Melbourne: ALIAS, 1994.

Premio 2 giugno. *Premio '2 giugno' Racconti.* Sydney: Consolato Generale d'Italia, 1999.

Rando La Cava, Rita. 'Alcuni aspetti della tradizione orale eoliana: fatti e misfatti raccolti presso eoliani emigrati in Australia e residenti nelle città di Melbourne, Sydney e Wollongong.' BA (Honours) Dissertation. Department of European Languages, University of Wollongong, 1983.

Rando, Gaetano. 'Italian Australian Poetry by First Generation Writers: An Overview.' *JASAL 5* (2006): 39–57.

——, ed. *Italo-Australian Poetry in the 80s.* Wollongong, NSW: Department of European Languages, The University of Wollongong, 1986.

——, ed. *Italian Writers in Australia: Essays and Texts. Incorporating the Proceedings of the Italo-Australian Poetry Reading (16 August 1981) and the National Seminar on Italo-Australian Narrative and Drama Writers (25–26 September 1982).* Wollongong, NSW: Department of European Languages, University of Wollongong, 1983.

Savoca, Carmelo. 'Italo-Australian Poetry: A Study of Selected Poets.' In *Italian Writers in Australia: Essays and Texts.* Ed. Gaetano Rando. Wollongong, NSW: Department of European Languages, The University of Wollongong, 1983, 81–102.

Tedeschi, Pietro. *I CAMMINANTI Quasi poesia di Pietro Tedeschi.* Wollongong, NSW: The Estate of Pietro Tedeschi, 1998.

——. *Le rime e le prose del maligno.* Wollongong, NSW: The Author, 1997.

Totaro, Paolo. *'Participation* Twenty-five Years Later.' Paper. International Conference on 'Minorities and Cultural Assertions – Literary and Social Diasporas.' University of Wollongong, Wollongong, NSW. 8 October 2004–10 October 2004.

——. *Storia patria: Opera aperta.* Naples: MeltingPot, 1996.

——. *Paolo poesie.* Sydney: The Author, 1981.

——. *Environment and Earthmoving.* Sydney: Fiat of Australia, 1971.

15

Two Approaches to Constructing 'Chinese' Cultural Identity: Australia's Authors with Chinese Ancestry[1]

Christine Sun

The 'Chinese' in Australia is a 'non-static and composite reality' (Lee, 578). Since the official abolition of the White Australia policy in 1973, Australia has taken in large numbers of migrants of full or partial Chinese descent from Malaysia, Singapore, Hong Kong, Taiwan, China, other South-East Asian countries and the rest of the world. These groups of newcomers have been nurtured within different versions of Chinese culture. As they settle and develop their new lives in Australia, significant divisions begin to appear within and between them. Political differences, socio-economic differences, urban/rural differences, gender differences, language and dialect differences and ethnic differences have emerged and are sometimes aggressively expressed. The result is the presence of considerably different types of 'Chinese' cultural identity in writings produced by Australia's authors with Chinese ancestry.

Identity, in the form of a reproducible set of cultural, political or class traits, affects not only the ways in which individuals, groups, communities and nations understand and represent themselves to others,

---

[1] This paper is an extract from Christine Sun's *Voices Under the Sun: English-Language Writings by Australian and Other Authors with Chinese Ancestry* (Melbourne: Taiwan.com.au Portal, 2007).

but also how they are recognised and treated by others accordingly. By examining how different types of 'Chinese' cultural identity are represented in writings produced by Australia's authors with Chinese ancestry, we are able to investigate how these authors comprehend and construct their perceived 'Chineseness' in writing. A critical analysis of these representations also enables us to understand how cultural stereotypes impose an identity to which individuals respond in different ways and under different circumstances. In a multicultural country such as Australia, multicultural policies have influenced the ways in which 'Chineseness' and different types of 'Chinese' cultural identity are formed and standardised and find circulation in mainstream society. Therefore, the cultural assumptions evident in writings produced by Australia's authors with Chinese ancestry are the most important sites in which their perceptions of the nature and significance of their 'Chineseness' may be explored adequately.

Constructing 'Chinese' Cultural Identity

Diana Giese (1997) points out:

> As Australian society was defining itself in the prosperous 1960s and 1970s, Chinese identity was preserved in a number of different ways. These included the eating of Chinese food, adhering to traditional belief systems and worshipping the Chinese way, and continuing to speak in languages and dialects. (140)

What Giese is suggesting is that 'Chinese' cultural identity is most commonly constructed and/or defined, in both mainstream Australian society and the Chinese-speaking world, in two ways – the ability to use a common Chinese language or dialect, and the adoption of common Chinese cultural practices (for example myths, superstitions, legends, foods, manners, behaviours and beliefs). Her phrase 'worshipping the Chinese way' reflects the common 'essentialist' belief that there is an 'orthodox' way in which the Chinese worship their ancestors and/or gods.

It seems to me that such an 'essentialist' approach to constructing 'Chinese' cultural identity is most visible in writings produced by those authors with Chinese ancestry who increasingly and often aggressively promote the importance of 'Chineseness' in defining the lives of individuals of Chinese descent. 'Chinese' cultural identity appears to be frequently portrayed by these authors as having a 'bonding power' over individuals and groups, in the same way that people may be restrained by the borders of geopolitical entities. The result is that 'Chineseness' is constructed in their writings as a concrete 'site' whose existence cannot be neglected and whose omnipresent influence can be felt in the lives of both Chinese and non-Chinese. Even more limiting, the 'boundaries' of this imagined 'site' that is called 'Chineseness' are represented as being extremely difficult to cross, for those who are defined within them and those who are assigned to be outside of them.

Common, particularly traditional, Chinese cultural practices are often considered to be important determinants of 'Chinese' cultural identity in both mainstream Australian society and the Chinese-speaking world. Singapore-born author Lillian Ng's *Silver Sister* (1994) provides ample examples of how traditional Chinese cultural practices are represented as markers that distinguish 'Chinese' individuals from their Australian counterparts. In this book, a disagreement takes place between the narrator ('I'), a Chinese domestic servant, and her young hostess 'Kim' who lives in modern-day Australia, on how to ease symptoms of allergy. Convinced that Western pills are 'too potent' for her system, the Chinese servant much prefers traditional Chinese medicine.

> I had brought some dried crocodile meat shreds, the Chinese traditional treatment for lung ailments, sealed in an envelope, which I didn't declare at Customs. When Kim was out, I brewed pork rib soup with a few shreds of crocodile meat. After that treatment, the sniffing and sneezing ceased. (*Silver Sister*, 265–66)

Such traditional Chinese cultural practice is one of many described in *Silver Sister*. As an author, Ng appears to be specifically dramatising contradictions between these traditional Chinese cultural practices and those existing in contemporary Australian society.

Another example of traditional Chinese cultural practices being considered as an important determinant of 'Chinese' cultural identity is found in Singapore-born author Ang Chin Geok's *Wind and Water* (1997). In this book, emphasis is repeatedly given to the power of *feng shui* in affecting and even regulating the lives of generations of Chinese individuals, even after their relocation to other countries far away from their homeland. For instance, Soo Teen, one of the three female protagonists in *Wind and Water*, begins telling her life story by suggesting that the Chinese believe 'the influence of natural topography and the directions of the compass could bless or blight the destiny of individuals, families, clans, ancestral groups and whole communities' (*Wind and Water*, 3). She continues:

> In my parents' country the landscape teemed with demons and spirits. People built winding paths and screens in front of their homes, and placed mirrors above their doors, to thwart these spirit beings who could travel only in straight lines … When my parents left their homeland the spiritual landscapes of their birthplace went with them, carried in their hearts and minds to be carefully transplanted into the strange, wild places where they now found themselves, so that although I was born many thousands of miles from the home of my ancestors, my life and fate were inextricably tied to the ancient beliefs of their country. I was only one of a multitude who inherited these old spiritual landscapes. (*Wind and Water*, 3–5)

In *Wind and Water*, Soo Teen's parents left Southern China in search of their fortunes in South-East Asia. She and her daughter, Peng An, live through the Japanese occupation to witness Singapore's birth as an independent nation after the Second World War. But even Peng An, who has received education from Western-style schools in modern-day

Singapore and who has learned not to be easily affected by the 'cultural categories' imposed on her (such as gender, race and socio-economic class), finds it difficult to escape from the seemingly omnipresent influence of *feng shui*. She laments:

> Eating bitterness was what her mother had done for most of her life, and eating bitterness was what my mother now did, her mother's sorrows as fresh as each difficult day which dawned, her blighted *hongsui* [feng shui] condemning her to repeat the boom-and-bust cycles of her parents. I cried every day. If this was what awaited us after all that hardship, all that struggling, why wait til I was old? Why not go now? (*Wind and Water*, 235)

Like Ng in *Silver Sister*, Ang in *Wind and Water* presents plenty of traditional cultural practices that are commonly ascribed to the Chinese. These include celebrating Chinese New Year and other religious events, practicing rituals of ancestor worship, and observance of various myths and superstitions. These two authors appear to have consciously included as many Chinese cultural practices as possible in their writings, in order to suggest the significance of these practices to all Chinese people. Their representations of the subjective experiences of their Chinese protagonists are predicable and almost stereotypical, as if to imply to their readers that these are typical and fundamental Chinese cultural experiences encountered by every Chinese individual in the world. In this sense, their writings may be considered as exemplary essentialist accounts of 'Chineseness'.

The danger of the essentialist approach to representing 'Chineseness' as something that is universal is obvious. As one proposes a global Chinese identity in terms of ethnicity and one's familiarity with certain cultural practices that are commonly ascribed to the Chinese people, one takes the risk of ignoring individual and local versions of Chinese identity formed and circulated within different types of Chinese culture all over the world. Since society abounds with cultural stereotypes, reductive and essentialist ways of representing Chinese cultural difference in literary texts may have the adverse effect of further reinforcing such stereotypes through fictive reproduction.

Challenging the 'Universal' in Chinese Cultural Identity

In his article 'Cultural Identity and Cinematic Representation' (1989), Stuart Hall develops two contrasting views on cultural identity. The first view defines cultural identity in terms of the idea of one shared culture, 'a sort of collective one true self' that provides unifying and unchanging points of reference and meaning. The second view defines cultural identities as being 'always constructed through memory, fantasy, narrative and myth … [They are] the points of identification … which are made within the discourses of history and culture' (Hall, 705). These two views explicitly illustrate the tension between what I refer to in this paper as 'essentialist' and 'non-essentialist' approaches to representing Chinese cultural identity in writings produced by Australia's authors with Chinese ancestry.[2] Essentialist authors such as Ng and Ang appear to be constructing a global version of 'Chineseness' in their texts, by portraying certain Chinese cultural practices as being 'fundamental' to the existence of every Chinese person in a cultural sense.

David Parker (1995), who studies the cultural identities of young Chinese people in Great Britain, criticises the essentialist approach to representing Chinese cultural identity as being 'too closed, unitary [and]

---

[2] Hall's article mainly deals with cinematic constructions and presentations of national identity in Caribbean countries, where new generations of native artists strive to create and express a 'Caribbean uniqueness' in films that may unify their people politically and culturally against a colonised past. However, Hall's conceptualisation of identity as self-produced continuity that designates what is said by whom and for what purposes is particularly useful for this paper, as we attempt to understand the formation and circulation of cultural identities through powerful public channels such as literature, music, photography and drama.

homogeneous'. According to Parker, whether or not the fundamental elements of Chinese culture (if there are any) should be emphasised in literary texts is beside the point. Rather, what matters

> is whether these [fundamental cultural elements] should be seen as unchanging and emanating from one source that has to be traced back by a unique narrative of origination … A more open sense of the diversity of stories could form part of an awareness of the multiplicity of narratives of experience, and which doesn't have to be collapsed into one all-encompassing myth of origin. (Parker, 34–35)

In other words, Parker's critique of essentialist assumptions in cultural expressions is directly relevant to a consideration of the ways in which Chinese cultural identity can find different and heterogeneous forms of expression in writings produced by authors with Chinese ancestry.

In sharp contrast to essentialist authors such as Ng and Ang, various 'non-essentialist' authors with Chinese ancestry in Australia share Parker's preference for open-ended cultural expression. These authors, including Malaysia-born Hsu-Ming Teo, Hong Kong-born Brian Castro and Malaysia-born Beth Yahp, are well read in literary and cultural theories. They are able to demonstrate evident knowledge of the multiplicity of narratives that construct a sense of cultural identity, as they seek to problematise the 'universal' in Chinese cultural identity with literary representations of diverse cultural experiences lived and cherished by different individuals of Chinese descent. To borrow Hall's words, these authors appear to be considering 'Chinese' cultural identity not as an 'essence', but as a 'positioning' (Hall, 707).

Hsu-Ming Teo's Love and Vertigo

In *Love and Vertigo* (2000), the thoughts and deeds of the three main protagonists, Grace Tay and her parents, are designed by Teo to reflect her views on Australia's multicultural policies as an author and academic. With a postmodern tone, Teo appears to be problematising the idea of a 'universal' version of 'Chineseness' by placing her protagonists in subjective and local environments where commonly accepted social norms such as traditions, morals and choices of life are constantly challenged. Certain cultural values such as children's love and respect for parents and the self-esteem of individuals, which are often taken for granted as natural facts, are designed to collapse so that the protagonists are forced to depend on their naked instincts of survival.

In *Love and Vertigo*, Grace's mother Pandora is portrayed as a victim of patriarchal Chinese culture. Having married a man who appeared to have a secure financial future, Pandora repeatedly questions herself as to whether she truly loves him. She submits to his frequent requests for sex, as a 'proper' wife would do, but secretly resents him to such a degree that she cannot feel joy or love for their unborn child.

> He invades her body and she has to make space for his colony ... She will never be human again until she expels this foreign 'I' inside her. She wants to carve her belly out, beat it and pummel it into flatness. Now she knows how her mother felt, carrying her all those years ago. (*Love and Vertigo*, 124–25)

According to Grace, pressures of patriarchal Chinese culture are not the only factor that contributes to her mother's (and therefore her) family tragedy. Cultural conflicts, parent-child disputes and her desire for intimate and trustworthy personal relationships are also reasons why Pandora is in despair. Having migrated to Australia so that she and her husband can be free of his mother's control and surveillance, Pandora constantly casts doubt on her ability to manage a new life in a foreign country as a wife and mother. Her children, Grace and her brother, who have to deal with their own problems such as racial discrimination at school, have tried desperately to understand her, but to no avail. Pandora turns to religion for faith and meaning of life, and falls in love with a married man from the local church. When she later finds out that he neither loves nor needs her, she 'just let herself go'. During a trip back to

Singapore, she leaps off the balcony of a tall building and kills herself. In short, Pandora is a character confined by a highly reductive account of her social roles, as daughter, daughter-in-law, wife, mother and lover. Therefore, her suicide may be seen as a desperate attempt to escape from all kinds of social and cultural duties that she as a Chinese woman is expected to endure, and to redefine her role as an independent human being who is free to do whatever she chooses.

Pandora decides to go back to Singapore because of a desire to return to 'the moment when she could have made another choice and life would have been completely different' (*Love and Vertigo*, 275). But when she realises that the country has changed dramatically during the decades since she left, that she can no longer find her childhood home, she loses the last bit of hope for life. Indeed, Pandora's limited view of herself, constructed around a rigid definition of what being a good Chinese woman, wife and mother means, becomes the prison from which she cannot escape. Consequently, her desire to return 'home', where her life began, may be interpreted as a wish to reflect on her 'Chineseness', something that she perceives to be so essential to her existence as a woman that the only way to escape from it is to die. This is a critique of the acute social and cultural pressure that patriarchal Chinese culture has placed upon women.

However, to Grace, who is raised and educated in Australia and has tried hard to fit into mainstream Australian society, her mother's 'home' is simply an Asian country that is strange and remote. She reflects:

> I was baffled that my mother could belong to these people. For the first time in my life I saw my mother in relation to her family and I did not recognize her anymore. Her carefully maintained English disintegrated and she lapsed into the local Singlish patois, her vocabulary a mélange of English, Malay and Chinese; her syntax abbreviated, chopped and wrenched into disconcerting unfamiliarity. These Singaporean roots of hers, this side of her – and probably of me too – were unacceptable ... I was determined not to belong, not to fit

in, because I was Australian, and Mum ought to be Australian too. The tug of her roots, the blurring of her role from wife and mother to sister and aunt, angered and frightened me. (*Love and Vertigo,* 2–3)

This reflection of Grace's is crucial because it tells us that *Love and Vertigo* as a book does not seek to reinforce the life-long sufferings of a woman under the pressures of patriarchal Chinese culture or the struggles of migrants to fit into mainstream Australian society. Rather, by illustrating Grace's love-hate relationship with her mother, Teo as an author criticises the social and cultural constraints imposed by 'essentialist' constructions of Chinese cultural identity and dramatises this in the form of Pandora's suicide. Grace, who grows up outside the Chinese-speaking world, is able to detect the negative impacts of these social and cultural constraints on her mother. However, she is angered and frightened by the fact that as a daughter she not only is unable to help her mother in the latter's attempt to escape from these constraints, but she may also become a victim of these constraints as a result of her Chinese ethnicity. That Grace is determined not to belong, not to fit into the Chinese society and culture represented by her mother, may be seen as a direct challenge to the 'essentialist' constructions of Chinese cultural identity.

Brian Castro's Birds of Passage

Castro is another one of Australia's authors with Chinese ancestry who challenge universal accounts of 'Chinese' cultural identity. In his texts, he appears to question the usefulness of identity itself as a cultural category constructed by some for the purpose of imposing it on others and judging them accordingly. This point is made clear through the words of Australian-born Chinese Seamus O'Young, the main protagonist of *Birds of Passage* (1983): 'People are always very curious about nationality. They will go to great lengths to pigeonhole someone. They think this knowledge gives them *power*' (*Birds of Passage,* 8). Castro himself emphasises the fact that prior to his relocation to Australia, he never had to use the word 'identity' except when displaying his bus pass in Hong Kong.

> The first time I was asked not *Who* are you, but *What* are you, was when I arrived in Australia [as an eleven-year-old] … It was the immigration officers who were convinced it was their sacred duty to keep Australia pure. Where I came from, I was more used to being asked 'What would you like to drink?'. (*Writing Asia and Auto/biography,* 7)

This reflection gives a hint to Castro's views on how external factors such as government policies and commonly accepted social norms are used by some to construct cultural identities as self-evident categories of assessing others. It also highlights the many ways in which different individuals may react to these constructed categories under different circumstances.

In *Birds of Passage*, the lonely and confused young man O'Young lives his life as a hybrid. Having accidentally discovered a diary written by Ah Shan, an educated Chinese who came to Australia during the goldrush days of the mid-1880s, O'Young becomes increasingly convinced that Ah Shan was his ancestor. He asks himself 'Who am I?' and begins a long journey of searching for an identity. O'Young confesses:

> I was aware that my appearance created around me a desolation, a metaphysical landscape as barren as the Sahara. Perhaps this was due more to my own penchant for isolation than to the boundaries marked out by reality. I saw myself as a foreigner, and this view pushed me into situations where it became fact. At the same time the feeling of being foreign evoked in me an almost obsessive curiosity about what I like to call 'the secrets of place'. It was in some way connected to the explosion of my sexual life, an internal, masturbatory instinct linked with the need to see, to gaze into the dark, secret places in houses, behind curtains, under covers, sheets, skirts – in short, inside the skull. Thus I became a voyeur. (*Birds of Passage,* 22)

As O'Young tries to find out who he is, he begins to question the value of having an identity. From his words quoted above, it is evident that O'Young acknowledges the fact that while individuals may be identified by others and judged accordingly, they can also become the victim of their own self-perceptions. To a certain degree, this may be seen as reflecting Castro's views on the flexible and ever-changing nature of cultural identity – there cannot and should not be a 'universal' version of cultural identity, because there are ample ways in which people's positioning may be adjusted, by others and/or by themselves.

O'Young's relating the idea of identity to that of 'places' containing 'dark secrets' inevitably leads him to doubt the nature of identity itself. On more than one occasion he observes the power embedded within certain invented and standardised cultural categories when they are taken for granted as facts and consequently find wide circulation within society. For instance, the following conversation takes place between O'Young and the manager of a fabric factory:

> 'My name is Seamus O'Young. I've come about the job'.
> 'Oh, yes. Vat ist you say your name?'
> 'Seamus O'Young'.
> 'Such a funny name for a Chinese'.
> 'I'm Australian'.
> 'Really. Hum. You haf some Chinese blod. I can see that. Your fater ist Chinese? Your mutter?'
> 'I don't know. I'm Australian'.
> 'That ist unfortunate … but ve try you out chust the same'. (*Birds of Passage*, 23–24)

This passage dramatises the difficulties faced by individuals in social communication in having to accommodate the cultural stereotypes circulating within society. Throughout the conversation the manager, possibly a German migrant, shares the view that was common during the days of the White Australia policy that Australians should be 'white'. Consequently, the manager simply concentrates on the 'fact' that O'Young is 'Chinese' and ignores the young man's repeated claim that he is Australian. Not only does the manager assert that he can see O'Young has 'some Chinese blood', he has also agreed to interview O'Young and to offer him a job because he was previously told that the young man is 'Chinese'. Such is the power embedded in the constructed cultural category 'Chinese', as it is commonly and stereotypically assumed that Chinese workers are diligent and resourceful. O'Young is believed to be a hard worker and hired on the spot simply because he looks 'Chinese'.

Reflecting on this episode, O'Young bitterly agrees that his getting the job may have resulted from 'the positive, active attributes of my nature', that is, his 'Chinese' nature. He soon begins to resent the imposition of such a 'nature' as he is abused by others who assume that because he is 'Chinese', they have the right to tell him what to do and he should obey their orders. In the words of O'Young:

> It was at that moment that I thought I heard a voice deep within me say: 'Compromise and resignation are traits that reach far back into your ancestry. They understood, those people, that freedom is economic, not ideological' ... I heard the roaring of my own hostility. (*Birds of Passage*, 26)

O'Young's inner rage as expressed in these lines provides a powerful critique of the violence imposed by an 'essentialist' view of Chinese culture, which is shared by others and himself. The 'roaring of his hostility' is not only at those who 'understand' his 'Chinese' nature and therefore abuse him, but also at himself who for a moment believes that he should tolerate such abuse because he is 'Chinese'.

In *Birds of Passage*, O'Young's journey of searching for an identity expands from Australia to countries in Europe, from the present to different moments in history, and from reality to dreams. Eventually he confronts Ah Shan in his imagination: 'Are you really my ancestor, bearing the mark of Cain, standing there with your pigtail pulled off, your face gaunt and haunting?' (*Birds of Passage*, 144) Intriguingly, with this confrontation O'Young is able to reconcile with Ah Shan, his other self in the past. Consequently, O'Young in modern-day Australia imagines that 'he was in the river watching the current ... uniting him with the human stream of which he had never been a part' (*Birds of Passage,* 151). Ah Shan of the mid-1800s learned that he would be hunted 'not in general terms as part of a race of people, but as an individual', as he fled Australia after killing, in self-defence, two white men who tried to murder him (*Birds of Passage,* 155). Finally free from the burden of having a collective 'Chinese' identity, both protagonists can now enjoy the freedom and joy of living in their own terms. This celebration of individuality takes the form of 'non-essentialist' literary representation of individual and subjective versions of Chinese cultural identity, as a direct challenge to the essentialist approach to expressing such identity as a 'universal/global' characteristic of all individuals of Chinese descent. The frequent change of narrators and the intentional distortion of timeline in *Birds of Passage* further support Castro's portrayal of cultural identities as points of positioning within various discourses of history and culture, rather than an essence.

Beth Yahp's The Crocodile Fury

In a similar way that Teo's *Love and Vertigo* and Castro's *Birds of Passage* showcase the different ways in which 'Chinese' cultural identity and subjective experiences of 'being Chinese' in Australia may be represented in literary texts, Yahp's *The Crocodile Fury* (1992) deals with the fluid and ever-changing nature of 'Chineseness' in the lives of different individuals. In this book, tales of a mysterious crocodile sneaking around in Malaysia's dense jungle are told by three generations of Chinese women – grandmother, mother and the narrator ('I'), the granddaughter. It is through these tales of ghosts, demons, legends and wonders that confrontations among the Chinese, local Malaysians and Western businessmen are portrayed. However, these tales are always told in different versions, by different people, and from different angles, so that the granddaughter soon becomes confused as to exactly which version reveals the truth – if any truth exists at all. Meanwhile, new tales keep emerging from old ones as Malaysia's histories – its colonial histories and national histories, as well as the personal histories of its Chinese residents – are constantly reconstructed and reinterpreted. The result is that the process in which these tales are generated, circulated and recorded as memories and/or histories become more revealing than the tales themselves. In Yahp's words: 'Stories are history. Stories are used by different people – governments and grandmothers – to present their points of view ... I grew up with sometimes conflicting versions of what was going on. One of my preoccupations is thinking about the truth.' (qtd. in Giese, 2) In an interview, she interprets *The Crocodile Fury* as the following:

> I think Malaysia, where I grew up, is a place where heaps of stories get told – for all kinds of purposes ... I guess telling the different versions of the story in the book is my way of trying to get a rounded picture ... I think there are many different kinds of truths. Put them together and you might get the picture of something you can work with, and you can live with. (qtd. in Giese, 43)

Based on these words, it is evident that Yahp, like Teo and Castro, intends to challenge an essentialist description of Chinese culture by focusing on the value of having multiple narratives of Chinese cultural experiences. Not only do these three authors affirm and further celebrate individual and subjective versions of 'Chineseness' by representing the lives of different Chinese people under different circumstances, they also seek to promote in their texts the concept of narrating real and fictive experiences of 'being Chinese' through dramatically different discourses of history and culture.

In this sense, as we recall Hall's views on cultural identity, the 'Chinese' identity of Malaysia's Chinese residents as represented by Yahp 'is a matter of "becoming" as well as of "being" '. In other words, Yahp appears to consider the 'Chineseness' of the Chinese in Malaysia to

> [belong] to the future as much as to the past. It is not something which already exists, transcending place, time, history and culture ... Like everything which is historical, [it undergoes] constant transformation [and is] subject to the continuous 'play' of history, culture and power. (Hall, 706)

It is therefore evident that Yahp's *The Crocodile Fury* is different from some of the writings produced by other South-East Asian-born authors who grew up among all kinds of 'Chinese' stories, myths and folk tales told by their parents and grandparents. Some of these authors, like Ng and Ang whose texts were discussed earlier in this paper, attempt to construct and express a global 'Chinese' cultural identity that transcends all subjective experiences of 'being Chinese'. However, Yahp seems to be arguing that none of these stories, myths and tales can be nor should be considered as having any universal influence over different individuals. Instead, these stories, myths and tales, as well as other versions of personal memories and official histories, need to be seen as constant reminders of the numerous cultural assumptions commonly made about the Chinese people and culture, to such an extent that a person's 'Chineseness' is frequently believed to be an encompassing cultural origin from which his or her beliefs and values have derived. As an author, Yahp challenges this myth of having only one cultural origin by portraying different stories, myths, tales, memories and histories as different kinds of narratives that construct different senses of cultural identity.

Conclusion

In this paper, I have briefly dealt with the representation of 'Chinese' cultural identity and subjective experiences of 'being Chinese' in writings produced by five of Australia's authors with Chinese ancestry. Lillian Ng and Ang Chin Geok adopt an 'essentialist' approach to constructing a 'universal/global' version of 'Chinese' cultural identity. In contrast, Hsu-Ming Teo, Brian Castro and Beth Yahp in their 'non-essentialist' approach choose to celebrate individual and subjective versions of Chinese cultural identity. By comparing how in their writings these five authors perceive the nature of 'Chineseness' and its significance for different individuals under different circumstances, we are able to detect how these authors are responding to the political, economic, social and cultural demands of their lives in Australia and/or elsewhere. We are also able to understand how different types of 'Chinese' cultural identity may be established and normalised and find wide circulation within a given society, and consequently have considerable impacts on how individuals and groups associate with each other in a cultural sense. As the diversity of literary texts discussed in this paper has demonstrated, 'Chineseness' in Australia is and will continue to be a site of contested meanings.

Works Cited

Ang, Chin Geok. *Wind and Water*. Milsons Point, NSW: Random House, 1997.

Castro, Brian. *Writing Asia and Auto/biography: Two Lectures*. Canberra: Australian Defence Force Academy, 1995.

——. *Birds of Passage*. 1983. St Leonards, NSW: Allen & Unwin, 1993.

Giese, Diana. *Astronauts, Lost Souls & Dragons: Conversations with Chinese-Australians*. Brisbane: University of Queensland Press, 1997.

Hall, Stuart. 'Cultural Identity and Cinematic Representation.' 1989. In *Film and Theory: An Anthology*. Eds. Robert Stam and Toby Miller. Malden, Massachusetts: Blackwell, 1999, 704–14.

Lee, Mabel. 'Chinese Writers in Australia: New Voices in Australian Literature.' *Meanjin* 57.3 (1998): 578–85.

Ng, Lillian. *Silver Sister*. Port Melbourne, Victoria: Mandarin, 1994.

Parker, David. *Through Different Eyes: The Cultural Identities of Young Chinese People in Britain*. Hampshire, UK: Ashgate, 1995.

Teo, Hsu-Ming. *Love and Vertigo*. St Leonards, NSW: Allen & Unwin, 2000.

Yahp, Beth. *The Crocodile Fury*. Sydney: Angus & Robertson, 1992.

16

RE-DEFINING PARAMETERS: GREEK-AUSTRALIAN LITERATURE[1]

HARICLEA ZENGOS

Con Castan (1983) has described Greek-Australian literature as 'a plant of recent growth and of even more recent flowering' ('Greek-Australian Literature', 24), an apt description when one considers that this literature did not really exist prior to 1950, but grew out of the mass migration of Greeks to Australia shortly after the Second World War, between 1950 and 1970, to be more exact. To carry Caston's plant metaphor a bit further, Greek-Australian literature is truly a seedling among the literatures of Australia; in fact, its relative novelty makes it difficult to define the term 'Greek-Australian' and to outline its parameters. To illustrate, consider just a small sampling of writers who may be categorised as writers of Greek-Australian literature: Vasso Kalamaras, a short-story writer who was born in Greece, has lived in Australia for over fifty years and writes in Greek; Angelo Loukakis, born in Australia to Greek immigrant parents, writes in English about what he knows first-hand – what it is like to be an Australian of Greek descent; and George Papaellinas, who like Loukakis is an Australian-born writer of Greek parentage.

---

[1] This was first published in *Reading Down Under: Australian Literary Studies Reader* edited by Amit Sarwal and Reema Sarwal (New Delhi: SSS Publications, 2009, 271–82).

The term Greek-Australian, then, is quite broad. To simplify matters, it might be best to narrow down two types of writers, two streams of literature: first, those writers who write in Greek and are migrants themselves, that is, those who are first generation, arriving in Australia as adults (like Kalamaras, who writes in Greek, often translating her own work into English) and the second generation, writers like Loukakis and Papaellinas who were born in Australia of Greek immigrant parents, or those who came to Australia as young children, such as the poet πO. This dichotomy in Greek-Australian literature also gives rise to a duality of theme. Often, in the writing of first-generation migrants, there is a preoccupation with exile, what the Greeks call *xenitia* (a word for which there really is no English equivalent – it is something akin to life in a foreign land coupled with nostalgia for the homeland), and with the lost homeland and the foreignness of the 'new world.' In the work of the second generation – writers like Loukakis and Papaellinas – there is also a sense of exile, but it is exile of a different nature. Many of Loukakis' and Papaellinas' characters question their ethnicity and are in search of identity and a sense of place. These characters are neither here nor there, neither 'dinkum Australians' nor Greeks. Thus, much of the work of the second generation writers explores the nature of hybridity and identity.

The Greeks in Australia: Post-World War II Migration

Greek migration to Australia dates back to 1827, but the vast majority of Greeks arrived between 1945 and 1982. In the 1940s, German, Italian and Bulgarian occupation during the Second World War (1941–44) and the Civil War (1946–49) had left Greece with a devastated economy and thousands of displaced people. In addition, people who sympathised with the communists defeated in the Civil War, or other people with leftist political views were oppressed by the ruling dictatorship. As a result, to escape their poor and ravaged homeland, thousands of Greeks migrated to Australia in the 1950s and 1960s as part of the Australian government's migration schemes. The most significant wave of Greek migration occurred in the 1960s, when approximately 140,000 Greeks came to Australia. By 1971 there were 160,200 Greek-born persons in Australia, and smaller numbers from Cyprus and Egypt. Nearly half of the Greek-speaking community of Australia settled in Melbourne; as a consequence, the city today is a 'small Greece' Down Under. Globally, Melbourne is said to have the third largest Greek-speaking population after Athens and Thessaloniki (Melbourne's sister city). Numbering approximately half a million today, the Greek community in Australia is the third-largest, non-English-speaking population after the Italians and the Vietnamese.

Greek-Australian Poetry

Belonging to the first-generation of Greek-Australian writers, Dimitris Tsaloumas was born on the Greek island of Leros and migrated to Australia in 1952. He has published several collections of poetry, primarily in Greek, earning him the reputation in Greece as an important poet of the post-Second World War period. Following the publication of his work in English translation, notably *The Observatory* (1983) and *The Book of Epigrams* (1985), Tsaloumas produced three collections of poetry written in English: *Falcon Drinking* (1988), *Portrait of a Dog* (1991), and *The Barge* (1993). Tsaloumas' English poetry draws on the Greek poetic tradition while also incorporating images from and allusions to Australia. 'Apocrypha Homerica', a poem from his collection *Stoneland Harvest: New and Selected Poems* (1999) that consciously rewrites Homer's *Odyssey* in terms of Tsaloumas' journey to Australia, is a case in point:

> Thus,
> blasted along the shores
> of Suckdem-Suckdem, past
> Arkademea fair in which
> the Kolophonics live,
> a pungent race; and on
> past Derridaea beyond
> the rock that sings ...

hit the parlous rocks
off Bondi Beach. And so,
thinking himself a goner,
he suffered deconstruction
and lost his loving Homer. ('Apocrypha Homerica', 23)

Living and writing across his two cultures, and published in both languages, Tsaloumas rejects the label 'ethnic' writer, preferring instead to be described as an Australian Greek author. In 1983 his poetry collection *The Observatory* broke new ground as the first bilingual book to be awarded the prestigious National Book Council Award for Australian Literature. It was a great achievement for multicultural Australia and for Dimitris Tsaloumas, the beginning of deserved recognition in his adopted homeland. *The Harbour* (1998) won the John Bray Award in 2000.

One of the more provocative and challenging poets to emerge in contemporary Australian writing is πO, one of the country's foremost 'performance poets'. Born Panagiotis Oustabasides in Katerini, northern Greece in 1951, πO migrated to Australia with his family when he was three years old and grew up in a working-class suburb of Melbourne, Fitzroy. In keeping with the trend toward assimilation of ethnic groups prevalent in Australia in the 1950s, πO's first name was changed to Peter. However, in the early 1970s, while a student at La Trobe University, Peter Outsabasides changed his name to the Greek characters πO. In *The Number Poems and Other Equations* (2000), he explains that he made the change 'to suit my mind i.e. into my Greek-Australian initials, in honour of Archimedes and Euler who I fell in love with' (qtd in Zervos, 'πO'. 261).

πO's poetry is highly experimental, challenging issues of style, representation, and presentation while also critiquing class distinctions, ethnic discrimination and literary elitism. Many of πO's collections of poems such as *Fitzroy Brothel* (1974), *Panash* (1978) and *The Fitzroy Poems* (1989) are about life in Fitzroy, the inner-city, working-class Melbourne suburb in which πO grew up. These poems represent the diverse voices of a multicultural community and capture the way non-native speakers of English employ the language. Using phonetic spelling that challenges the English-speaking reader, πO documents the dialect of the working class, non-Anglo European Australian population as evidenced in the following lines from *The Fitzroy Poems*:

> *Wotz*
> *goot for dis kuntri*
> *kum?*
> *Dai bai dai*
> *Dai bai dai*
> *wayt to*
> *gon in da*
> *g-rewn?*
> *Awl mai kitz*
> *Layborus*
> *layk*
> *mi!*
> *ekzaakli*
> *ekzaakli mai'*
> *ekzaakli*. ('Two Men in a Corner', 56–57)

πO's interest in concrete poetry (composed of typographic elements) and visual poetry (that makes use of significant amounts of non-text imagery and/or text as visual image) is evident throughout his publications, as for example in *The Number Poems and Other Equations* where all the poems are made up of numbers that often form grids that make recognisable images; in other words, πO replaces words and letters with numbers, achieving a startling effect. He is also well known as a performance poet, having delivered stirring, passionate performances of his work internationally.

Greek-Australian Fiction

Vasso Kalamaras belongs to the first group of writers, whom Castan calls the 'dying generation' of Greek-Australian writers who write in Greek. Kalamaras' work in Australia has appeared in Greek-English bilingual texts, a sign of the growing Australian interest in multiculturalism. Considered one of the most published and translated Greek authors outside Greece, Kalamaras writes poetry, plays, short stories and novels. For her outstanding literary achievements, she has received numerous awards including the Western Australian Premier's Award for Fiction in 1990. In 1951, Kalamaras migrated to Western Australia where she and her husband worked on a tobacco farm. The stories in her first collection, *Other Earth: Four Greek-Australian Stories* (1977), grew out of her experiences as a woman in Australia. The protagonists of the four short stories are women who, because of the hardships of the homeland, are forced to migrate to Australia. Kalamaras explores the double burden of being a woman and a migrant in Australia. Australia offers hope for a better future, but the sacrifices that women must make to achieve this place a strain on their mental and physical wellbeing. Kalamaras' vision is a tragic one. Her women suffer pain, exploitation and abuse but endure. These women have traded the cruelties of the homeland for the cruelties of exile.

In 1976 Kalamaras privately published six short stories in Athens written in Greek under the Greek title *Pikres*. This collection became available to English readers under the title *Bitterness: Six Short Stories* (1983), once again in a bilingual edition. As in *Other Earth: Four Greek-Australian Stories*, migrant women and their struggles figure in these stories. 'May the Virgin Grant Her Going', for example, tells the tale of Avgoula, a poor Greek girl from a small fishing village. The hardships of the village force Avgoula to find an escape; her solution is migration to Australia. 'She will escape, the poor girl!' one villager remarks, 'Better for her to go to Australia' (33). The story ends on an ironic note, particularly when one considers the fates of Kalamaras' *Other Earth: Four Greek-Australian Stories* protagonists. What Avgoula and the villagers do not realise is that Australia may not exactly be the great escape they envision. It can, in fact, be a land of bitterness.

Many of the works of second-generation Greek-Australian writers concern the seemingly unbridgeable cultural gap between immigrants and their offspring, and the progeny's search for a sense of identity, themes apparent in the short stories of Loukakis and Papaellinas. Loukakis writes of the ambiguous identity of the second generation, who are neither Greeks to the Greeks nor Australians to the Australians; they are hopelessly alienated from both cultures. All of the stories in Loukakis' first collection, *For the Patriarch* (1981), deal with Greek migrants and their experiences. In 'Dancing', for example, Australian-born youth tire of their Greek parents' ethnic 'wog' dancing and instead head to the nearest disco. In 'Anastasia Panos', the title character, an ethnic dance instructor, attempts to teach young Greek-Australians the dances of 'their' people, but comes up against their desire to learn jazz and ballet instead. All the characters of *For the Patriarch* question their sense of self and suffer from isolation and dislocation.

In another collection of short stories, *Vernacular Dreams* (1986), Loukakis expands his vision to explore the lives of other Australians besides those of Greek immigrants. However, the more successful stories of this work are those which concentrate on the migrant experience. In 'Only the Truth', Loukakis subtly critiques Australian-born people of Greek descent for whom ethnicity is just a passing fancy or fad. The main character, Peter Dracopoulos, decides to write an oral history on postwar migrants. He begins his project by taping an interview with his mother. Peter tells his friends, Jilly and Sonya that he is interested 'only in the truth' (99). Though he claims that he wants to make the 'injustices to the migrants' known to society, Peter, in truth, edits his mother's responses when they are, in his opinion, too emotional or too personal. In essence, he censors the migrant experience to suit his own vision of it and silences the voice of his mother, who represents other immigrants and their pains and hardships. Jilly is biting in her criticism of Peter's research methods. She claims that the 'bits' he will finally choose for his book 'will be the ones that suit [his] own advancement' (98). 'Where would you be if you didn't have your migrant heritage to trade off?' (99) she questions. Peter tries to cash in on his ethnicity rather than truly learning about his ethnic background.

In 'This Wizened Creature', Loukakis manages to highlight Greek and Australian cultural and ethnic tensions and generational conflict. The story is narrated by Cleo, a seamstress enlisted by a Greek mother to design a coming out dress for her daughter. Cleo finds these 'ethnics' (127) a tacky lot; their 'gigantic ornate sofa and armchairs, done in crimson velvet, and *drapes* hiding the windows' (130), their 'kingsize pictures' (130), and their 'really *Greeky*' (131) worry beads are, in her opinion, beyond the realm of bad taste. Cleo is a stereotypical example of ethnic prejudice. 'They come over here from their villages or whatever, and the next thing they're *wanting* everything' (130), she complains to a friend. 'I don't understand how they think – how can they be something they're not?' (130). Cleo lacks understanding and tolerance; she cannot value cultural and ethnic differences, choosing to accept as truth the negative stereotype of the Greeks as uneducated and unassimilable foreigners. What Cleo fails to recognise is that save for the Indigenous peoples of Australia, the Aborigines, all others living in Australia are descendants of immigrants and are as 'foreign' to Australia as she thinks the Greeks are.

Like Loukakis' Peter Dracopoulos, Peter Mavromatis of George Papaellinas' *Ikons* (1986) is a young Australian-born Greek with shallow cultural and ethnic allegiances. The icons of the title refer to the sacred religious images of the Greek Orthodox, which Peter's classics professor calls 'poor parodies' (27) of old Byzantine forms. In a sense, this is what Peter is: an icon of sorts, a poor parody of a Greek, a pale imitation.

Ikons follows the lives of the Mavromatis family. The eight short stories of the collection are told from each member's point of view. For example, 'A Merchant's Widow' is narrated by Peter's elderly grandmother while 'Christos Mavromatis is a Welder' is told from the vantage point of Peter's father, Christos. Regardless of point of view, Peter dominates every story. The varied narration helps to develop Peter as a character; we learn much about him through his family. For instance, in 'A Merchant's Widow', Peter's grandmother is well aware that her grandson is ashamed of his ethnic background and immigrant family. She recalls that when Peter was a child, she used to pick him up from the neighbourhood playground. He would 'pretend that he did not understand her language' (10) and he would walk 'slightly apart from her in her black, black clothes' (10). Peter pretends not to understand Greek because knowledge of the language would identify him with his grandmother and her ethnicity; it would marginalise him or make him an outsider to the dominant Anglophone society. Peter, even as a child, understands that appropriation of language defines the relationship of the individual to his culture. In showing his friends that he speaks and understands only English, Peter is trying to earn Aussie identity.

In the story 'In Which Peter Mavromatis Lives Up to His Name', Peter ironically finds success as an ethnic photographer. As his sponsor states, Peter's exhibition is 'timely'. 'There's a bit of interest up now in … ah … in … um … multiculturalism … the film industry has done the bush like a dinner' (192). Peter's photography mentor, Gary, tells him that his technique is superb, but it is obvious to all – including Peter – that the photographs lack feeling for his Greek subjects. As his parents clearly see, 'Pete went to Greece, but he never went home' (196).

As both a poet and prose writer, Antigone Kefala has made an impact on contemporary Australian writing. Born in Romania of Greek parents, Kefala has lived in Romania, Greece, New Zealand and Australia. Given her own experiences of migration, Kefala writes poignantly of exile, dislocation, estrangement, and identity. In her novellas *The First*

Journey (1975), *The Boarding House* (1975), and *The Island* (1997), the central narrators are displaced and alienated individuals engaged in a search for meaning and belonging that usually ends fruitlessly. Critic Helen Nickas (1994) has suggested that Kefala's prose work should be read autobiographically as offering in fictional form Kefala's own journey from Romania to New Zealand and Australia. *Alexia: A Tale of Two Cultures* (1984), which explores the traumas of migration from the perspective of its young protagonist, is certainly a retelling of Kefala's own experiences of displacement as a migrant child.

Loukakis, Papaellinas and Kefala write of their roots, the problems of identity, alienation, acculturation, assimilation, and of cultural barriers and misunderstandings, particularly misunderstandings which divide families which consist of immigrant parents and children either born or brought up in Australia. Their main concerns are ethnicity and assimilation, and their meaning and implications for Australian society. For most of their characters, ethnic is a term of marginalisation; as 'ethnics', these characters often feel that they are outsiders or outside of mainstream Australian society. As Loukakis and Papaellinas dramatise in their short stories, ethnically distinct groups like the Greeks were expected (particularly in the 1950s and 1960s) to assimilate into Australian society. Loukakis and Papaellinas, who were born in the 1950s and know well the effects of assimilation on second-generation Australian-born Greeks, directly challenge the ideology of assimilation by either showing or implying that ethnic differences are powerful and enduring, and give an individual's life coherence, meaning, and identity.

Like Loukakis and Papaellinas, Christos Tsiolkas also explores identity and cross cultural conflict, but from the perspective of a homosexual protagonist, Ari Voulis, in his novel *Loaded* (1995). Ari's homosexuality places him on the periphery of both Greek and Australian culture, as both expect males to conform to standards of masculinity and heterosexuality. Tsiolkas has said that in this novel he was 'keen to upset simplistic categorization of sexuality, of ethnicity, of nationalism'. Thus, in

Loaded, Tsiolkas offers a queer reading of multiculturalism, ethnicity and identity, finally drawing the conclusion that the only way to have an identity is to resist making one.

In *Loaded*, Melbourne is a city divided by racial, class and ethnic differences. In the twenty-four hours that frame the story, Ari cruises the suburbs and city of Melbourne searching out clubs, drugs and anonymous sex. The novel is divided into four sections – East, North, South and West – each representing the four 'territories' of Melbourne. As Ari provides a running commentary on his life, he also produces a politically loaded map of the city which reflects not only his deep understanding of the hierarchies of class, race, and ethnicity but also his ambivalence concerning his sexuality and desires.

In his exploration of the city and self, Ari deconstructs the myth of solidarity, whether of the family unit, the religious, ethnic, or sexual group as well as the idea of Australian multiculturalism. In his inability to identify with any part of the city or any of its communities, Ari proves to be an alienated modern individual who refuses to conform to society's 'normative' patterns of behaviour, largely because such assimilation comes with a price – subservience to and complicity with a prejudiced society. Ari's resistance to definitions is due to his belief that words and expressions are loaded with meaning and have the power to define and confine; hence, he resists being labelled: 'I'm not Australian, I'm not Greek, I'm not anything' (Tsiolkas, *Loaded*, 114). Tsiolkas has said in an interview that 'identity always remains elusive and malleable', and this is the main theme that he explores in the novel through Ari's abhorrence of and resistance to labels.

While Ari is intent on de-scribing the reductive identities that society so oppressively inscribes on humans, he ironically is complicit with some of them, particularly heteronormative masculinity. Ultimately, the struggle to resist identity does not prove to be liberating for Ari; rather, it is a tyranny of its own because the collective sense of belonging is replaced by displacement, as the novel's urban cartography emphasises. *Loaded* was critically acclaimed and made into a film, *Head On* (1998).

Tsiolkas' 2005 novel, *Dead Europe*, tells the story of Isaac, an Australian-born photographer of Greek descent, who travels to Greece for an exhibition of his work, which receives little attention but is an opportunity for him to visit with family and friends. He is dismayed to find them disillusioned by and uninterested in politics, having instead embraced racism and consumerism. He decides to travel to Europe's major historical and cultural centres, such as Paris, Prague, Berlin, London and Cambridge, where he chronicles through his photography the racism, poverty, displacement and anti-Semitism of post-communist Europe. The multilayered plot moves between a tale set in a Greek peasant village during the Second World War, Isaac's travels through Eastern Europe to Amsterdam and Britain, and his reflections on his life in Australia as part of an immigrant family.

Greek-Australian Drama and Performance Poetry

In addition to writing poetry and fiction, Vasso Kalamaras is also an accomplished playwright. *The Bread Trap* (1986) dramatises the story of the large community of migrant tobacco farmers in Manjimup. Although the play is not autobiographical, Kalamaras did draw on her own experiences (she was one of many migrant women involved in tobacco farming in Manjimup from 1950–61) to create an intimate portrait of a Greek family who struggle to come to terms with their new lives, a new country, different values and changing economic realities. The play, set in 1961, focuses on the hardship and deprivation of the migrant workers and the ruthlessness of the corporate world while also exploring cultural and generational conflicts.

In 'Karagiozis Down-Under' (1992), Kalamaras borrows from traditional Greek shadow-puppet theatre to examine contemporary Australian realities. The protagonist, Karagiozis, is a Greek migrant who manages to get a position as an interpreter to the prime minister of the country, Mr 'Vulture'. This is not so much because of his real ability, but because he is a member of one of the largest minority groups, and hence a source of votes for the government. Karagiozis is joined by all the main characters of the traditional shadow-puppet theatre: his long-suffering wife, Aglaia; his children the Kollitiria; Hatziavatis, the quintessentially subservient type who bows continually in front of the prime minister; Barbayiorgos who wants to return to his village in Greece to find a bride; Stavrakas, the tough streetwise guy, and others. By adapting the old tradition of Greek theatre and by writing her work in Greek first, subsequently translating it into English (as is true of all of her work), Kalamaras succeeds in perpetuating and promoting Greek art and language in Australia.

Kalamaras' recent play, *Olympias: Mother of Alexander the Great* (2001), published first in book form in both Greek and English, dramatises the life of the legendary queen of ancient Macedonia, and pays tribute to her as a woman who fought courageously against the male dominance of her day, liberating women, encouraging education and increasing salaries for men in the army and in public office.

Since 1998, Christos Tsiolkas has worked as a playwright. His first play was the AWGIE award-winning collaboration (co-written with Andrew Bovell, Patricia Cornelius, Melissa Reeve and Irini Vela), *Who's Afraid of the Working Class?* (1998), for Melbourne Workers Theatre, and he subsequently worked with the same team on the play *Fever* (2002). His other plays include *Elektra AD* (1999), *Viewing Blue Poles* (2000) and *Dead Caucasians* (2001). His most recent play, *Non Parlo di Salo* (co-written with Spiro Economopoulos), about the controversial Italian film director Pier Paolo Pasolini's last film, was staged by Melbourne Workers Theatre in July 2005.

πO has established a reputation as one of Australia's notable performance poets. In 1991, πO teamed up with nine fellow performance poets (Billy Marshall-Stoneking, Nigel Roberts, Grant Caldwell, Amanda Stewart, Jas H. Duke, Jenny Sheard, Grant Caldwell and others) to create, direct and produce the first ever, poet-performed, directed and produced, dramatic verse play. Entitled *Call it Poetry/Tonight* (1991), the show was made up entirely of the poems of the poets who were performing and involved unusual presentations of their work, including several poems broken up into dialogues between the poets themselves. The performance was neither a poetry reading nor a play, but a combination of both with a touch of mime, cabaret and jazz thrown in.

A Brief Look at Other Greek-Australian Authors

Fotini Epanomitis was born in Australia in 1969, the year her parents migrated from Greece. She received a Bachelor of Arts (Hons) and a Master of Arts in Literature from Curtin University where she later taught as a lecturer. In 1993 Epanomitis burst into the limelight as the winner of one of the most prestigious young writers awards for her novel *The Mule's Foal*, namely the Australian/Vogel Literary Award as well as the Victorian Premier's Award. *The Mule's Foal* belongs to the genre of magic realism. Set in a Greek village, it tells the story of three houses – the house of Stefanos, the house of the Vaias, and the house of sin. The lives of the people in each of these houses intersect in a multitude of ways which generate more and more stories. The voice of the storyteller belongs to Mirella, a prostitute whose storytelling creates a world in which anything can and does happen. Stefano's wife Meta transforms herself into a man in order to be released from prison and later becomes a woman again; their son Theodosios marries Vaia, the daughter of Yiorgos and Stella, and they produce a gorilla-like child, Yiorgos the Apeface; a woman is transformed into a bear and eats her mother-in-law; a house is taken over by sand; and the sterile mule gives birth to a foal. Incredible events such as these are woven into the fabric of daily life and death in a small village. *The Mule's Foal* was adapted and directed on stage by Alan Becher for the Perth Theatre Company in 2000.

Jim Sakkas was born in 1954 on the Greek Island of Lefkas and came to Australia with his family at the age of seven. He grew up in Melbourne, studied Arts at Monash University and later studied for a Diploma of Education at La Trobe University. From 1980 Sakkas taught English to adult migrants. In 1987 he won the Australian/Vogel Literary Award with *Ilias* (1987), the story of Ilias, a migrant from Greece who arrived in Melbourne in the 1920s seeking financial security far from home. His second novel *Stella's Place* was published in 1998 and (according to the book's dust jacket) is a tale about 'loneliness and marginalisation so often experienced by migrants, but is also an exploration of human spirit and of the nurturing qualities of friendship and of the earth'.

Born in Richmond, Melbourne, of Greek parents and possessed of a science degree, Komninos Zervos is one of Australia's most entertaining performance poets. His performances in schools, trains, pubs, street corners, prisons, clubs and factories, in which he rants about everyday life, suburbia and migrants amongst other things, are legendary. He is author of *The Komninos Manifesto* (1985), *Sophisticated Souvlaki* (1986), *The Second Komninos Manifesto* (1986), *The Baby Rap* (1992), and *The Venus of Marrickville* (1993).

Born in Sydney to a Greek father and Australian-born mother, Timoshenko Aslanides published his first collection of poetry, *The Greek Connection*, in 1977, winning the British Commonwealth Poetry Prize for best first book of poetry in English. As he notes on his website, Aslanides considers himself an Australian poet, not an ethnic writer, emphasising his 'determination to celebrate Australia and Australians' in his work. His recent poetry collections include *Australian Alphabet* (1992), *A Calendar of Flowers: Selected Poems 1975–2000* (2001), and *Occasions for Words* (2006).

Conclusion

Greek-Australian literature has undergone profound developments in the last two decades, evidenced both by the impressive number of new, younger Greek-Australian writers writing in English as well as the academic and scholarly interest in this literature, particularly within the fields of Diaspora and Multicultural Studies. Also, given that many contemporary authors, such as Christos Tsiolkas, have had their works accepted by 'mainstream' publishers, Greek-Australian writers have become a part of the Australian literary scene.

Not surprisingly, categories such as 'Greek-Australian writer' and 'Greek-Australian literature' are being redefined, if not challenged, by scholars and writers. Initially, 'Greek-Australian literature' identified an early generation of migrant writers whose texts challenged conceptions of Australian national and cultural identity that were firmly rooted in the Anglo-Celtic tradition. These 'ethnic texts' called into question the exclusionary nature of Australian literature and culture, and encouraged scholars to redefine and review the canon to include 'ethnic minority' voices. In the 1980s, a large number of second- and third-generation Australian writers of Greek descent emerged whose literary concerns were no longer limited to migration, but tended to focus on the problems of hybridity and assimilation (specifically the impossibility of reconciling conflicting national and cultural identities). It was at this time that scholars and writers began to question the adequacy of terms such as migrant, ethnic, multicultural, Greek-Australian, and considered their potentially marginalising and homogenising effects.

Innovative contemporary Greek-Australian writers such as πO and Christos Tsiolkas are redefining the parameters of Greek-Australian literature. Their work scrutinises multicultural Australia and the mores of Anglo-Celtic as well as Greek-Australian life. What does it mean to be Greek or Australian? What does 'Australia' and 'being Australian' currently mean? In *Framing Marginality* (1994), Sneja Gunew's observation aptly applies to contemporary Greek-Australian writers:

> Quite often, and rightly so given their current conditions, writers object to the special pleading they perceive as inherent in the label 'ethnic' or 'multicultural' writer. Understandably, they wish to be considered as Australian writers. (14)

In focusing on 'the contemporary lived experience of "Being in Australia" ' (Leishman, 99), the work of today's Greek-Australian writers has moved from the margins to the mainstream where it belongs.

Works Cited

Aslanides, Timoshenko. *Occasions for Words: Poems for Birth, Marriage, Death and Much Between*. Kent Town, SA: Wakefield, 2006.

——. Timoshenko Aslanides' Website. 2006. [Accessed 25 March 2007]. timoshenko.actewagl.net.au/.

——. *A Calendar of Flowers: Selected Poems 1975–2000*. Wollongong, NSW: Five Islands, 2001.

——. *Australian Alphabet*. Springwood, NSW: Butterfly, 1992.

——. *The Greek Connection*. Canberra: The Author, 1977.

Castan, Con. 'Greek-Australian Literature.' *Journal of the Australasian Universities Language and Literature Association* 59 (1983): 5–25.

Epanomitis, Fotini. *The Mule's Foal*. St. Leonards, NSW: Allen & Unwin, 1993.

Gunew, Sneja. 'Introduction: From Migrant Writing to Ethnic Minority Literatures.' *Framing Marginality: Multicultural Literary Studies*. Melbourne: Melbourne University Press, 1994, 1–24.

Head On. Dir. Ana Kokkinos. Prod. Jane Scott. Strand Releasing, 1998.

Kalamaras, Vasso. *Olympias: Mother of Alexander the Great*. Melbourne: Owl, 2001.

——. 'Karagiozis Down-Under.' Old Customs House Theatre, Fremantle, WA. 6–29 February 1992.

——. *The Bread Trap*. Box Hill, Victoria: Elikia, 1986.

——. *Bitterness: Six Short Stories*. Trans. Vasso Kalamaras and Reg Durack. Perth: Artlook, 1983.

——. *Pikres: Diegemata*. Perth: The Author, 1976.

——. *Other Earth: Four Greek-Australian Stories.* 1961. Trans. Vasso Kalamaras and Reg Durack. Fremantle, WA: Fremantle Arts Centre Press, 1977.

Kefala, Antigone. *Summer Visit: Three Novellas.* Artarmon, NSW: Giramondo, 2002.

——. *Poems: A Bilingual Edition.* Melbourne: Owl, 2000.

——. *Absence: New and Selected Poems.* Alexandria, NSW: Hale & Iremonger, 1998.

——. *The Island.* Alexandria, NSW: Hale & Iremonger, 1997.

——. *Alexia: A Tale of Two Cultures.* Sydney: John Ferguson, 1984.

——. *The Boarding House.* Sydney: Wild & Woolley, 1975.

——. *The First Journey: Two Short Novels.* Sydney: Wild & Woolley, 1975.

Leishman, Kirsty. 'Australian Grunge Literature and the Conflict between Literary Generations.' *Journal of Australian Studies* (December 1999): 94–102. Expanded Academic ASAP. [Accessed 19 March 2007]. find.galegroup.com.ezproxy.lib.monash.edu.au

Loukakis, Angelo. *The Memory of Tides.* Sydney: HarperCollins, 2006.

——. *Vernacular Dreams.* St Lucia: University of Queensland Press, 1986.

——. *For the Patriarch.* 1981. St Lucia: University of Queensland Press, 1987.

Nickas, Helen, ed. *Mothers from the Edge: An Anthology.* Melbourne: Owl, 2006.

——. *Dimitris Tsaloumas, A Voluntary Exile: Selected Writings on His Life and Work.* Melbourne: Owl, 1999.

——. *Migrant Daughters: The Female Voice in Greek-Australian Prose Fiction.* Melbourne: Owl, 1992.

Nickas, Helen, and Konstantina Dounis, eds. *Re-telling the Tale: Poetry and Prose by Greek-Australian Women Writers.* Melbourne: Owl, 1994.

Papaellinas, George. *Ikons.* Melbourne: Penguin, 1986.

Π O. *The Number Poems and Other Equations.* Melbourne: Collective Effort, 2000.

——. et al. *Call it Poetry*/Tonight. Sydney Theatre Company, Studio
    Theatre, Wharf, Sydney. 1991.

——, ed. *Off the Record*. Ringwood, Victoria: Penguin, 1985.

——. *The Fitzroy Poems*. Melbourne: Collective Effort, 1989.

——. *Panash*. Carlton, Victoria: Collective Effort, 1978.

——. *Fitzroy Brothel*. Melbourne: Strawberry, 1974.

Sakkas, Jim. *Stella's Place*. Sydney: Allen & Unwin, 1998.

——. *Ilias*. Sydney: Allen & Unwin, 1987.

Tsaloumas, Dimitris. *Stoneland Harvest: New and Selected Poems*.
    Nottingham: Shoestring, 1999.

——. *The Harbour*. St Lucia: University of Queensland Press, 1998.

——. *The Barge*. St Lucia: University of Queensland Press, 1993.

——. *Portrait of a Dog and Other Classical Bagatelles*. St Lucia: University
    of Queensland Press, 1991.

——. *Falcon Drinking: The English Poems*. St Lucia: University of
    Queensland Press, 1988.

——. *The Observatory: Selected Poems of Dimitris Tsaloumas*. St Lucia:
University of Queensland Press, 1983.

——. *The Book of Epigrams*. Macedonia, Greece: Nea Poreia, 1980.

Tsiolkas, Christos. *Dead Europe*. Melbourne: Random House, 2005.

——, and Spiro Economopoulos. *Non Parlo di Salo*. Dir. Andrea James.
Melbourne Workers Theatre, Trades Hall, Carlton, Melbourne, 15–30 July
2005.

——. *Fever*. Dir. Julian Meyrick. Melbourne Workers Theatre, Trades Hall,
Carlton, Melbourne, 18 September 2002.

——. *Dead Caucasians*. Dir. Roland Manderson. Social Division, The
Courtyard Studio, Canberra Theatre Centre, ACT, 25 January–3 February
2001.

——. *Elektra AD. 1999*. Dir. David Branson. La Mama Theatre, The Carlton
Courthouse, Melbourne, 2000.

——. *Viewing Blue Poles*. Dir. Lauren Taylor. Fitzroy Gallery, La Mama
Theatre, The Carlton Courthouse, Melbourne, 1999.

——, Andrew Bovell, Patricia Cornelius, Melissa Reeve, and Irini Vela. *Who's Afraid of the Working Class?* Melbourne Workers Theatre, Trades Hall, Carlton, Melbourne, 1998.

——. *Loaded.* Milsons Point, NSW: Vintage, 1995.

Zervos, Komninos. 'Π O' *Dictionary of Literary Biography: Australian Writers 1975–2000.* Vol. 325. Ed. Selina Samuels. New York: Thomson Gale, 2006. 260–65.

——. *The Venus of Marrickville.* Backspace Theatre, Hobart, Tasmania. 1993.

——. *The Baby Rap and Other Poems.* South Melbourne: Oxford University Press, 1992.

——. *Sophisticated Souvlaki.* The Studio, Victorian Arts Centre, Melbourne. 1986.

——. *The Second Komninos Manifesto.* North Melbourne: Fat Possum, 1986.

——. *The Komninos Manifesto.* North Melbourne: Fat Possum, 1985.

CONTRIBUTORS

Alison Bartlett is Professor of Women's Studies and also teaches English and cultural studies at the University of Western Australia. She publishes regularly in literary and feminist journals, is co-editor of *Australian Literature and the Public Sphere* (1999) and author of *Jamming the Machinery: Contemporary Australian Women Writers* (1998). In addition to literary studies her research has included postgraduate supervision and feminist pedagogy, fictocriticism, reading embodiment and more recently modes of activism (including writing). She edits the online journal *Outskirts*.

Mary Besemeres is a Research Associate at the Australian National University. A founding co-editor of the journal *Life Writing*, she is the author of *Translating One's Self: Language and Selfhood in Cross-Cultural Autobiography* (2002) and co-editor of *Translating Lives: Living with Two Languages and Cultures* (2007).

Anne Brewster teaches at the University of New South Wales, Sydney. Her books include *Literary Formations* (1995) and *Reading Aboriginal Women's Autobiography* (1996). She co-edited, with Angeline O'Neill and Rosemary van den Berg, an anthology of Australian Indigenous writing, *Those Who Remain Will Always Remember* (2000).

Scott Brook is Assistant Professor of Writing at the University of Canberra. His research on Vietnamese-Australian cultural heritage and politics has been published in various Australian and international journals and magazines.

Konstandina Dounis lectured at RMIT for many years, during which time she convened a series of conferences on aspects of Greek-Australian literature and identity. Her publications include the anthology *Retelling the Tale* (1994) and *From Sapfo to Sappho* (1994), both concerned with women writers. She is currently carrying out research for her Ph.D. at La Trobe University. She is also a literary translator and creative writer working on her own collections of poems and short stories.

Debra Dudek is a Lecturer of English Literatures at the University of Wollongong. She has published internationally on postcolonial studies, Canadian and Australian literature, and children's literature.

Nijmeh Hajjar is a Senior Lecturer and Chair of the Department of Arabic and Islamic Studies at the University of Sydney. Her research interests include gender issues in modern Arabic culture, literature and cinema. Her publications include *The Politics and Poetics of Ameen Rihani: The Humanist Ideology of an Arab-American Intellectual and Activist* (2010) and *Living Arabic in Context* (2005).

Dennis Haskell is the author of five collections of poetry and twelve volumes of literary scholarship and criticism. His *All the Time in the World* won the Western Australian Premier's Prize for Poetry in 2007 and is being translated into French and Italian. Haskell was co-editor of *Westerly* from 1985 until 2009 and is Professor of English and Cultural Studies at The University of Western Australia. He is also currently Chair of the Literature Board of the Australia Council. His *Acts of Defiance: New and Selected Poems* will be published by Salt in 2010.

Sissy Helff teaches English and postcolonial literature as well as media and gender studies at the Universities of Frankfurt and Paderborn. She studied German and English literature at the universities of Bristol and Frankfurt and was a research fellow at Leeds University in 2007–08. More recently she has been working on a postdoctoral project focusing on the representation of strangers in media and literature. Her publications include the three co-edited volumes *Facing the East in the West: Images of Eastern Europe in British Literature, Film and Culture* (2010), *Transcultural Modernities: Narrating Africa in Europe* (2009) and *Transcultural English Studies: Theories, Fictions, Realities* (2008).

Deborah L. Madsen is Professor of American Literature and Culture at the University of Geneva, Switzerland. Her books include *Rereading Allegory: A Narrative Approach to Genre* (1994), *Allegory in America: From Puritanism to Postmodernism* (1996), *American Exceptionalism* (1998), *Feminist Theory and Literary Practice* (2000), *Understanding Contemporary Chicana Literature* (2000), *Maxine Hong Kingston* (2001), *Chinese American Literature* (2002) and edited volumes on post-colonialism and American literature. She is currently president of the Swiss Association for North American Studies.

Igor Maver is Professor at University of Ljubljana, Slovenia where he holds a personal Chair in Literatures in English. His research and teaching interests include literature in English, postcolonial, diasporic literature, and American literature. He is the author of almost two hundred scholarly articles, two monographs in English on Australian literature (1997 and 1999) and co-author of two books of essays (2000 and 2005). In 2006 he published a book of essays *Critics and Writers Speak: Revisioning Post-Colonial Studies*.

Sonia Mycak is an Honorary Research Fellow in the School of Letters, Art and Media at the University of Sydney and an Adjunct Senior Research Fellow in the Centre for the Book in the School of English, Communications and Performance Studies at Monash University. Her early work was in Canadian literature and literary theory and she is author of *In Search of the Split Subject: Psychoanalysis, Phenomenology, and the Novels of Margaret Atwood* (1996). More recently Sonia's research has focused upon the multicultural literatures of Australia and Canada. She is author of *Canuke Literature: Critical Essays on Canadian Ukrainian*

Writing (2001) and edited *I'm Ukrainian, Mate! New Australian Generation of Poets* (2000) and *Australian Mosaic: An Anthology of Multicultural Writing* (with Chris Baker, 1997).

Hoa Pham is an author, playwright and psychologist. She is completing a doctorate of creative arts at the University of Western Sydney. Her publications include *Silence* (2010), *Vixen, 49 Ghosts, No one like me* and *Quicksilver*. She is also the founder of *Peril Magazine,* an Asian arts and culture on-line magazine at www.peril.com.au.

Robert Pickering holds the Chair of Contemporary and Modern French Literature at Blaise Pascal University, Clermont-Ferrand (France). A specialist of symbolism and post-symbolism (Mallarmé-Valéry), his publications also cover a wide range of nineteenth- and twentieth-century French and European literature.

Gaetano Rando holds degrees from both Italian and Australian universities and is Associate Professor in the School of English Literatures, Philosophy, and Languages at the University of Wollongong. One of his major research interests is in the area of Italian-Australian studies, the latest volume length publication in this field being (*Migration and Literature: The Italo-Australian Case*) *Emigrazione e letteratura: Il caso italoaustraliano* (2004).

Amit Sarwal is Assistant Professor at the Department of English, Rajdhani College (University of Delhi), New Delhi, India. He was an Honorary Visiting Scholar (2006–07) at Monash University as an Endeavour Asia Award winner (2006). His areas of interest include South-Asian diaspora literature, Australian literature and popular fiction. He has co-edited *English Studies, Indian Perspectives* (2006) with Makarand Paranjape and Aneeta Rajendran; *Australian Studies Now* (2007) with Andrew Hassam; *Fact & Fiction: Readings in Australian Literature* (2008), *Creative Nation: Australian Cinema and Cultural*

Studies Reader (2009) and *Reading Down Under: Australian Literary Studies Reader* (2009) with Reema Sarwal.

Christine Sun received her PhD from Monash University's School of Languages, Cultures and Linguistics in 2004. She is the author of *Voices under the Sun: English-Language Writings by Australian and Other Authors with Chinese Ancestry* (Melbourne: Taiwan.com.au Portal, 2007). She is now an independent scholar and web manager of Taiwan.com.au portal.

Hariclea Zengos has been a Professor of English and American Literature at The American College of Greece since 1989. She received her PhD in English from Tufts University, Boston in 1989. Her research and publications focus on Greek writers of the diaspora (with a specific interest in Greek-Australian writers), travel writing about Greece, as well as colonial and postcolonial fiction. She is currently completing a book-length study on white colonial European women's construction of Africa in their autobiographical fiction.